D1735974

© 1983 AT&T

Injury and Litigation Prevention
Theory and Practice

Stanley H. Freeman

Department of Environmental Health
School of Public Health and Community Medicine
University of Washington

VNR VAN NOSTRAND REINHOLD
_____ New York

Copyright © 1991 by Van Nostrand Reinhold

Library of Congress Catalog Card Number 90-22785
ISBN 0-442-23847-9

All rights reserved. No part of this work covered by
the copyright hereon may be reproduced or used in any
form by any means — graphic, electronic, or
mechanical, including photocopying, recording, taping,
or information storage and retrieval systems — without
written permission of the publisher.

Printed in the United States of America.

Van Nostrand Reinhold
115 Fifth Avenue
New York, New York 10003

Chapman and Hall
2-6 Boundary Row
London, SE1 8HN, England

Thomas Nelson Australia
102 Dodds Street
South Melbourne 3205
Victoria, Australia

Nelson Canada
1120 Birchmount Road
Scarborough, Ontario MIK 5G4, Canada

16   15   14   13   12   11   10   9   8   7   6   5   4   3   2   1

Library of Congress Cataloging-in-Publication Data

Freeman, Stanley H.
    Injury and litigation prevention: theory and practice/by Stanley H.
Freeman.
        p. cm.
    Includes index.
    ISBN 0-442-23847-9
    1. Industrial safety.   I. Title.
T55.F74   1991
685.3'82 — dc20

90-22785
CIP

For Helen, Doug, and Harry—
Long May They Wave.

To Herb and Helen—
The Ties That Bind.

To my departed family, who would have been proud—
Jack and Mary, Harry and Goldie,
Clyde and Betty.

Contents

PREFACE

During the construction of the transcontinental railroad the yardmaster said to Howard Hamblen, a newly hired hand, "Get your dinner first, there's no use getting killed on an empty stomach." It was the year 1888 when 2070 railroad workers were killed and 20,148 injured on this one project. This was the first year that statistical records were kept by the railroad on work-related injuries.

Today, slightly over one hundred years later, injuries, while not with the same frequency as that rail project, still kill and maim in all walks of life with frequent litigation as an additional consequence. In spite of no-fault compensation insurance, court calendars many times require a one- to three-year wait before personal injury suits can be heard. Personal injuries are still a significant hazard to life and limb but a relatively little researched and poorly managed problem in our society.

This book provides usable, easy-to-read, personal injury and litigation prevention information to all those involved, or who want to avoid involvement in the litigation process. This includes owners of retail establishments, manufacturers, engineers, lawyers, public servants, insurance companies, injured parties, judges, product designers, product distributors, administrators, service providers, worker's compensation administrators, rental companies, consultants, accident investigators, general contractors, sub-contractors, loss control managers, inventors, risk managers, educators, safety professionals, and industrial hygienists.

This volume is not written from a lawyer's point of view, where the letter of the law is reviewed and explained. Rather it presents practical advice from a safety professional who has participated in a significant number of personal injury cases as an expert witness. This experience indicates that any type of business, profession, or public agency can employ relatively simple and often inexpensive techniques to avoid causing personal injury to their customers, clients, employees, and subcontractors. Obviously, when personal injury is avoided, litigation is almost always prevented.

Although there are many actual cases described, this book is not intended to be a source of case law. (However, see the Appendix for captions and cities of origin for most cases presented here.) The purpose of liberally using case material is to effectively illustrate the principles of litigation prevention.

Some of the techniques described in this book are not sophisticated, but are well known, and do not require complicated computation. Yet these or other methods were not used by even some of the nation's largest businesses to reduce the injury-causing potential of their products or operations. In many third-party suits in which I have been involved, defendants could not say that they critically examined their product, operation, or facility for safety to the user. Most times the defense was based on contributory negligence of the plaintiff or in the case of prime contractors, disclaiming responsibility. Although accepted as standard, these types of defense are not as cost effective by an order of magnitude as well-planned analysis, prior preparedness, and concerned corrective action. This book explains the how and why of these more effective approaches to litigation prevention.

If you are an attorney, this book can be of assistance by helping you to determine your approach to the prosecution or defense of a personal injury lawsuit. If you know what should have been done in terms of accident prevention by either the plaintiff, the defense, the employer, the general contractor, or the owner, that knowledge could influence the way you handle your case in court.

Part I deals with the philosophical issues that confront juries when they must decide liability in a personal injury case. Some of the more important litigation-prevention principles involved with these issues will be covered in more detail later in the book. It is recommended that the reader become well acquainted with these issues, since they are vital to the general understanding of the litigation-prevention process from a professional safety point of view.

For example, should a designer make a machine or environment "idiot proof?" Is there a definable line where a plaintiff's actions can be judged unreasonable, thus relieving the machine designer, architect, manufacturer, or facility owner/manager from incorporating accident-prevention criteria or devices? The response to these pivotal issues can help form the litigation-prevention model for the designer, the attack or defense plan for a trial lawyer, and the information required to prevent litigation in general.

You may wonder why this book also concerns itself with employer safety programs in Part III, when worker's compensation laws give employers immunity from litigation brought by their employees. The answer is that in twenty-seven states there have been successful lawsuits brought by employees against employers who were previously aware of the hazards that resulted in serious employee injuries. Two states where such litigation is routine are California and New Jersey, and the trend appears to point to an increase in such actions.

Professional-quality employer programs will also enable avoidance of litigation with OSHA for contested citations and penalties.

Very complete indexing will enable the reader to extract information that may be required to satisfy many litigation-prevention needs.

ACKNOWLEDGMENTS

I want to acknowledge the following persons who assisted me with material and/or inspiration.

First and foremost my wife, Helen, who created and maintained the atmosphere that made it possible for me to write this book.

Dr. Barry Dunphy, former Medical Director of the Boeing Company, who did the original groundwork on the Management Decision Point Analysis. Also, John LaLonde, a colleague and counterpart Safety Manager at Boeing whose interest in philosophical safety issues, particularly "dependence on safe practice," served as inspiration for my own research in this area.

Dr. Sheldon Murphy, now deceased, Chairman of the Department of Environmental Health at the University of Washington while most of the manuscript was being prepared, who gave me needed "official" encouragement to produce a scholarly work. Also at the University of Washington, Dr. Gilbert Omenn, Dean of the School of Public Health and Community Medicine, who by his own example creates a climate where achievement is rewarded and encouraged.

I am grateful to the many attorneys and legal associates whom I have worked with, particularly Rob Williamson, who critiqued the entire manuscript and gave valuable input to the last chapter; Doug Hofmann, who contributed thought-provoking material and editorial assistance for the chapter on construction safety; and Bob Davis, for his legal insights.

Gerald van Belle, Chairman of the Department of Environmental Health, was very helpful with the content and editing of the chapter on probability.

Dan Ericson, who ploughed through the initial manuscript and gave invaluable assistance with the grammar and terminology.

The crew at VNR—Steve Zollo, Cindy Savaglio, Rima Weinberg, Liz Geller, and the editing staff—have been very helpful in getting me through the hurdles of publishing; particularly Bob Esposito, who first contacted me and pointed me in the right direction.

Harry Philo—his advocacy of safety expertise gave me added incentive to fill a niche in the attorney–expert relationship.

Deane Cruz, now a senior vice-president of the Boeing Company, who, when he was Director of Manufacturing, showed me how and why safety was meant to be integrated into company operations.

Jim Vinson, friend and associate, now Corporate Safety Director for Boeing, helped me to understand the human side of occupational safety.

Chapter 1

Introduction

USING THIS BOOK EFFECTIVELY

In the following paragraphs, we examine the tasks and circumstances under which the reader would find this text useful. In all cases users should familiarize themselves with the philosophical safety issues in Part I, acquire an understanding of the author's perception of risk assessment, and examine Tables 7-1, 7-2, and 7-3. These tables will help readers determine the correct form of safety analysis and provide a pathway to corrective action.

The material in this book should enable the reader to:

1. Gather information on appropriate corrective measures for personal injury hazards in products, facilities, construction sites, and public and private organizations.
2. Research a product design for hazards to the user for routine and foreseeable use.
3. Research a facility (premises) for hazards in routine and foreseeable use.
4. Help prepare trial strategy for the plaintiff in a personal injury lawsuit.
5. Help prepare trial strategy for the defense in a personal injury lawsuit.
6. Assess a safety program's effectiveness, and if not effective, develop a safety program for a manufacturing or service organization.
7. Assess a construction site safety program's effectiveness, and if not effective, develop a safety program that is.
8. Develop a program to train management, engineers, and others to search out and correct product and facility hazards before the product is marketed or the facility opened.
9. Determine whether the current safety program in a public institution is adequate.

10. Determine whether the accident experience report is effective.
11. Determine whether your organization, business, or product is particularly vulnerable to litigation.
12. Effectively use one of six types of safety analysis to discover and correct incipient hazards.
13. Improve the number, type, and meaning of product warnings.
14. Decide whether or not to authorize epidemiological studies, product substitution research, and improved customer warnings for a widely used product that may be harmful to users.
15. Provide a text in a graduate curriculum in safety and industrial hygiene programs, law, business, or industrial engineering.

Example 1. Product Defect.   A manufacturer of a part revolution punch press wants to determine what, if anything, should be done to provide customers with up-to-date safety information to help reduce injuries to press operators.

Knowing that safe practice or rigorous training may not be depended upon to eliminate unsafe practice during production runs, the manufacturer conducts a hazard effects and control analysis and a management decision point analysis.

Both analyses show that double tripping is a continuing hazard, and that indeed there are reports of amputations involving its punch presses as well as those of other manufacturers.

The problem of double tripping is researched by the engineering staff and a retrofit kit is developed, which when installed will eliminate double tripping. The availability and details of kit installation are circulated to all press owners of record, including second, third, and fourth owners, if known.

Example 2. Product Defect.   The manufacturer of an electric can opener has received a few reports of electrical fault current from customers. A fault tree analysis shows that if a user vigorously attempted to open a rimless can and the can opener was powered by a non-GFCI-controlled circuit, a dangerous ground fault could occur. If this happened, it could be followed by serious injury, including, under the right conditions, electrocution.

A product recall is initiated at great cost but at far less cost than a lawsuit.

Example 3. Trip and Fall Hazard in a Restaurant.   A restaurant owner, dismayed by stories of other restaurant owners concerning lawsuits brought by injured patrons, decides to research the problem. A management oversight and risk tree (MORT) analysis is conducted. The analysis shows that to avoid customer injuries a number of management systems need to be set up, including warnings to customers, a program of inspection, and a training program for employees.

The day after the inspection system is initiated, a tear in the carpet is brought to the attention of the restaurant owner who has the tear repaired at a cost of $58. Compare this to $25,000 for the plaintiff and $8,000 in other costs associated with a customer injury from a trip and fall.

Example 4. Attorney Prepares Product Liability Case for Plaintiff.
During discovery, the plaintiff's attorney finds:

1. The company that designed and built the baby carriage purchased by her
   client had learned of a basic defect in the brake system whereby the brakes
   would fail if the product was on a hill and also loaded with heavy packages
   such as food bags.
2. This knowledge had come to them in the form of complaints from
   customers.
3. The company had assumed that the standard brake design would be
   adequate for this new, heavier, deluxe model baby buggy.
4. The complaining letters were not circulated to appropriate management
   personnel and the letters were not filed.
5. One company manager did see two of the four letters, but he had either
   forgotten to bring the matter up or had purposely ignored them.

The plaintiff was able to show the jury during trial that if the company had
performed a management oversight and risk tree analysis (MORT) or a
hazard effects and control analysis (HECA), they would have determined the
catastrophic nature of the hazard and taken steps to correct the problem in
existing as well as production models of the baby buggy. The MORT analysis
would detail what systems should have been in place to properly respond to
reports from the field that show product defects, and the HECA would have
revealed the defects before the product was marketed.

Example 5. Attorney Prepares Product Liability Case for Defense.   A
lessee fell from a scaffold that he had rented from a local rental company and
was permanently disabled. He sued the rental company for damages, claiming
that the scaffold was improperly maintained. During trial the rental company
was able to show how they used the hierarchy of prevention to eliminate the
inherent instability of the scaffold by supplying outriggers. They were also
able to show that the customer declined training in scaffold erection, which
would have included the installation of the outriggers. Had the outriggers
been installed the scaffold would not have tipped.

Example 6. Safety and Industrial Hygiene Program Development.
An owner of a medium-sized business (350 employees) is dissatisfied with the
current safety and industrial hygiene program now in operation. Before
coming to this conclusion, she examines the criteria for an effective safety
program. Using these same criteria she is able to adopt the administrative and
operational aspects of an effective program. By consulting the information on
staffing, and the material on adjusting program effort to company size, she is
also able to operate effectively and economically.

*Example 7. Safety and Industrial Hygiene Program for a Construction
Site.*   A construction manager is tired of being in a position where he cannot
deal with subcontractors on safety subjects in the same way that he deals with
them regarding the quality of their work. The manager knows that if he takes
obvious control of safety on the entire construction site it will increase his

company's liability in case of a civil suit. He wonders if neglecting safety in this way is the right thing to do.

After reading Part III, he is convinced that if he takes complete safety control, as general contractor he will be in a better position to control accidents and injuries and also to deal with liability if a lawsuit should arise.

He examines the blueprint for construction site safety and sets up the required organization, giving appropriate responsibility to his foremen, safety professionals, and subcontractors.

Example 8. Manufacturing Company Safety Training Program. This manufacturing company produced nine types of machine tools used in the wood and metal fabrication industries. The company had already had two product liability lawsuits and the CEO was concerned that his subordinate managers and engineers were insufficiently committed to customer protection.

Using this book as a text and with the company law firm providing an attorney as instructor, a course was developed entitled "Injury Control and Litigation Avoidance by Design." Some of the subjects (page numbers available in index) included were:

A. The Customer and Safety
    1. Dependence on Safe Practice
    2. The Hierarchy of Accident Prevention
    3. The Credo of Safe Design
    4. Accident and Injury Foreseeability
    5. The Accident/Injury Continuum
    6. Our Products as Part of a System
    7. How to Avoid Repeating Our Litigation Experience
B. Risk, Probability, Harm, and Danger
C. Methods of Product Safety Analysis
    1. Management Oversight and Risk Tree Analysis (MORT)
    2. Fault Tree Analysis (FTA)
    3. Task Hazard Analysis (THA)
    4. Management Decision Point Analysis (MDPA)
    5. Hazard Effects and Control Analysis (HECA)
D. Controlling Customer Injuries by Design
    1. Interlocks
    2. Guarding Principles
    3. Effective Warnings
    4. Retrofit
    5. Substitution
    6. Operation Manual Design
    7. Truth in Advertising
    8. Electrical Safety

Example 9. Employee Safety in a State Institution for the Mentally Disabled. Many in the safety profession, let alone the general public, are unaware that injury frequency in mental hospitals is usually above that in the normally high-rate industries of construction, mining, and logging. This is due in large part to patient-inflicted injuries to the staff. These institutions are also chronically understaffed and the staff undertrained, partially because of high turnover.

Because they are also generally insufficiently organized for safety, accident experience becomes a chronic problem. A manager of such a facility who wishes to reverse this condition can use Part III of this book to determine the appropriate safety structure and principles.

Example 10. Monthly Accident Summary.   The safety manager of a large multinational company is dissatisfied with the acceptance of the accident experience summary. Its current limited readership exhibits almost no response, and she can never find it on anyone's desk or in any file. One of her colleagues has jokingly told her that the accident summary is classified BBR (burn before reading).

If the safety office is to be taken seriously she knows that this situation must be reversed. By reading the section that deals with accident summary design she learns that the following attributes are necessary to the design of an effective report.

1. Goals and objectives.
2. Show names of reporting organization managers.
3. Hazard rate each organization.
4. Use exposure headcounts to determine populations.
5. Achievement rate each organization.
6. Use of the publication for manager safety accountability.

After reorganizing the summary format, convincing top management to establish safety goals and objectives for the company, and including the other listed features for an effective report, she now receives calls from management before the report is published asking for preliminary information on its contents.

Example 11. Recreational Ski Area.   The owner and operator of a large (average weekend patronage, 14,000) recreational ski area wants to be certain that the ski facility is as safe as possible for his patrons. He knows that there is already a considerable investment in personnel and equipment devoted to skier safety, but he has some uncertainty about the effectiveness of their safety program.

Using the chapter on management oversite and risk tree (MORT) analysis, he is able to develop an optimum safety program that makes the best use of existing equipment, facilities, and personnel. See Figure 1-1 for a sample page from this program.

Example 12. Demonstration to a Jury in a Product Liability Case.   In an actual case a worker was caught in an unguarded pulley station on a huge conveyor system used in a pulp mill [see Fig. 7-2(a)]. As part of preparing the case for trial the plaintiff's expert composed a task hazard analysis (THA) for demonstration to the jury.

The analysis showed that in the manufacturer's design, wood chips would periodically accumulate at the pulley station, which was surrounded on three sides by a 36-in.-high concrete wall. When chips reached a certain depth it

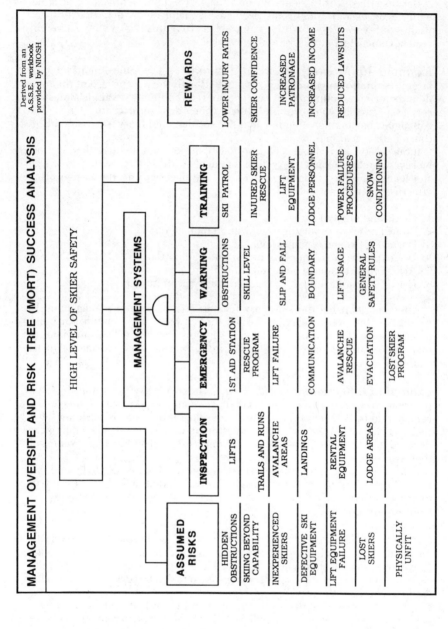

Figure 1-1. MORT analysis of a recreational ski facility.

was necessary for a worker to enter the pulley station to shovel chips onto the conveyor while it was running. After completing his task the worker must exit the pulley station.

It is at this point that the analysis would show the definite possibility that the worker could boost himself to the top of the concrete barrier by placing a foot on the bed of the conveyor. Of course, this is what happened on the occasion that the worker's left foot was caught in the conveyor and his leg torn off.

Task hazard analysis (THA) is a commonly used method in the safety profession, and this demonstration would clearly demonstrate to the jury the steps that should have been taken by the manufacturer before placing the product in the commerce system.

Example 13. Portable Hand Grinder Manufacturer is Sued for Failure to Warn.   A lawsuit was filed against the manufacturer of a hand grinder when the operator attached an underrated grinding disk. The normal operating speed for the grinder was 12,000 rpm, and the worker unknowingly attached a grinding disk with a maximum operating speed of 7000 rpm. The disk subsequently disintegrated and injured the user.

The plaintiff complained that the grinder lacked an explicit warning that dealt with its rated speed and the fact that it was possible to place a lower rpm-rated disk on the grinder's shaft. Such a warning could read:

```
WARNING!
OPERATES AT 12,000 RPM.
USING A DISK WITH A LOWER
RPM RATING WILL CAUSE
SERIOUS INJURIES.
```

Placing an explicit warning of this type both on the tool itself and in the operating manual would have been a reasonable and prudent action by the manufacturer. It does not necessarily mean that all users would heed the warning, but it shows that the manufacturer went as far as reasonably possible to avoid injury to an inexperienced or reckless operator. Such an action would also have probably prevented court action. Criteria for appropriate warnings are covered in Chapter 6.

Example 14. Fiberglass, The Next Asbestos?   In the early years of the twentieth century, asbestos, occurring naturally and in quantity, was considered to be the answer to many manufacturer's needs where fire resistance and insulating values were required. Today we know that asbestos is carcinogenic and a producer of a chronic, deadly disease.

Tracing the history of asbestos use, we know that in the early years it was considered only a nuisance, placing it in the same category as household dust. Although we are currently examining fiberglass with greater scrutiny, this material is a common substitute for asbestos, is probably even more widely used, and is generally considered benign by most users.

In the chapter on management decision point analysis (MDPA), we concluded that if Johns Manville, a huge manufacturer of asbestos products had performed such an analysis, the asbestos problem could have been corrected much sooner. It may be logical to extrapolate this reasoning to Fiberglass, and insist on an MDPA or more rigorous analyses that could result in the protection of the buying public before serious disease becomes manifest.

Example 15. Requirements for a Safety Textbook. The following subjects are covered in sufficient detail to provide a foundation for didactic material.

I. Accident prevention plan for all industry except construction (see the table of contents). This includes:
   A. Safety program integration
      1. Structure
      2. Functions
   B. Accident experience summary
   C. Operational criteria
   D. Safety office responsibilities
   E. Program size matrix
   F. Staffing criteria
II. Accident prevention plan for the construction industry.
   A. Responsibilities of the construction manager
   B. Responsibilities of the subcontractor
III. Insights into over thirty-five personal injury torts and their prevention.
IV. Descriptions of six methods of safety analyses and their application.
V. Philosophical basis of accident prevention. Both the industrial and nonindustrial situations are emphasized.
VI. How the business owner/manager can avoid personal injury litigation.

PART I

Safety Issues Important to Litigation Prevention

Compared with medicine, law, and even industrial hygiene, the safety profession is an emerging discipline with relatively little active research and fewer universally recognized philosophical "truths." There is controversy in all professions, but in the established disciplines mentioned earlier there are great volumes of traditional and accepted criteria that guide the actions of its professionals.

In the safety discipline, on the other hand, even something as straightforward as accident prevention training does not have, in my opinion, a firm role in the lexicon of the safety professional. Many in the profession feel it is the only and best answer to all safety problems; a large number of others, including myself, feel that training is important but that it is only a secondary—not a primary—prevention modality.

For example, if training is relied upon as an exclusive remedy what is to prevent the wrong information from being passed from an employer to a worker? Or, in a more practical example, if a worker panics when the work binds between the blade and fence of a table saw, will training alone prevent injury if the guard is not in place? If training is the sole source of protection for persons exposed to hazards, can society rely unswervingly on learned safe practice for protection?

Part I of this book deals with these questions by examining six philosophical safety issues that show how the thoughtful application of existing, recognized, and established accident prevention principles can be useful in injury and litigation prevention. Included with each issue are examples of its preventive role.

Chapter 2

Preventing Injury and Litigation

Preventing litigation is not an extremely complex issue. It demands that those who want to avoid harming others because of design deficiencies, mismanufacture, improper business layout, use of improper materials, omission of guarding, inappropriate corporate decisions concerning the safety aspects of their products, failure to warn, or other acts of omission or commission, understand some relatively simple principles that are included in this section. Once these principles are understood, some equally uncomplicated prevention techniques can be employed to counteract litigation-producing conditions. It is important to understand that litigation prevention involves an overt, scheduled effort to be successful.

Juries that decide on liability often must consider a confusing array of opinion and fact that may lead to an uninformed decision. If juries had a more complete understanding of the accident-prevention process and the elements of accidental injury, they would be in a better position to make an informed decision.

In the following actual case*, in which the plaintiff could have been judged as "careless"—indeed the jury argued for "carelessness" during their deliberations—the plaintiff was instead awarded an amount greater than he had requested.

Case Study 2-1

The plaintiff had purchased a 10-in. radial arm saw from a well-known retail outlet. The saw came with standard equipment, which did not include the lower blade guard that was offered in the catalog and in the

---

Hallman v. *Sears Roebuck*. See Appendix.

11

saw manual as optional equipment. On the day of the accident the plaintiff was using the saw at home and was cutting a board in the "rip mode," that is, cutting a board lengthwise. While in the rip mode a radial arm saw is in its most dangerous configuration because it often requires operators to bring their hands close to the point of operation (see Fig. 2-1). If the board binds or the operator is distracted, a hand could be drawn into the point of operation and a portion of the hand amputated.

On this occasion the saw operator's right hand was moving close to the blade, pushing a 1 × 6 board through the saw when his brother came to the room's entrance. The brother was leaving for the grocery store and asked the plaintiff if he wanted to go with him. Distracted, the plaintiff turned to face his brother, and in so doing rotated his right hand into the in-running blade, amputating four fingers. It was shown in testimony and by demonstration that a lower saw guard would probably have prevented this injury.

The jury in this case had to decide whether the seller of the saw had a right to assume that a home operator, or any operator, would always work safely and not commit the involuntary act just described. They also

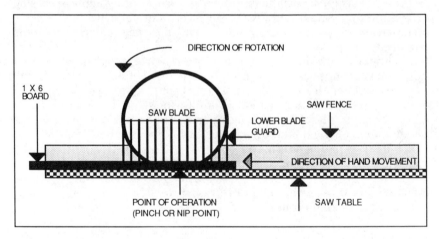

Figure 2-1. Radial arm saw. In this front view of a radial arm saw the rotating blade creates a nip where the saw blade meets the table. If the operator touches the blade, the hand can be drawn through the point of operation and an amputation will take place. While the lower blade guard is designed to retract as the work piece pushes against it, the guard will protect the operator against side penetration into the point of operation. In the case described the operator would have been protected against the results of his unsafe but unplanned movement.

had to consider the alleged negligence of the seller in not providing as standard equipment a relatively inexpensive lower blade guard when such a guard most likely would have left the plaintiff with an intact hand.

These considerations are discussed in this section under the title The Dependability of Safe Practice. Also discussed are six issues that I feel must be addressed when attempting litigation prevention; these are:

1. *The systems approach to hazard identification.* When analyzing a task, facility, or product for hazards each involved component, such as the man and machine, interacts with other components and therefore individual elements should not be isolated.
2. *The dependability of safe practice?* If all persons worked safely all the time, there would be far fewer accidents, little personal injury litigation, and probably no need for this book.
3. *The accident-prevention hierarchy.* Many persons, including some safety professionals, consider training the first and primary technique for preventing accidents. The accident-prevention hierarchy suggests otherwise.
4. *Responsibility for safety.* Considering the employee, employer, general contractor, subcontractor, owner, designer, manufacturer, and regulatory agency, what are their relative safety responsibilities? Juries must often decide for themselves.
5. *Should machines be "idiot proofed"?* Where does one draw the line between justifiable and outrageous behavior in the machine operation? The outcomes of many personal injury trials depend on clear thinking here.
6. *The mentality of accidents.* Does the way in which we perceive and measure accidents cause us to regard them as only a small threat to our health and welfare? Is the consequence of this perception that it promotes inaction until a serious problem occurs? These issues are at the very heart of why and how we, both as potential plaintiffs and potential defendants, act in behalf of accident prevention and why human nature many times must be overcome if litigation is to be avoided.

Information on how each of these issues can be used to promote litigation prevention will be included at the end of each discussion.

THE SYSTEMS APPROACH TO HAZARD IDENTIFICATION

A fundamental error that is often made when applying hazard-control methodology is to consider separately or to omit full, integrated consideration of all three major components involved with accidental injury. These components are *the persons involved, the environment,* and *the tools or equipment* (see Fig. 2-2). In the science of epidemiology these

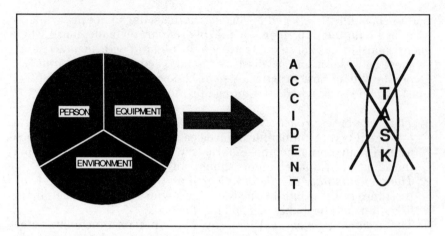

Figure 2-2. System diagram. In this diagram of a system (person, equipment, and environment) the introduction of an accident interferes with task accomplishment. Task accomplishment is dependent on the harmonious interaction between all three system components. By analyzing the system for hazards, persons interested in avoiding accidents that may lead to litigation can take prior action to eliminate or safeguard against events that can harm system components and prevent interruption of the task. Failure to deal with the components as a system can lead to inadequate or inappropriate accident-prevention measures.

elements would be known as the host, environment, and agent, respectively. For our purpose of litigation prevention these components are always considered to be operating together to perform a task, and this combination of elements is known as a *system*. To effectively prevent the injuries that ultimately produce litigation there must be an understanding of how system components interact.

For example, when assessing the safety merits of a truck that is to be used for delivery of steel angle iron, it is important to consider in addition to the truck itself (the equipment), the training, experience, and physical characteristics of the driver (the person), as well as the type of road and weather conditions (the environment) that will be encountered. If the truck is to deliver steel to Prudhoe Bay, Alaska, in the winter, failure to consider the driver and environmental requirments of this *delivery system* may result in the purchase of a vehicle incapable of negotiating Alaskan roads in winter, placed in the hands of an inexperienced or otherwise unqualified driver. It is plain that the truck alone is not the sole contributor to a probably very hazardous situation.

The safety of any system is dependent on the harmonious interaction of the three system elements: person, equipment, and environment. When a malfunction (accident) occurs to one or more elements, then the

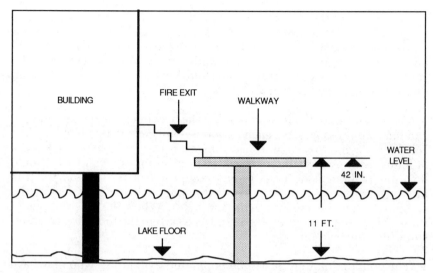

Figure 2-3. Drowning accident. The walkway depicted here represents a lethal hazard if it is not protected by a permanent rail. Once a victim falls into the water there is no assurance that rescue is possible, since in this case there was no rescue equipment, and no possibility of the victim being able to reach and hang on to the walkway from the water. In the winter the water temperature is 53°F, which can easily disable an accomplished swimmer. Because the hazard is so severe and because there cannot be any assurance that no person will ever fall from this open-sided platform, a prudent building owner or architect would install a 42-in. rail on both sides of the walkway.

entire system may be impaired, rendered unable to function, or even destroyed, and the accomplishment of the task prevented.

This principle can be illustrated in an actual case* in which a grandmother and her grandchild drowned in a lake.

Case Study 2-2

The grandmother was visiting her son, who lived with his family in a 70-unit condominium built out from the shoreline of a large lake. A walkway (see Fig. 2-3), constructed over deep water next to the building, was originally intended to be a pier, but for economic reasons was ultimately used as a fire escape path from the water side of the building to shore. The walkway was approximately 70 feet long, 10 feet wide, had no provision for tying up boats, and was open sided on both sides.

*Wrenn v. Spinnaker Bay. See Appendix.

It was a winter day when the grandmother and her grandchild decided to fly a kite from the walkway. After a time the child fell into the water and, because the walkway was 42 inches above the water level, he could not reach it to hang on to it. The grandmother, who was considered a good swimmer, dove in to rescue the child, but the water was so cold that neither person survived.

As the case unfolded it revealed that the architect, the owner, and the condominium association each at some point before this incident had considered what to do about the walkway. It was at those times that the building and its surrounding facilities, including the walkway, should have been thought of as a system, composed of the *equipment* (the building and walkway), the *persons* (the people living in or visiting the complex), and the *environment* (the lake). When the interactions of these three components are assessed as a system the following relationships become evident.

1. The condominium is or can be populated by families who may have nonswimmers as well as small children who will probably be nonswimmers. Visitors may also include nonswimmers. (The *person* component.)
2. Falling from the walkway could present a lethal hazard to nonswimmers or even to strong swimmers when the water is cold in winter. (The *environmental* component.)
3. The walkway is accessible to all tenants and guests. (*Equipment* component.)
4. As a fire escape it would be probable that in a panic situation at night, tenants escaping a fire could rush onto the walkway and be pushed into the water with lethal consequences. (The entire *system*.)
5. The walkway needs to be protected, at minimum, by a 42-in.-high guardrail. (The *solution* when considering the entire *system*.)

The preceding relationships were developed intuitively, which in this case was not difficult and well within the capability of the architect, owner, and the condominium association. There are somewhat more complex techniques within the discipline of systems safety analysis that would give a higher degree of confidence that appropriate analyses and corrective recommendations would be developed. These techniques are covered in Part II.

How the Principle of Systems Safety is Related to Litigation Prevention

Treating individual components as a system enables the visualization of how each component interacts with other system components to produce the problem. Simultaneously, this method permits the correct application of more comprehensive and effective solutions, since there is less chance of overlooking consideration of important component relationships. Litigation success for a plaintiff is far less likely when the defendant has used modern accident-prevention techniques to protect potential plaintiffs, because the protection is generally more effective. The bottom line is that where a systems approach has been used for accident prevention the defendant's actions are far less likely to be found negligent.

THE DEPENDABILITY OF SAFE PRACTICE

No matter how many times we may tell a child to look both ways before crossing a street we know that we cannot depend on that child being eternally vigilant in this regard. To augment their instructions parents still insist on well-marked crosswalks, laws that give pedestrians the right of way, traffic signals, adult guards at school crossings, etc. These and other similar controls compensate for a child's normal behavior, which parents instinctively know will many times keep their child from being watchful while crossing the street.

There is a lesson here for adults. Unquestionably, adults are usually more disciplined than children, but we need to consider the motivations that are present in the adult community. For example workers and their supervisors are encouraged to produce more product, at a faster pace, at less cost, with more quality. Promotions, pay, and transfer to more satisfying jobs often depend on how successfully workers perform relative to these demands. Add to these the stresses and priorities originating in the home environment.

The correlation is that just as a child's agenda makes it inappropriate for parents to depend only on consistent safe practice from their child, an adult's normal agenda makes it equally inappropriate to expect only safe practice. Adults do not want to be injured, but their daily routine includes varying degrees of successful risk-taking that is reinforced by the fact that it is successful (e.g., crossing the street where there is no crosswalk, with no resulting accident or injury). However, when risk-taking combines with poor design, unsafe facilities, unsafe conditions and equipment, then litigtion-producing injuries will occur.

If we are to create a climate for reduced litigation potential, we must augment the adult's normal desire to remain injury-free and compensate for risk-taking behavior with the application of controls such as guarding, restraint devices, protective equipment, warnings, safe design, training, and elimination of hazardous conditions. These controls compensate for the *normal* risk-taking human behavior that must be anticipated by those who wish to avoid litigation. Controls must be designed and applied to the full extent of the current state of the art if effective prevention is to be realized.

The implications of this principle are that designers, manufacturers of tools and equipment, and all those who are interested in litigation prevention must anticipate the consequences of unsafe practice in the use of their machines and facilities, and integrate state-of-the-art worker and consumer protection as a design component. Employers and general contractors that control worksites must design and implement safety programs with this principle in mind. Those of us who invite clients to use services or purchase food and products must also recognize that clients and customers will not always behave as we wish them to behave.

If it is certain that all persons can be expected to do the unexpected, then the rule must be that those of us who are in control, who manage, who design, who administer, must anticipate personal injury problems that may arise from the combination of unsafe practice and unsafe condition or design. The general rule is that *safe practice may never be relied upon.*

Once the principle of nonreliance on safe practice is accepted what follows must be careful analysis of possible hazardous situations along with the application of reasonable and prudent preventive action. The general types of risk analyses that can be made to determine accident vulnerability are described in Chapter 4. The specific types of prior analysis and corrective actions that can be taken are described in Part II.

How the Principle of Not Relying on Safe Practice Is Related to Litigation Prevention

Many defendants that I have observed became defendants because they assumed that their customers, clients, employees, or subcontractors would behave in a manner that would not place them in danger. Even when some defendants became aware that their customers, clients, etc., were not behaving rationally with respect to the defendant's products or facilities no action was taken until it was too late.

The principle of nonreliance on safe practice suggests that those who wish to avoid litigation should develop a "what if" strategy. That is, to determine at an early time how unsafe, unauthorized, or other unorthodox practices in the handling of products, facilities, or tasks will result in injury to those who engage in the irrational behavior. Once these determinations are made reasonable precautions can be taken before an injury occurs.

Case Study 2-3

Consider the case* of a machine that was designed to apply glue to wood slabs prior to the application of laminate. The machine was automatic in

---

Woodward v. Dusphol. See Appendix.

operation, and since the point of operation was well guarded, if operators followed the manufacturer's recommendations, they would never
be exposed to the powerful in-running rolls (see Fig. 2-4).

The machine needed to be cleaned at the end of operation each day.
Operators soon found that the device was easier to clean with the guard
removed and the rolls in motion. But the designers of the machine had
anticipated this and had placed an electrical interlock in the guard so
that the machine could not be energized when the guard was removed.

Unfortunately, despite this wise application of the "what if" ("what if
the guard is removed to clean the machine?") technique, employees still
routinely cleaned the machine in its unguarded and operating mode by
using a bent paper clip to defeat the interlock. One day an operator, in a

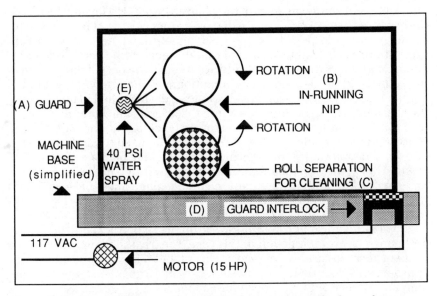

Figure 2-4. Glue-machine accident. This diagram shows the hazard to
workers who have access to the moving rolls. If a worker were to be caught
in rolls of this power, a fatal injury could occur. The guard (A) is interlocked
at (D), but the interlock can be easily defeated with a wire bent in the shape
of a U. By separating (C) the rolls, the nip point (B) is eliminated. This
would be a very satisfactory solution if the separation were protected by a
difficult to defeat interlock. The best solution from a safety and production
point of view would be the addition of an integral cleaning mechanism as
shown in (E). This would enable workers to effectively clean the machine
with pressurized water with the guard in place, thus eliminating the time
required for guard removal and restoration. The diagram is simplified to
show many ways of safeguarding.

hurry to get out of the plant before stores closed, was doing last-minute paperwork that she was instructed to complete after the machine was cleaned. When her supervisor suddenly appeared, she grabbed a rag, and without looking started to wipe the moving roll. Her right hand was grabbed by the in-running nip and subsequently had to be amputated.

A lawsuit against the manufacturer was initiated. During discovery it was found that the guard interlock was easily defeated by inserting a paper clip bent in the form of a U into the female side of the interlock. Also, the manufacturer's representative while on a plant visit had suggested to the operators that they clean the machine while it was running and with the guard removed, and had demonstrated how to defeat the interlock.

The manufacturer had correctly foreseen the removal of the guard by anticipating the desire to clean the machine more rapidly. Where it failed (the suit settled in favor of the plaintiff) was: (1) The interlock was too easily defeated. (2) To assure that operators would not be exposed to an unguarded nip point, the interlock should have depended on roll separation. Such an interlock could be designed to be very difficult to defeat, and this arrangement would accomplish the best of both worlds: the rolls could be cleaned while in motion and the nip point would be eliminated. (3) To help accomplish what the designer had in mind when the guard interlock was integrated into the original machine, all persons who had reason to contact the customer, such as the manufacturer's representative, should have been trained in the need for and use of the interlocked guard. (4) Recognizing that the machine needed to be cleaned daily, the best means for litigation prevention in this case was to provide for integrated automatic cleaning that would have enabled rapid cleaning with the guard in place. This latter solution is best both from a production and safety viewpoint.

The manufacturer and designer were on the right track, but did not go far enough to avoid litigation in this case. Clearly the plaintiff's actions could be termed careless or even negligent, but if the machine had been appropriately guarded, then these kinds of careless but predictable human actions would have been forestalled.

HIERARCHY OF ACCIDENT PREVENTION

Once a hazard is identified, hazard control must take place to avoid litigation. Fortunately, there is a sensible generic blueprint for an approach to hazard control: the hierarchy of accident prevention. Because this blueprint looks like common knowledge, it is difficult for a defendant to justify misapplication or omission of hierarchy principles. Experience shows, however, that many defendants become defendants because they only partially apply, incorrectly apply, or omit this type of hazard control altogether. The accident prevention hierarchy, as outlined below, is composed of five steps in order of preference.

I. *Primary Accident Prevention Techniques*
   1. Eliminate the hazard
   2. Safeguard the hazard
II. *Secondary Accident Prevention Techniques*
   3. Warn (at point of danger)
   4. Train and instruct
   5. Provide protective equipment

Persons who are untrained in accident prevention and sometimes even safety professionals will identify training as the first and most important method for accident prevention. While training is important and should not be omitted, it must not be relied upon as the sole or most effective source of accident prevention. To rely exclusively on training violates the previously discussed fundamental principle of accident prevention, *do not depend upon safe practice.*

The first and most effective methodology is to eliminate the hazard. For example, if there is an interface between pedestrians, cars, and railroad trains at a crossing, the most effective way to reduce or eliminate the possibility of fatal accidents is to construct a tunnel for cars and a protected walkway for pedestrians. If this is not feasible because of cost, ground water, or other reason, then the crossing can be safeguarded with a guard tower, or automatic gates equipped with visual and audible signals. Warning signs would also be appropriate, but exclusive reliance on training pedestrians, drivers, and railroad engineers on correct behavior at rail crossings obviously would be ineffective because of the futility of relying on safe practice.

As a general rule the secondary accident-prevention techniques are applied along with the primary techniques, but should not be selected as the sole prevention method unless the primary techniques would be infeasible or relatively ineffective. A typical case where a secondary technique would be exclusive is the marketing of a chemical for consumer use. Here the only accident/illness prevention methodology available to the manufacturer is number 3, "Warn at the point of danger."

How the Hierarchy of Accident Prevention is Related to Litigation Prevention

In personal injury cases, the prevention hierarchy fixes priorities, establishes optimum accident-prevention methods, and can serve to identify incorrect or inappropriate approaches to accident/injury prevention. The following is an illustration of hierarchy use.

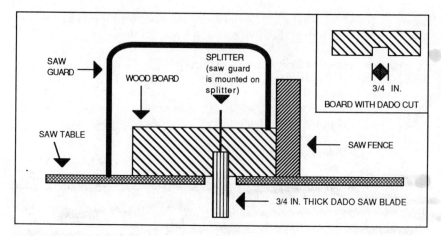

Figure 2-5. Guarding a dado blade. The splitter is a vertical piece of metal about 1/16 in. thick. Its purpose is to separate the two sides of a board as the board runs through the saw blade. This is particularly important when ripping a warped board that may bind and pinch the blade. If the blade is pinched, a dangerous kickback can occur. When the splitter is fixed as shown in this diagram a dado cut obviously cannot be made unless the splitter and the attached saw guard are removed. However, when the splitter is retractable it can be adjusted out of the way below the surface of the saw table. A specially designed guard can then be used with the dado blade.

Case Study 2-4

In a school shop case*, a student amputated three fingers on her right hand while using a table saw. The saw was purchased with a special guard and a retractable splitter that enabled the guard to be used in a dado cut (see Fig. 2-5). The instructor had removed the guard, however, and instructed students to dado cut without the guard on the pretext that dados could not be cut with a guard because of the splitter. In his deposition the instructor stated that he felt that since students would most probably not use guards when working with table saws outside the school shop, he felt that they should not use them while in the school shop. He further stated that guards were a nuisance, because they increased the time it took to complete each cut on the saw.

From the point of view of possible injury, the instructor was inviting disaster for his students. From the point of view of litigation, he was

*Altick v. Kent. See Appendix.

inviting disaster for himself and the school district. In order to properly instruct students he needed to emphasize that the use of guarding is an integral part of accomplishing the job rather than an impediment that could be discarded. If he had strictly followed the hierarchy of prevention, which is critical on so dangerous a machine as a table saw, he would have determined that the hazard required safeguarding. Instead of using the unique protection supplied with the saw, the instructor relied on his demonstration of saw use and verbal cautions on the serious nature of saw injuries. These are two secondary prevention methods—"warn," and "train and instruct." This accident-prevention methodology could not hope to succeed in the school shop environment, where relatively untrained students work with one of the most dangerous of woodworking machines.

Chapter 3

Responsibility for Safety

We often hear a manager state or write, "Everyone is responsible for safety." What does this really mean? Surely assigning safety responsibility to all employees or to all managers has to be a good thing. Or is it? If we examine this statement more closely, it is clear that what it really means is that no person is responsible for safety. The manager (or parent, or chief designer, or supervisor, etc.) has successfully off-loaded safety responsibility to everyone else and therefore feels no ownership or need to develop and conduct a viable safety program. What generally happens instead is that injuries and illness are unaffected by planned preventive action and can become rampant. The ultimate consequence of this brand of leadership is personal injury litigation.

Understanding who or what entity is responsible for safety is vital to the establishment of liability. *Understanding the factors that influence the establishment of liability is vital to litigation prevention.* Juries are often faced with conficting feelings when they must decide if the plaintiff, the employer, the general contractor, the industrial safety/ health professional, or the machine designer and manufacturer is liable in some degree for an injury. In some cases regulatory agencies have been assigned liability because of their failure to discover an existent hazard during an inspection. The fact that liability is often an issue illustrates that there is not a clear separation of responsibility when more than one entity is involved in an injury situation. The following section contains a brief general description of the safety responsibility of the six entities previously mentioned.

SAFETY RESPONSIBILITIES

The Plaintiff

Plaintiffs as a class have the responsibility to avoid injury to themselves, but strong consideration must be given to their normal life situations; for example: (1) to produce as much product as possible, in the least possible time, with superior quality and at the least cost attainable; (2) to carry out their normal daily routines with an overlay of personal problems arising from relationships, economics, and their current tasks; (3) the normal rigors of being a child; (4) temporary or permanent physical or mental impairment.

To ignore these stresses is to place potential plaintiffs in a superhuman role, one which they often cannot or will not play. The ultimate result is that vulnerability to litigation is greatly increased when the human side of the equation is ignored. The temptation to place prior blame on workers or customers (e.g., "only a stupid person would operate the machine without a guard," or "why didn't she look where she was going?") to avoid application of accident-prevention devices and methods is a trap that is often sprung in the courtroom.

The Employer

The employer has the primary responsibility for worker safety. This involves:

1. Maintaining a safe workplace (when the workplace is under the employer's control)
2. Establishing a viable safety program and participating in that program
3. Integrating safety and industrial hygiene criteria into normal operating routines of the company or agency. This refers to the use of safety accountability systems
4. Assessing the effectiveness and effort level of the safety program
5. Developing and implementing an accident-illness-prevention program plan

Part II contains a much more comprehensive description of an employer-developed-and-operated safety program.

The General Contractor

General contractors are responsible for the safety of their own workers and for the employees of the subcontractors to the extent that they (the general contractors) exercise overall control of the worksite and the planning, sequencing, approval, and completion of the job. When subcontractors are employed on a construction worksite, it is important that the general contractor hold preconstruction conferences with their subcontractors where they should discuss pertinent and specific safety matters.

The responsibility of general contractors requires a great deal of attention because they do not enjoy immunity from litigation brought by subcontractor employees. In fact, they are a target of opportunity for subcontractor employees who sustain injuries on a general-contractor-controlled jobsite. Often such a lawsuit will result in much greater recovery for the employee than would worker's compensation.

General contractors and owners depend on contractual language for tort protection. For example, if a general contractor hires a roofing subcontractor to reroof a building, a contract will most probably be drawn that contains clauses designed to protect the general contractor from a third-party suit in the event a roofer is seriously injured. The safety provisions in the contract are also designed to encourage the subcontractor to employ and monitor safe practices on the job. Some of these clauses are listed below.

1. Hold harmless agreements, where the general contractor is indemnified by the subcontractor for any injuries sustained by subcontractor employees.
2. The subcontractor will comply with OSHA and state safety and health regulations.
3. The subcontractor will comply with the general contractor's safety and health regulations, which may be contained in a document as large as 250 or more pages.
4. The subcontractor will submit an approved safety plan before work begins.
5. The subcontractor's employees will receive safety orientation from the general contractor before work begins.
6. The subcontractor and/or the subcontractor's employees are subject to dismissal by the general contractor if safety violations are observed.
7. The subcontractor is subject to scheduled or random safety inspections by the general contractor or owner.
8. The owner may also dismiss any subcontractor whom the owner feels is working unsafely.

These contract provisions are impressive, but they may not be as good as they look because they are subject to individual interpretation and generally vary widely in implementation. In court these clauses can work against the general contractor who is relying upon them for protection.

As but one example, take a closer look at clause 5, the object of which is to create a uniform level of knowledge of construction site hazards and, if necessary, to be able to show in court that the subcontractor was made aware of the nature of construction hazards by the general contractor.

To determine how this provision is often misused and why it is ineffective as an accident- and litigation-prevention device, consider the use of prior orientation on a roofing subcontractor's employees. Typically, to facilitate the orientation process, many general contractors develop a videotape covering construction site hazards and requires each subcontractor employee to view it. Many times, however, the description of specific hazards to which roofers are exposed are either missing or inadequately covered in the tape. Further, information on hazards that are peculiar to the current job may be omitted, such as the precautions that must be taken when "twenty roof holes are cut at varying times by another subcontractor."

If, by showing the program the general contractor assumes that each roofer who views the presentation becomes knowledgeable of the most severe roofing hazards that will be encountered on the job, and will perform the necessary safe practices to avoid serious injury during the life of the job, the general contractor has made an error that may have serious and negative consequences in court.

If, for example, a roofer suffers a catastrophic injury from a fall through one of the previously mentioned roof holes, and he (or his estate) sues the general contractor for failing to maintain a safe workplace, clause 5 will work against the defendant because the orientation did not cover the specific life-threatening hazards to which each roofer would be exposed. The general contractor incorrectly assumed that the roofing subcontractor would know and follow safe practice.

The general contractor's orientation for employees of the roofing and hole-cutting subcontractors should have covered (1) detailed protection of workers on high workstations such as roofs, (2) the methods and equipment for safeguarding roof holes, and (3) the specific safe practices that would be expected of subcontractor employees during each construction phase of the project on which they were hired. Three of many examples of such instructions follow.

1. All roof holes will be framed, covered, with covers nailed and marked immediately after the holes are cut.
2. The procurement of materials for framing and covering roof holes will be the responsibility of the hole-cutter subcontractor.
3. No subcontractor employee will abandon an uncovered roof hole for any length of time without covering and marking the opening.

While this example is important to an injury-free workplace the key element is that job-related roof safety issues are specifically addressed. Not only will such treatment convince a jury that roofing workers were given appropriate instruction, but the instruction itself will serve to prevent accidents and relieve all parties from litigation.

In this example the general contractor should not assume that the subcontractor understands how to prevent injury to its employees. Instead, the general contractor must assume that the subcontractor will most likely shortcut safe practice, even in the event the subcontractor understands how to conduct the job safely.

It is hard for juries to understand why a general contractor will monitor and control subcontractor employees when they are behind schedule or when they mess up a job, but will deny any responsibility for monitoring and correcting unsafe subcontractor actions. By controlling the subcontractor's safe practice the general contractor is recognizing the reality of the workplace and is not handling safety any differently than job performance and quality. This is what a jury would expect and why juries will many times not permit a general contractor to be protected by contractual clauses, particularly when the jury realizes that they were not conceived in good faith or were boilerplate provisions not meant to be enforced until a problem arose.

The Safety Professional

The safety professional is responsible for convincing management of management's role in the safety program and for guiding management in the exercise of its safety responsibility.

To those uninitiated in the mechanics of occupational safety, the safety professional is the likely candidate for total safety responsibility. This view is shared by many members of the management community, and even by some safety professionals, but it is a mistake from which companies and agencies will suffer inferior results.

Responsibility for safety belongs to the management hierarchy. It does not belong to the safety professional, or the union, and it is not the exclusive domain of the first-line supervisor.

When management states that it will build 2000 product units per month, it must set up and track the necessary workers, funding, and facilities to accomplish the job. Similarly, when management states that the company will operate a safe and healthful work environment (and only management can state this and make it work), it must set up and track similar resources. Unfortunately, this simple rule eludes many company officials, particularly when they must decide how management will exercise its safety responsibility.

Where safety programs fail, management has placed responsibility for the safety of its work force in the hands of a safety professional and has charged that person with total responsibility for the discipline. To many managers this is a logical approach, since they feel uncomfortable with safety and are only too glad to hand it over to a "professional" who can take this nebulous and unproductive detail off their hands. Unfortunately, what usually follows this basic organizational defect is listed below:

1. The safety professional is asked to correct hazards over which he or she has little or no control.
2. Safety is treated as a separate entity and is routinely excluded from normal operational functions such as budget development, scheduling, and performance reviews.

3. The safety professional is often expected to control unsafe practices that occur on the factory or office floor in organizations not under his or her supervision. These unsafe practices usually occur at widely separated locations and at varied time intervals. This is like trying to cover a football field with a napkin.
4. Limited resources are available for significant hazard correction, since safety is not part of the company or agency standard budget development process.
5. A profound disillusionment sets in, resulting in little accomplishment, a set of ulcers for the safety professional, and a feeling by the managers that something is wrong, but they are not quite sure what it is. Managers seldom consider their own management styles.

The Machine Designer and Manufacturer

These individuals are responsible for anticipating misuse of their equipment, and with this in mind, designing state-of-the-art safe equipment, plus warning of danger in the most appropriate manner. Failure to do so opens the door to litigation, sometimes decades after the device is sold to the customer.

Consider the following case* involving the binder jack, a well-respected, widely used device in the logging industry that is used to bind chains around a load of logs that are being transported on a logging truck. The jack is simple in construction and principle of operation. When chains encircle the loaded logs the binder jack is attached to the two loose ends, the handle is pulled, and the chains are drawn taut around the logs (see Fig. 3-1).

Case Study 3-1

An experienced log truck driver was in the process of binding his load, and had just tightened one of three rings of chain. Suddenly the jack explosively opened, hitting the arm of the driver with excruciating force. The injury was severe and permanently disabling.

The design of the binder jack was defective in that in the fully tightened position the handle protruded somewhat from the body of the jack. If the protruding part of the handle encountered an irregularity such as a bump on a log the handle could be forced back and the jack would open with explosive force.

A close examination showed that a minor change in the design of the body of the jack would prevent the handle from protruding, thus eliminating this hazard.

The designer of the binder jack undoubtedly was familiar with the tremendous forces involved with binding a load of logs. An analysis

---

*Case not filed; defendant settled.

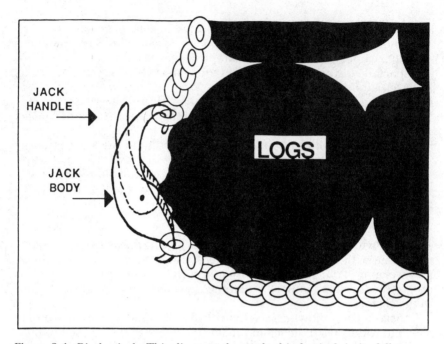

Figure 3-1. Binder jack. This diagram shows the binder jack in its fully locked position. Notice how the bulge in the handle pushes against the log. In this configuration it is possible for the protrusion on the log surface to push back the jack handle so that the jack releases with explosive force. Changing the shape of the jack body as shown by the crosshatched section would prevent any portion of the jack handle from contacting the log surface. This correction made in the design phase of the jack would have prevented litigation over thirty years after initial marketing of this useful product.

should have been made before marketing this product to determine whether those forces could be accidentally unleashed, and design corrections accomplished.

As it turned out this case was quickly settled out of court.

Sample analyses that could have been made, such as hazard effects and control analysis and fault tree analysis, are described in Part II.

Regulatory Agencies

Regulatory agencies such as the Occupational Safety and Health Administration stimulate voluntary compliance with OSHA standards through random inspection of workplaces, the imposition of monetary fines, and coordination of employee safety and health-related criminal codes with the Justice Department.

Both plaintiff and defense will attempt to use OSHA standards to buttress their cases. In product liability cases and others where negligence is an issue OSHA standards have no direct application since they directly apply only to the employer. OSHA does not approve products, but they do stipulate how products are to be safeguarded, and in some cases will formulate performance standards (standards that describe how a machine should perform relative to safety, as opposed to standards that describe how a machine should be configured to achieve the same level of safety).

Other than OSHA there are many safety criteria and standards-producing agencies that can affect the litigation process; These include the American Society for Testing and Materials (ASTM), Underwriters Laboratories (UL), the Society of Automotive Engineers (SAE), and the National Institute for Occupational Safety and Health (NIOSH).

HOW RESPONSIBILITY FOR SAFETY IS RELATED TO LITIGATION PREVENTION

These guidelines for safety responsibility should be used by potential defendants to determine the quantity and quality of their accident-prevention activities. In the example of the machine that applied glue to wood slabs (Chapter 1), the designer did not go far enough to protect machine operators against anticipated misuse even though the misuse was against the manufacturer's recommendations. Had the designer understood the importance of making the interlock difficult to defeat or better yet, understood that designing an integral cleaning device would eliminate the hazard [better to eliminate than safeguard a hazard (see hierarchy of prevention)], a damaging lawsuit would have been avoided.

A general contractor who feels he can totally depend on the safety knowledge and safe practice of a subcontractor is extremely vulnerable to a third-party lawsuit. The eight guidelines listed earlier in this chapter advise general contractors to determine the hazards to which its subcontractors will be exposed, and to preplan the elimination or safeguarding of those hazards before the job begins.

Once a potential defendant has recognized the criteria for safety responsibility, meaningful litigation-prevention activities can be implemented.

Litigation prevention is an overt action considered and planned by persons who by the nature of their role in life are responsible for this activity. This would include managers, parents, designers, manufacturers, lawyers, safety and health professionals, risk managers, and consultants. Their efforts are most effective before accidents and injuries occur; their efforts are least effective when they or their agents must appear in the courtroom pleading or defending a personal injury lawsuit. Recognition of litigation-prevention responsibility is therefore an important first step in the litigation-prevention process.

Chapter 4

Idiot-proofed Machines and the Mentality of Accidents

A question that juries often consider is, How far must a machine designer go to protect a machine operator who flagrantly misuses the machine?

Case Study 4-1

Consider the case* of two automatic panel saw operators who operated a machine together and who had established a routine for cutting ends off residential doors. Operator one would place the door in the saw in the correct position and then notify operator two, who was positioned at a remote-control station, that the saw was ready and safe to operate. When operator two pressed the start button an hydraulically controlled clamp would actuate to hold the door in position. The saw would travel downward to automatically cut the end off the door and then return to its original position. The saw blade turned in a groove in the underside of the clamp, preventing operator access to the revolving blade (see Fig. 4-1).

An examination of the operation revealed that the signal that operator one gave operator two was sometimes verbal and sometimes a hand signal. This operation was carried out without incident for eight years, when a misinterpretation occurred and the saw was started when operator one, stationed at the saw head, had his right hand in the wrong place. It was caught by the clamp and was subsequently taken off by the traveling saw blade.

Lytikainen v. *Rodgers Machinery.* See Appendix.

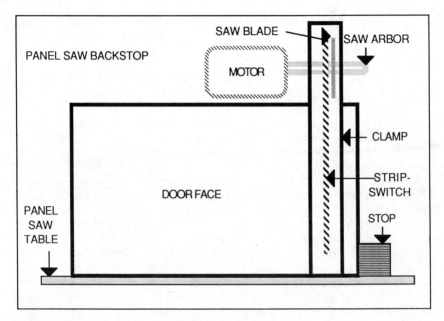

Figure 4-1. Panel saw accident. Plan view of the panel saw involved with the hand amputation described in the text. The motor, arbor, and saw blade, located behind the backstop, travel automatically down and back when actuated. The saw blade runs in a groove in the bottom of the clamp and therefore the operator is protected from access to the running blade in normal operation. When the operator's hand was caught in the hydraulically operated clamp, he could not extracate himself or shut off the machine without the stripswitch (which was missing at the time of the accident).

There were three major problems with this situation:

1. The saw design was inherently unsafe in that it did not provide a shut-off switch for operator one, in the event that he was trapped by the clamp while the saw was running in the automatic mode. A strip switch running the length of the top side of the clamp would have filled this function.
2. The method of signaling between the two operators was subject to misinterpretation, and would eventually lead to accidental actuation of the saw. It took eight years in this case, but it did happen.
3. The operation had been run successfully for eight years, and this reinforced the idea that it was a safe operation and a safe design. The fact was that neither the operation nor the design was safe.

Particularly when a machine is designed for operation by more than one operator, the designer must provide all the operators with a way to shut the machine down in an emergency situation. The designer must not depend on the consistent safe practice of the operators. In this case, the operators and their employer had a false sense of security because of the eight-year, accident-free record.

This analysis reveals some important considerations. Despite the fact that workers cannot be depended upon to work safely 100 percent of the time, they will work injury-free *most* of the time. This is true because hazards will seldom result in an accident each time the hazard is encountered, unsafe practices will result in accident and injury infrequently, and accidents occur much more frequently than accidents with injuries, particularly serious injuries. These relationships reinforce risk-taking behavior, and a prudent designer of machinery therefore recognizes these realities of machine use and does not define persons that may be injured on his/her machine as "idiots."

There are times when a worker is negligent and where the machine designer cannot compensate for unreasonable behavior by the operator. An example of this is when the designer of a machine provides an interlocked guard where the interlock is difficult to defeat. If an operator removes the guard, defeats the interlock, and operates the machine in this condition, the designer cannot be expected to have compensated for this unreasonable act. However, if the machine is much easier to operate, or clean, or is significantly more productive in the unguarded mode, the machine should be redesigned initially so that it is far less desirable to operate the machine without the guard. In any case suitable warnings must be provided at the point of danger.

HOW THE QUESTION "SHOULD MACHINES BE IDIOT-PROOFED?" RELATES TO LITIGATION PREVENTION

A popular defense against personal injury litigation is that the plaintiff acted unreasonably or recklessly and was the primary cause of his or her own injury. While this defense is sometimes successful, the human factors and ergonomic (human engineering) considerations often place the burden on the designer and manufacturer to compensate for the human component. Those interested in avoiding litigation cannot reasonably rely on proving the negligence of the plaintiff (you may not rely on safe practice) and will not be required to do this if the initial design is correct.

The Mentality of Accidents

What we are concerned about here are the reasons why potential plaintiffs and potential defendants will assume the risk of accidental injury when the consequences of such injury can be physiologically and economically devastating. Why will a person who has just purchased a radial arm saw operate that saw without instruction or even consulting the manual? In just such an incident the operator, a high school English teacher, had three fingers of his right hand amputated the first time he used his new saw. The teacher was confident he could operate the saw from prior observation and from "common sense."

Why will a manufacturer of a beer bottling machine design a lever that requires a worker to place his or her hands within one inch of an unguarded and lethal point of operation. In this case,* the operator's hand and arm were drawn into the point of operation and amputated. The machine's designer was not aware of the need for guarding the points of operation and was not schooled in the various safety analysis techniques open to him.

Why would the project manager of a 22-million-dollar factory-remodeling project be unconcerned about how roof holes are covered after they have been cut? This oversight resulted in a catastrophic 26-foot-fall injury to an installer of the ventilation equipment that fit into the holes.† When questioned why he did not feel responsible for this problem, the project manager stated, "Everyone on my staff was responsible for safety."

Many psychologists agree, and most of us know, that behavior that is positively reinforced is behavior that is likely to continue. When a worker shortcuts a job, has an accident but no injury; when a restaurant has a badly placed step-down for its patrons that creates accidents but no injuries; when a housewife cuts vegetables the wrong way and the knife slips but no injury occurs—all these events reinforce the idea that it's okay to do it the wrong way. As you will see in the next few paragraphs, studies have shown that we are not "taught lessons" by accident experience; but usually have our poor practices reinforced.

The latter condition has personal application to those of us who wish to prevent litigation. With respect to accident experience it says that the realities of everyday living, on or off the job, encourage risk-taking, undervalue the threat of accidents, and encourage the occurrence of accidental injury. In this context consider the following:

1. Heinrich, an early pioneer in the field of accident prevention, developed a well-known relationship between injury-producing and non-injury-producing accidents (see Fig. 4-2). He said that for every lost-time injury there will be 29 accidents with minor injuries and 300 accidents with no injury! The correct interpretation of Heinrich's rule is that for a single individual who experiences 330 similar accidents, there will be only one major injury, 29 minor injuries, and 300 incidents with no injury. We can conclude from this, even if Heinrich is off the mark by 25 percent, that on a personal level accidents are hardly a threat.

A study similar to Heinrich's was conducted by safety philosopher,

*Brown v. Crown, Cork, and Seal. See Appendix.
†Wilkie v. Carnation. See Appendix and Chapter 11.

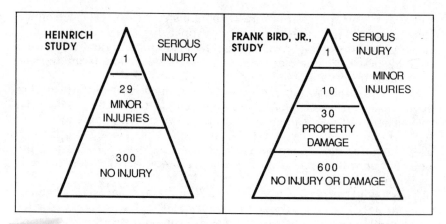

Figure 4-2. How injuries and accidents relate. (*Left*) As reported by Heinrich, an individual experiencing 330 similar accidents would sustain one serious injury. This relationship is important because it relates to the influence that accident experience has on whether or not persons perceive accidents as a threat. Here accidents appear relatively benign because the chance of serious injury is only one in 330 incidents. We conclude that on an individual level, occurrence of accidents do little to stimulate accident-prevention activity. We must keep in mind that this relationship is deceptive, in that accidental injuries pose a very significant, but veiled threat. (*Right*) In 1969 Frank E. Bird, Jr., analyzed 1,753,498 accidents reported by 297 companies. The relationships shown here are not dependent on similar occurrences, nor do they deal with the same individual as in the Heinrich study. The relationship does indicate that accidental injuries pose even less of a threat than indicated in the Heinrich study. However, the inclusion of the property damage component can cause a change in perception of the effects of accidents, particularly if the damage is costly to repair. The threat, however, is real (see text).

researcher, and professional, Frank Bird, Jr. His findings, described in Figure 4-2, give even more support to the notion that accidental injury is a rare occurrence.

2. The construction industry is well known for its high injury rate, which in the latter half of the 1980s varied between 14 to 16 reportable injuries per 100 employees. This means that a typical project superintendent with a crew of 50 will see about 7 lost-time injuries in a year's time. If that superintendent is as busy as most, it is questionable that such an injury experience will cause a flurry of accident-prevention activity, or stimulate him (or her) to examine the way that safety is transacted. Also, the array of protectionist contract provisions gives still more credence to a sense of security.

A remarkable aspect of the construction industry accident experience is that it is not true that the nature of the work makes a high accident frequency inevitable. Companies such as DuPont Construction have achieved consistent rates of below one to three injuries per 100 employees doing heavy construction. The secret is hard-nosed enforcement of programmed, preplanned safety measures and integration of safety into daily operating routines. In Part III, I discuss techniques for effective safety programming for the construction industry.

3. There are psychological factors at work that cause us as humans to treat accidental injuries with less respect. The following letter, well-known in the "folklore" of occupational safety, illustrates what can happen to a worker who may not have been as skilled or lucky as he should have been. The point of using this letter, ostensibly from a brick-layer in Barbados to his contracting firm, is to illustrate that accident situations many times tickle our funny bone, but the ultimate injury can be deadly serious.

Respected Sir, when I got to the building, I found that the hurricane had knocked some bricks off the top. So I rigged up a beam with a pulley at the top of the building and hoisted up a couple of barrels full of bricks. When I had fixed the building, there were a lot of bricks left over.

I hoisted the barrel back up again and secured the line at the bottom, and then went up and filled the barrel with extra bricks. Then I went to the bottom and cast off the line.

Unfortunately, the barrel of bricks was heavier than I was and before I knew what was happening the barrel started down, jerking me off the ground. I decided to hang on and halfway up I met the barrel coming down and received a severe blow on the shoulder.

I then continued to the top, banging my head against the beam and getting my finger jammed into the pulley. When the barrel hit the ground it bursted its bottom, allowing all the bricks to spill out.

I was now heavier than the barrel and so started down at high speed. Halfway down, I met the barrel coming up and received severe injuries to my shins. When I hit the ground I landed on the bricks, getting several painful cuts from the sharp edges.

At this point I must have lost my presence of mind, because I let go of the line. The barrel then came down giving me another heavy blow on the head and putting me in the hospital.

I respectfully request sick leave.

The authenticity of this letter may be subject to doubt, but to many of us it is a funny story that creates a vivid picture of an oscillating bricklayer and barrel. The letter also illustrates another human problem. That is, that we as humans tend to treat accident situations with humor and that may help encourage a correspondingly light treatment of accident prevention.

4. Why would a soldier run onto a battlefield where random bullets are flying and his comrades are falling dead or wounded all about him? Is it superpatriotism or overwhelming hate for the enemy? I think these may be only a small component of what drives the soldier onto the battlefield. Primarily I believe his action is motivated by another aspect of human nature that also contributes to a reduced concern for accident prevention, that is, risk-taking behavior inspired by the idea that "It won't happen to me." This human trait has obvious and detrimental application to the frequency and severity of accidental injury, and is another reason why the mentality of accidents is an important aspect of causation.

How the Mentality of Accidents Relates to Litigation Prevention

This chapter is devoted to the premise that although accidental injury is a grave threat to the well-being of the U.S. population, the population, being subject to human traits, tends to disregard the threat, as illustrated by generally complacent behavior toward accident reduction. Although accidents represent as great a threat as disease, both in frequency and severity of harm, we spend 300 times more for disease research than for accident-prevention investigation.

An extract from the Executive Summary of "Injury in America, a Continuing Public Health Problem," written by the Committee on Trauma Research, the Commission on Life Sciences of the National Research Council, and the Institute of Medicine, states:

1. Each year, more than 140,000 Americans die from injuries, and one person in three suffers a nonfatal injury.
2. Injury is the last major plague of the young. Injuries kill more Americans aged 1–34 than all diseases combined, and they are the leading cause of death up to the age of 44.
3. Injuries cause the loss of more working years of life than all forms of heart disease and cancer combined.
4. One of every eight hospital beds is occupied by an injured patient.
5. Every year more than 80,000 people in the United States join the ranks of those with unnecessary, but permanently disabling, injury of the brain or spinal cord.
6. Injuries constitute one of the most expensive health problems, costing $75–$100 billion a year directly and indirectly, but research on injury receives less than 2 cents out of every federal dollar spent for research on health problems.

On top of all this civil court dockets in large metropolitan areas are filled, with 1- to 3-year waiting lists for courtroom availability for personal injury cases. The Yellow Pages of the Seattle metropolitan area, which services a population of about 1.5 million, contains 52 pages of attorney listings. While not all of these attorneys are engaged in personal injury cases, we have to assume that there is a direct relationship between the number of attorneys and the number of cases.

All six issues important to litigation prevention direct your attention to the fact that it is human nature to have relatively copious quantities of accidental injuries, it is human nature to be complacent about these injuries, and it is human nature to avoid concentrated and studious application of accidental-injury control. To prevent litigation it is necessary to recognize this problem and make a conscious effort to control hazards. It is with the control of litigation-producing hazards that this section and the other sections of this book are concerned.

Chapter 5

Risk and Danger: Their Meaning and Control

It is important at the outset for readers to understand the meaning of the terms associated with risk assessment. These terms are, *danger, risk, hazard, probability, accident,* and *harm.*

Danger can be defined as a condition that has the ability to cause harm. Regarding litigation there are two significant ways of dealing with danger: (1) we may increase or decrease the ability of a condition to produce harm, or (2) we may increase or decrease the amount of harm a condition may produce. In both instances we are affecting the degree of danger. If we place a guardrail on the edge of a 100-foot cliff, we are reducing the chance that someone or something will go over the cliff. This would decrease the ability of that condition—the unguarded cliff—to produce harm. We can decrease the amount of harm that would occur to a person or thing that fell from the cliff by exchanging sand for rocks at the bottom of the cliff or raising the lower surface so that the fall distance is decreased in a meaningful way. In both of these examples we have decreased the danger of the cliff edge.

Risk has been defined as the probability that damage of a specified nature to specified system components (see Chapter 2 for a definition of *system*) will occur over a defined time period. An example of an expression of risk would be "a construction worker is three times as likely to sustain a fatal fall as a machinist."

To many individuals risk and danger are synonymous, since if you increase risk you also increase the ability of a system to cause harm or damage. There is greater risk to life and limb in falling from a sixth-floor window than from a second-floor window. There is also greater danger from the sixth-floor fall. If we place a guard over the sixth-floor window, we decrease both danger and risk to the tenant. It is important, however, to consider the probabilistic nature of risk; important because for purposes of litigation prevention it is necessary that probability be de-emphasized and that danger be the prime factor for the determination of corrective action. A judgment as to the acceptability of risk is always subjective, even when highly sophisticated methods are used to objectively determine risk. When danger is high and a judgment is made to do nothing because of an expectation of remote or extremely remote probability of occurrence, the stage is set for future litigation. See the paragraphs on Probability of Occurrence for a more detailed discussion of this issue.

A *hazard* is a specific agent that under defined circumstances would cause damage to a system element. Every dangerous situation would contain one or more hazards. In the open window example the hazard would be the fall from one level to another. The defined circumstance would be that the person who is harmed must fall out of the open window. It is important to note that hazards may be unsafe conditions or unsafe practices.

Instead of the open window let us say that the window was protected by ordinary window glass and two teenage boys were roughhousing in the room. During their struggles one boy is thrown against the window, crashes through, and falls to the ground. The roughhousing would be classified as a hazard.

Hazards are often a combination of unsafe conditions and practices. Consider the classic case of the landing gear actuation lever that is of similar design to the flap actuator and is positioned in the cockpit where it can be mistaken for it. Then after many flawless takeoffs and landings, the pilot mistakenly retracts the landing gear while the plane is sitting on the ground. The unsafe practice of the pilot has combined with the hazardous design to severely damage a system component.

A safety analysis would clearly point out that the landing gear lever must be easily distinguishable from other levers, located in its own special place on the console, and the gear itself must be interlocked so that it is normally not capable of being retracted while the airplane is on the ground. The correction of hazards is a primary task in the control of litigation.

Probability deals with the likelihood that a hazard will cause an accident, the likelihood that the accident will cause harm, and with the variation in the severity of the damage. Probability may be expressed as an event over time, such as "failure of a system component will occur in X hours of operation," or with the time factor implicit, such as "the failure of the valve is highly (or remotely) probable." In this book we will deviate from the norm in the treatment of probability to accomplish effective litigation prevention.

An *accident* is defined as an unplanned event that *may* result in damage (harm) to a living or nonliving structure (system component). The accident is the center component in the hazard–accident–harm continuum (see Fig. 5-1). This continuum indicates that harm (inter-

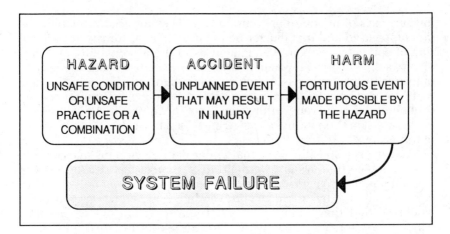

Figure 5-1. The hazard–accident–harm continuum. The important point to consider in this diagram is that seldom do accidents result from an unsafe condition alone or an unsafe practice alone, but usually result from a combination of the two. Also, an accident may occur without injury (harm or damage). The text will increasingly concern itself with the operational and administrative means for controlling hazards so that the hazard–accident–harm continuum is interrupted and both system failure and litigation are prevented.

changeable with injury or damage) results in system failure, which could mean that a living component of the system is injured or killed while the equipment component is still capable of operating and producing, or vice versa. For litigation-prevention purposes this would not be an acceptable condition.

Harm is damage to a system element. The hazard classification matrix that is described later in this section enables the analyst to define and identify the amount of harm that will most probably occur when an accident-producing hazard exists.

In the world of commerce, risk/danger must be controlled if litigation is to be prevented. A central problem is that the business owner, general contractor, machine designer, etc., may not perceive danger at the appropriate time, that is, before an injury has occurred.

In the following composite case, restaurant patrons were exposed to a routine sort of danger that often exists in establishments that have parking facilities. The restaurant owner was completely unaware of the continuing problem with her facility, which made her vulnerable to litigation on a daily basis.

Case Study 5-1

A patron drove into the parking lot of a Mexican food restaurant at night. It was exceptionally dark and rainy, and to avoid getting wet she pulled into a poorly marked parking stall as close to the restaurant entrance as possible. As she emerged from her car and walked toward the entrance, which was about 30 feet away, she tripped on a cement parking berm. The berm (low cement barrier) had been shoved into the place between the cars where she would be normally expected to walk. This twenty-five-year-old mother of two was severely injured and required a long hospital stay as well as surgery.

The testimony during the litigation that followed revealed that:

1. According to the standards of the Illuminating Engineering Society, there was insufficient lighting in the parking lot and in the path from the parking lot to the restaurant entrance. The measurement (made on a nonrainy night) was only 0.3 footcandle, while the standard required 2.0 footcandles, nearly seven times the existing illumination.
2. The berm was not only out of its normal position but was a dark gray color that blended in with the background, making it all but invisible.
3. There was no clearly lighted path leading from the parking spaces to the entrance of the restaurant. This forced the plaintiff to walk the dangerous route where she fell and was injured.

The obvious remedy to this situation was to: (1) paint the berms a visible white or yellow and provide well-lighted walkways from the parking lot to the restaurant entrance; (2) provide good general lighting in the entire parking facility; and (3) secure the berms to the pavement so that they could not be moved into areas where restaurant patrons normally walk. Good restaurant management also demands that the redesigned parking lot be consistently maintained.

Following this accident the customer, who sustained a broken hip and pelvis, spent fourteen days in the hospital, where her family visited her every day. Medical costs were over $25,000 plus costs incurred by disruption of normal living schedules. Then there was the pain and suffering of a broken hip and pelvis and the disability that left her with a permanent limp and an inability to perform her job.

The restaurant owner spent many hours answering interrogatories, consulting with her attorney, giving a deposition, worrying about the increase in her insurance premiums, and concerned about why this had happened to her. Unquestionably had she been given a choice to avoid the problems the accident had created by spending 30 minutes performing some type of accident-prevention analysis, she most certainly would have made that choice.

The question is, how does the restaurant owner get from the dangerous configuration of the parking lot that existed before the accident to a
reduced-risk situation where customers can safely negotiate the distance between their cars and the restaurant entrance? The answer is
risk assessment and control. Figure 5-2 describes in general terms how
the process of risk assessment and control can work for litigation
prevention. The procedure is straightforward, involving no mathematical wizardry, but at the same time it is necessary to participate in all the
steps if litigation prevention is to take place. Using the restaurant case
and Figure 5-2 we can model a typical approach to risk assessment and
control.

RISK ASSESSMENT AND CONTROL

Hazard Identification

Hazard identification, also called *discovery*, will be covered in detail in
two places in this book. The first is at the beginning of Chapter 6, and the
other is in Part III, Chapter 10, which contains a model accident
prevention plan.

Before undertaking hazard identification it is best to define the

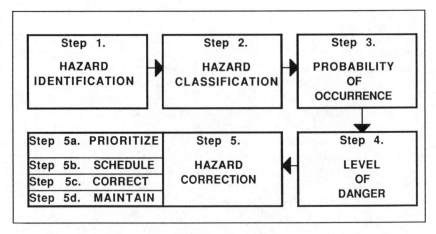

Figure 5-2. Risk assessment and control. Those of us who become
defendants in a personal injury litigation have many times failed to assess or
control risks to our business, job, facility, or product, or have failed to follow
through on corrective action. The road to risk reduction requires a
step-by-step process described in the text where hazards are analyzed,
prioritized, and corrected. This process need not be complex and laborious,
but requires the interest and attention of those who wish to prevent
litigation.

restaurant system, that is, to determine the nature of the equipment, the characteristics of the environment, and the person or persons who will interact with the equipment and environment.

In Case Study 5-1 we can establish the restaurant itself and its parking lot with incoming and outgoing vehicles as the equipment, the climatic conditions including lighting both indoors and outdoors as the environment, and the restaurant patrons and employees as the persons.

For the purposes of this example we will focus on the parking lot and restaurant entrance. The same procedure would apply to the restaurant interior if we wished to include that as part of this analysis. Using the techniques described in the next section, we can list the hazards in the parking lot and entrance as follows:

Hazard 1. The berms are dark concrete in color, blend in with the parking facility background color, and therefore may be a tripping hazard to restaurant customers.

Hazard 2. The berms are not secured to the pavement and can be pushed by cars into places where restaurant patrons must walk to gain access to the restaurant.

Hazard 3. The lighting appears to be inadequate, which could contribute to falls. This becomes particularly hazardous during inclement weather, which occurs frequently during the winter.

Hazard 4. There is no clear path to the restaurant entrance from the parking facility, forcing patrons to take circuitous, poorly lighted paths to access the restaurant.

Hazard 5. The many displaced berms and the hard-to-see striping indicate poor parking lot maintenance.

Hazard Classification

There are a number of hazard classification matrices available, but the one that is most descriptive and usable in a systems approach is the hazard classification matrix used for failure modes and effects analysis (FMEA). Figure 5-3 shows the four classes of hazard in this matrix. When classifying hazards it is correct to assume the most serious injury that can be reasonably anticipated if the hazard were to result in a systems failure (harm to one of the system's components). For example, if a person were to get a hand caught in the drive gear of a large, powerful, motorized conveyor belt, it is most likely that an amputation or death would occur rather than the possible minor injury. The resultant classification of the exposed drive gear would be *catastrophic*.

Referring to the list of five hazards discovered in the restaurant parking lot in Case Study 5-1, we can classify each according to Figure 5-3.

Hazard 1: Because they are on the same level as the hard surface, the dark, noncontrasting berms will cause tripping, which can result in

Hazard Class 1 - **SAFE**	Hazard Class 2 - **MARGINAL**
FAILURE WILL NOT RESULT IN MAJOR SYSTEM DEGRADATION AND WILL NOT PRODUCE SYSTEM FUNCTIONAL DAMAGE OR PERSONAL INJURY.	FAILURE WILL DEGRADE THE SYSTEM TO SOME EXTENT BUT WITHOUT MAJOR SYSTEM DAMAGE OR MAJOR PERSONNEL INJURY. THE FAILURE CAN BE CONTROLLED.
Hazard Class 3 - **CRITICAL**	Hazard Class 4 - **CATASTROPHIC**
FAILURE WILL DEGRADE THE SYSTEM CAUSING PERSONNEL INJURY, SUBSTANTIAL DAMAGE, OR RESULT IN AN UNACCEPTABLE HAZARD REQUIRING IMMEDIATE CORRECTIVE ACTION.	FAILURE WILL PRODUCE SEVERE DEGRADATION OF THE SYSTEM, OR DEATH, OR MULTIPLE DEATHS OR INJURIES.

Figure 5-3. Failure modes and effects analysis hazard classification. This classification system is a valuable tool for identifying hazards and prioritizing their correction. For example, if a system contains two hazards, one in Class 3 and the other Class 2, the Class 3 hazard should have precedence even if the probability is lower that the Class 3 hazard will cause an injury.

broken limbs or serious head injury. The classification here would be *critical*; that is, the system will be degraded and system personnel could be injured in a substantial way. The hazard should be corrected immediately. The implication of the critical classification is that the system will no longer be functional, that it will be unable to perform as intended. Certainly if a restaurant patron were to break a leg or sustain a concussion, the restaurant could no longer expect to serve her a meal.

Hazard 2: Also classified as *critical*, since the displaced berms can cause an interruption in stride that can result in a fall to a hard surface. When considering the "persons" component of the system, it is important to remember that restaurant customers can be elderly or disabled, which can intensify the problem, even to the point of increasing the classification to *catastrophic*. Elderly persons may not survive a broken hip, even with today's medical expertise.

Hazard 3: The combination of poor lighting, unexpected obstructions, and a dark rainy night is a perfect setting for a fall. Rain is the rule rather than the exception in this part of the country; therefore, the classification is clearly *critical*.

Hazard 4: Because of the parking lot layout patrons are forced to take a hazardous route to reach the restaurant entrance, one where they are subject to relatively hidden tripping hazards. This hazard must be classified as *critical.*

Hazard 5: Maintenance of the restaurant's parking facility appears to be chronically poor, especially since it consistently fails to correct critical hazards. Supporting evidence are the poorly marked stalls, the displaced berms, and the burned-out light bulbs. This in itself is a *critical* hazard.

Probability of Occurrence

So far we have established the existence of five critical hazards. The next step is to determine the probability of occurrence. Probability of occurrence is an element of risk, but as stated earlier, probability should not be the major determinant for hazard control. While it is necessary to determine probability, this step should not be considered as important as establishing and classifying possible system failures. This is because probability is affected by so many variables that change over time, that probability of occurrence of a failure is essentially unprovable.

For example, an electrical circuit breaker is tested in the laboratory and is subsequently rated at 500,000 actuations before failure can be expected. If that breaker is used as a switch to restore power to a continuous ground fault, the contacts may be degraded and fail long before the rated number of actuations. As a matter of fact, such a failure, which involved considerable arcing within the breaker, did occur in the following actual case.*

Case Study 5-2

A defectively wired advertising sign, mounted outdoors, tripped the circuit breaker, which was continuously switched back to the "on" position by a person or persons unknown. Because no one ever tried to determine the cause of the problem a teenage employee was electrocuted when he tried to change the sign's letters while the sign was in operation. The ground fault caused by the defective wiring had electrically energized the metal housing. Also, the circuit breaker had fused closed and was therefore unable to stop the flow of electricity.

In this case the probability of failure of the sign system was regulated by unreasonable negligence and could not be predicted by ordinary means. The standard methods for the accurate calculation and use of probability are highly dependent on low variability in the behavior of system

---

Reich v. *A&B Rentals.* See Appendix.

components. As illustrated in the many case examples in the text, we see that injuries that result in litigation occur during periods of unexpectedly high variability in the behavior of system components. Therefore, for purposes of injury and litigation prevention it is best to eliminate or safeguard *critical* and *catastrophic* hazards, particularly in the design phase of a product, facility, or task, without demanding high probability of component or system failure.

However, the determination of estimated probability can be useful for setting priorities for correction. For example, if a restaurant owner is confronted with five critical hazards, the one with the highest probability of causing injury should receive the highest priority for correction.

To simplify the determination of probability we will depart from the standard mathematical approach, which can be confusing, subject to error, and misleading to the analyst. For example, using the hard numbers approach the probability of failure statement may be expressed as "one failure in 10,000 hours of operation." The derivation of these data may be from word-of-mouth information, laboratory experimentation, articles published in trade journals, trade association data, and possibly from actual failure accounts from the field. Even using this revealing information the mathematical development of failure probability is a complicated struggle of compromises and Boolean algebra.

However, this same type of information can still be used by analysts to develop an estimate of probability based on the preceding factors (if they are available), as well as on personal knowledge of the job, facility, task, or product. The object of the proposed estimation method is to simplify and de-emphasize, but not eliminate, the role of probability in the determination of danger.

Table 5-1 shows the three levels of probability. Note that probability of system or component failure is an *expected* outcome. Failure can and does still occur even if *not expected*. The decision on the probability of occurrence of failure should be based on a reasonable expectation by the analyst. If, for example, it is easier to operate a machine without a guard, or more accuracy can be obtained without use of a guard, then there may be a high expectation that system failure will occur in the form of an amputated finger. Conversely, an electronic component, which if damaged or altered will materially affect system safety, can be embedded in plastic to prevent tampering. There may be no expectation of failure due to tampering in this case, but it still does not mean that someone will not take extraordinary measures to destroy or alter the component. Level of danger development allows for this anomaly by requiring corrective action when in the view of the analyst no expectation of failure exists but the hazard classification is extreme.

An actual example of this type of thinking is the design of commercial aircraft hydraulic systems. These systems are composed of highly tested and extremely reliable components. The possibility of the failure of the hydraulic system is very remote. However, because the survivability of

Table 5-1 Probability of Occurrence

Probability Level	Probability Description
A	There is no expectation that the identified hazard will result in a system failure
B	There is low expectation that the identified hazard will result in a system failure
C	There is high expectation that the identified hazard will result in a system failure

Note: It is important to remember that even when, in the opinion of the analyst, there is no expectation of failure, that failure may still occur. This fact permits a reduction of the effect of probability on the level of danger. This is necessary because in order to effectively prevent litigation, the approach must be conservative. We must not place too much credence in an estimate that cannot be proved and is random in its fulfillment. The three levels of probability are used in conjunction with hazard classification to determine a level of danger (see Fig. 5-4).

the entire aircraft system (passengers and aircraft) at any altitude above ground is so highly dependent on the hydraulic system, modern aircraft contain three and sometimes four redundant hydraulic systems. Even so, there have been hydraulic system failures with fatal consequences involving bizarre, unforeseen circumstances. The driving force therefore must be the hazard classification and not the probability of occurrence.

Using the three probability levels described in Table 5-1, it is possible to estimate the probability that each of the hazards identified in Case Study 5-1 will precipitate an injury-producing accident. Since all of the hazards are similar, and they all involve a fall to the same elevation, we can assign the same probability of occurrence to each hazard.

If the restaurant in Case Study 5-1 were open only for breakfast and lunch, that would mean no patron would be exposed to the poor parking facility at night. This would indicate a *low expectation* of system failure (probability level B). However, this particular restaurant was closed only from 2 A.M. to 6 A.M. every day of the week. This would result in a *high expectation* (probability level C) that each of the hazards that have been identified and classified will result in system failure. Specifically, it means that restaurant patrons are very likely to fall, and some of those that do fall are likely to be seriously injured. In the next paragraphs a specific level of danger will be identified to guide the analyst to appropriate and timely corrective action.

Level of Danger

The level of danger designation is made possible by combining the hazard classification with the estimate of probability of occurrence. Using these parameters the simple matrix in Figure 5-4 provides a guideline to the danger inherent in the restaurant parking facility, in its stated configuration, in Case Study 5-1. If the system is *dangerous* or *extremely dangerous*, corrective action is required.

HAZARD CLASS ▼	PROBABILITY OF OCCURRENCE		
	A	**B**	**C**
	DANGER LEVEL		
1. SAFE	D1	D1	D1
2. MARGINAL	D1	D2	D2
3. CRITICAL	D2	D3	D3
4. CATASTROPHIC	D3	D3	D3

DANGER LEVEL	DANGER LEVEL DEFINITIONS
D1	THE OPERATION OF THIS SYSTEM IN ITS PRESENT CONDITION POSES LITTLE OR NO DANGER TO THE LIVING OR INANIMATE SYSTEM COMPONENTS **CORRECTION** CORRECTIVE ACTION, IF ANY, CAN BE ACCOMPLISHED ON A ROUTINE BASIS
D2	THE OPERATION OF THIS SYSTEM IN ITS PRESENT CONDITION IS DANGEROUS TO THE LIVING OR INANIMATE COMPONENTS OF THE SYSTEM **CORRECTION** CORRECTIVE ACTION SHOULD BE ON AN 'AS SOON AS POSSIBLE' BASIS AND HAZARDS SHOULD BE TEMPORARILY SAFEGUARDED UNTIL CORRECTED
D3	THE OPERATION OF THIS SYSTEM IN ITS PRESENT CONDITION IS EXTREMELY DANGEROUS TO THE LIVING OR INANIMATE SYSTEM COMPONENTS **CORRECTION** CORRECTION MUST BE ACCOMPLISHED IMMEDIATELY AND PROCESS SHUT DOWN OR SAFEGUARDED UNTIL CORRECTED

Figure 5-4. Danger level matrix.

All five hazards in our restaurant parking lot fall into the 3C matrix position and therefore have a danger level of D3. The indicated definition is *extremely dangerous*. At first thought it is hard to accept that a parking lot in a restaurant can be classified as extremely dangerous. Should not this category be restricted to table saws, scaffolds, powerful in-running rolls, and punch presses? If you consider, however, that an elderly person can lose his or her life from a broken hip, this classification is not a difficult position to take. In fact, if you wish to prevent litigation from such a situation, you must expeditiously correct this level of danger no matter where it exists or how mundane the circumstance. In the actual trial the jury was impressed with the danger of the parking facility and found for the plaintiff.

Hazard Correction

There are four relatively simply and inexpensive corrections that can be derived from this analysis of Case Study 5-1. They are:

1. Paint berms and parking stalls a contrasting color.
2. Secure berms to asphalt.
3. Increase lighting in parking facility to code.
4. Provide well-lighted and marked pedestrian walkways to restaurant entrance.

All corrections can be accomplished in the same time frame so that prioritization may not be necessary. However, the restaurant owner, whether or not she plans to do the work herself, should schedule each correction. Also, a program of regular maintenance should be installed to maintain the paint, lighting, and the integrity of the walking surfaces.

Had these corrections been accomplished before the accident, there would have been a greatly decreased probability of occurrence, from *high expectation* to *no expectation*. If the accident had occurred in spite of these reasonable precautions, the case would most probably have been successfully defended.

PART II

Methods of Analysis

By now you should have an understanding of how this book is organized; that it is developed around the idea that if readers want to stay out of the courtroom, they must be willing to discard preconceived notions about accidents and injuries. Readers should not wishfully think that because a facility, product, organization, etc., has been accident-free for x number of years that "we must be doing something right." If you want to be more confident that a lawsuit is not waiting in the wings or that you can successfully defend yourself in court, you must choose to critically examine your operation or product in much the same way that we assessed risk for the restaurant in Case Study 5-1. Part II will describe six methods that can be used to quickly analyze this type of situation and even more complex problems without waiting weeks, months, or more for results (a system safety analysis of a complex missile system took fifty engineers and two years to complete). A matrix will be provided that will suggest when to use a particular form of analysis.

Safety analysis during the planning, design, or operational phase of a product, job, or facility operation has many litigation-prevention advantages for a potential defendant. It provides an opportunity to discover safety and health hazards before such problems can injure and at a point when there is usually ample time for correction. Obviously, it is far less costly to correct a problem before completion of a project, marketing a product, or operating an establishment than it would be to retrofit after an injury occurs. Finally, if by some chance there is litigation due to claimed negligence, the jury can be told and shown that the planner, designer, or owner acted with forethought at the conceptual and/or operational stage of the project. Many times this latter advantage can be vital to a successful defense.

The six analysis methods in this part enble prudent anticipation of safety and health hazards involving tasks, products, and facilities. Each method has been modified to facilitate the litigation-prevention process.

The six methods are fault tree analysis (FTA), hazard effects and control analysis (HECA), hazard control analysis, management oversight and risk tree analysis (MORT), management decision point analysis, and job safety analysis (JSA). All but two of these techniques—hazard control analysis and management decision point analysis—are well-known, proven techniques for hazard discovery and control. However, some of the known techniques have been altered to facilitate their development and utility.

Each of these methods has advantages either for qualitative analysis, to determine the type of hazard, or for quantitative analysis, to determine the number and degree of the hazards. Some methods do well both quantitatively and qualitatively. The description of each method will show how to use each technique to the best advantage.

Chapter 6

Hazard Effects and Control Analysis, and Task Hazard Analysis

HAZARD EFFECTS AND CONTROL ANALYSIS

Hazard effects and control analysis (HECA) is one type of systems safety analysis that is derived from the similar and more traditional failure modes and effects analysis (see Chapter 2 for description of a system). Differences between the two are not significant, but were made to increase the utility and reliability of the technique as a litigation-prevention tool.

The name hazard effects and control analysis is very descriptive of the way in which this technique accomplishes its purpose. It examines how the identified hazard causes system components to fail, then considers the effects of that failure on other system components as well as on the entire system, and finally leads to consideration of appropriate controls. The technique requires the analyst to answer seven questions on the system being examined (see Table 5-1):

1. What hazards are present?

The hazard can involve a component, can be hardware, or can be a failure to perform an operation (human failure) or perform the operation correctly. The analysis will determine whether or not the hazard or component failure will harm any other part of the system and what the extent of that harm will be. A typical expression of failure would be: *an electrical switch failed in the open position.* This would mean that the switch could not be closed or the circuit completed. A sample effect would be that a pump or light or bell could not be turned off.

Table 6-1 Hazard Effects and Control Analysis Format

Identify Hazard	Hazard Source	Effects on Other Components	Hazard Class	Probability	Danger Level	Correction
What action, inaction, component failure, or condition can produce harm?	How did component fail? How did hazard occur?	What happens to other components in the system as a result of this failure?	Safe? Marginal? Critical? Catastrophic?	Expectation of failure: None? Low? High?	Danger level: Low? High? Extremely high?	What action will prevent failure?

Specific Corrective Action: What specific actions must be taken to correct the identified hazards? Be specific. Example: "Purchase 12 half-mask respirators with organic vapor cartridges."
Note: This is a modified type of failure modes and effects analysis form. It is useful for examining a single component or an entire system. Once completed, with the danger level identified, this technique can help point to safety and health problems inherent in almost any type of hardware or activity. The format also identifies the more serious hazards in terms of potential harm, and can lead to the development of corrective action. The procedure is straightforward, but practice is necessary to use this technique to its best advantage.

As this column of the HECA is developed, the analyst will usually see a pattern of interrelatedness between human and hardware failures.

An excellent illustration of interrelated design and human failure occurred at Three Mile Island during the near meltdown of the nuclear reactor. A pressure-operated relief valve (PORV) had automatically opened because of an overpressure condition in a pressurizer tank that was part of the coolant system. This valve and tank were in the normally radioactive area so that no personnel could be on hand to observe the action of these units, but condition reports were of course made through sensors in the core and corresponding instruments in the control room. The open PORV permitted coolant water to escape the system into a nearby drain vessel.

At the same time, because of the loss of coolant the reactor shut down when control rods automatically dropped into the reactor core and the fission process was halted. However, the leftover fission products in the core continued to heat the core, though at only 6 percent of the rate of the fission process. However, coolant water would still be necessary to keep the reactor from eventual meltdown even at this low rate. This would mean that the PORV had to close to permit coolant to enter the core.

The PORV was designed to automatically close after remaining open for 13 seconds, and indeed the indicator panel in the control room showed that a "close" signal had been sent to the PORV. Although the signal had been sent, the PORV was stuck in the open position; thus coolant continued to drain, permitting the control rods in the core to become progressively more exposed and risking meltdown.

The PORV remained open for 2 hours and 20 minutes without the knowledge of control room personnel, draining well over 32,000 gallons of coolant water from the system, one-third of the system's entire capacity. The loss of this amount of coolant and the subsequent damage to the reactor resulted in a billion dollar repair and cleanup bill, downtime of well over one year, permanent reactor loss, and a significant contribution to the demise of the nuclear power industry in this country.

What were the significant human, hardware, and design failures that were primarily responsible for this catastrophic accident? Without relating the enormous amount of accumulated data that serve as backup information, we can list four major failures, some of them compound failures.

1. The PORV failed in the open position, which caused loss of a major amount of reactor-core coolant (hardware failure).
2. The indicator that showed that the valve received a "close" signal was not connected to the valve itself and therefore could not indicate the stuck open condition. The indication that a close signal was sent misled control room personnel into thinking that the valve had closed (design failure). The sensor should have been designed to detect

valve condition, open or closed, not whether or not a close signal had been sent.

3. Control room personnel did not realize that the PORV was stuck in the open position until 144 minutes into the accident (human failure). Had they sensed the stuck-open condition, they could have closed a backup valve that would have stopped the loss of coolant and restored the entry of coolant into the core.

4. Control room personnel also did not notice a red light that indicated that the emergency feedwater lines were blocked by a closed valve (human failure). Another red light that also would have warned that the emergency feedwater system was blocked by a closed valve was covered by a maintenance tag (human failure).

If a hazard effects and control analysis had been made prior to the accident, these four failures would have been listed in the first column, and then subsequently analyzed in the other columns to the point of determining corrective action.

Let us now continue with the questions asked by the HECA.

2. How did the component fail?

Identify the way the component will look or perform in the failed condition. For example, did a valve fail open or closed? That is, if it failed closed, once the valve was closed it would not open. If a human failure, what was done or not done? For example, using a Class A rated fire extinguisher on an oil fire will not control the fire. The fire will continue to burn at the same or even an increased rate.

3. What effects can this failure have on other system components?

Failure of a resistor in an electronic circuit can cause other resistors or circuit components to fail. Failure to sound an alarm in itself may not be harmful, but it certainly can have an effect on the functioning of a factory building if, because of this failure, the building is destroyed by fire. After this question the HECA moves to the quantitative aspect. That is, we will determine the degree of harm the various possible failures can generate.

4. What is the hazard classification of this failure?

Consult Figure 5-3 for the appropriate hazard classification of the identified component failure. This is the first step where the analyst determines degree of danger. This is significant because degree of danger is the prime motivator of corrective action.

5. What is the probability of this failure?

Consult Table 5-1 for the symbol that best describes what, in your opinion, is the most fitting probability of occurrence for this failure. Your expectation should be based on your own experience and knowledge of the condition as well as on that of others that you may consult.

Previous chapters have discussed the problems associated with the use of probability levels. It is important for the analyst to understand the limits of this element of risk assessment.

6. What is the danger level associated with this failure?

Using Figure 5-4 and the results obtained in the latter two questions you can develop the danger level that will occur as a result of the identified failure. Danger levels D2 and D3 will give you the sense of urgency required to proceed with the corrective action that is the key ingredient for effective litigation prevention and a believable defense.

7. What corrective action will prevent this failure?

Once you are to the point where corrective action is mandated you must follow through as suggested in steps 5a, 5b, 5c, and 5d in Figure 5-2, which requires prioritization of the hazard corrections, scheduling of correction, accomplishment of the corrective action, and finally maintenance of the correction. Once an effective control is installed it would be counterproductive to let it lapse because of mismanagement.

In the following actual product liability case* a supervisor was injured on a device that fed sheet metal into a punch press. We will construct a HECA that could have been developed by the machine's developer during the design phase of this product.

The developer of this sophisticated feeder was not an engineer, not even a university graduate, and the original machine was put together in a garage. These facts do not preclude the use of HECA or any of the analysis techniques suggested in this book! The only thing required is the desire to avoid injuring prospective users and the willingness to spend several hours to improve product design. In other words, to exercise one's responsibility for safety. A comparison of the time and money expended by the machine's manufacturer as a result of this suit to what would have been required to do the appropriate initial analysis and design modifications to ensure an appropriate degree of safety would be the same as comparing a trip to the planet Mars to a trip around the world.

My experience has shown that the safety of customers or users is usually more dependent on the orientation of the responsible person than on that person's level of education. It is generally accepted that schools of business, engineering, industrial arts education, and so on, do not include accident prevention in their curriculums in a meaningful way; therefore, whether the persons who are responsible for safety are educated or not the public, unfortunately, still must depend on tort law for protection.

Meyer v. *Coe Machinery.* See Appendix.

Case Study 6-1

The Accident and Injury

The plaintiff in this case was a supervisor in a small fabrication shop in the state of Washington. The feeder was brand new and was designed to automatically feed sheet metal into a punch press. The device was keyed to the ram of the punch press so that when the ram was on its upward stroke the mechanism would feed in a fresh blank from a roll of galvanized metal sheet.

The feeder used electricity to power the sheet metal grippers and plant air for the back-and-forth movement of the rear gripper. Also contained within the device, but hidden from view, was an air reservoir that maintained the required pressure and volume of air necessary to operate the rear gripper. When the machine was set up, the handle that operated the manual dump valve for the air reservoir was missing and was not mentioned in the setup instructions. Figure 6-1 shows two views of the general configuration of the feeder.

When the punch press is making a part the upper ram is descending and the stationary gripper on the feeder is in the closed-jaw position, holding the metal rigidly. At the same time the traveling gripper is in the rearmost position on the feeder with its jaws open. After the two halves of the die interlock and the part is made, the ram and upper die travel upward, while the jaws of the stationary gripper open and the jaws of the traveling gripper close. The traveling gripper then moves forward, carrying a fresh section of sheet metal into the press.

Fabrication of parts, as just described, had been going well and it appeared that the new feeder was becoming a valuable aid to production. No one suspected that the device was defectively designed in any way or that it had been misassembled. There were no warnings on the machine that indicated the danger (ablity to harm) that was contained within, in the form of the pressurized air reservoir.

On the day of the injury, the sheet metal had become canted in the metal track and refused to feed into the press. The supervisor was called to restore the feed. He was a generally cautious man, and before attempting to unjam the machine, he did what he thought would eliminate risk to his person. He first shut off the electrical power on the machine itself, then at the electrical main switch, after which he shut down the plant air supply at the valve that controlled the airflow to the feeder. At this point he was convinced that the feeder was safe to be repaired.

The supervisor grabbed the sheet metal, which had jumped the track, and forced it back on track. As soon as the metal was free to move, the residual pressure in the air reservoir, which was still pressurizing the system, forced the traveling gripper to slam into its forward position. In the moment it took for this to occur, the supervisor's left hand was struck and punctured by the traveling gripper, which had an adjustment screw

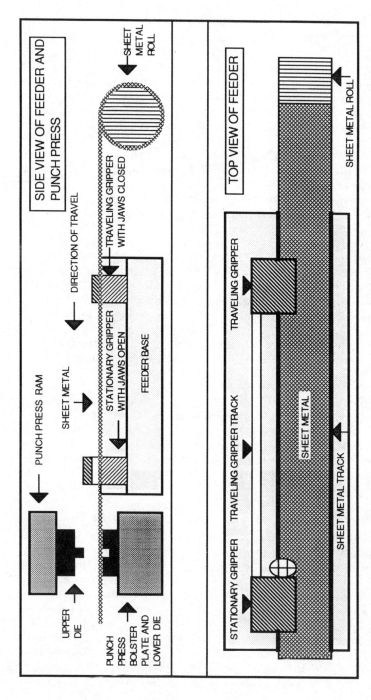

Figure 6-1. Sheet metal feeder for use with a punch press. *Top:* Side view of feeder and punch press. *Bottom:* Top view of feeder. These two views of the sheet metal feeder show how the device was functioning when the accident occurred. The traveling gripper had slammed forward under the residual pressure in the air reservoir and punctured the hand of the victim where a symbol ⊕ is located. The text shows how a prior hazard effects and control analysis would most likely have avoided this problem and the subsequent litigation.

protruding from the front. The injuries received were severe and permanently disabling.

The Trial

At the trial the owner and developer of the feeder, who was from the Midwest, appeared and testified in his own behalf. His testimony was unable to shake the plaintiff's argument that the feeder was negligently designed, fabricated, and manufactured. What the jury believed was:

1. The feeder had a hidden hazard in the form of the air reservoir that continued to maintain pressure to the system after both electrical and air power were turned off.
2. There were insufficient warnings on the machine and in the instruction manual relating to the retention of residual pressure after the feeder was shut down.
3. The instructions in the manual and on the machine itself were insufficient as they related to the assembly of the feeder at the customer's establishment. There should have been warnings in the manual to assure the installation of the pressure dump lever, since it was not installed at the factory. There also should have been a red tag on the pressure dump shaft to further ensure proper installation of the lever.
4. There were insufficient instructions in the manual relating to unjamming the feeder. Those warnings that were in the manual were ineffectively expressed.

The trial outcome was in favor of the plaintiff and the jury awarded him in excess of $300,000. This was a larger amount than expected, considering the extent of the injuries. The jury was later questioned and stated that they felt the designer and manufacturer had omitted any consideration for the safety of the user in the feeder configuration as well as in the manual. They were hoping to send a message that this was inappropriate behavior.

The Analysis Technique

Now comes the moment of truth. What should or could the designer of the sheet metal feeder have done in consideration of user safety before the feeder was placed in the stream of commerce? This question is important for at least two reasons. First, the manufacturer wants to avoid injuring anyone, particularly a customer. Litigation could certainly result from such an injury if the design or manufacture was in any way defective. Secondly, if the machine is heavily built and does its job well, it will be sold and resold over a period of many years. During this time the original instruction manual will undoubtedly be lost and subsequent buyers will be denied any safety benefit from this source. The manufacturer, if locatable, is still vulnerable to a lawsuit if the original design can be proved negligent or if a dangerous modification made by any user was foreseeable.

If the machine designer and manufacturer had an inexpensive, reliable, relatively simple, and quick method of analyzing their product for safety to the user, then such an analysis could have been made in the design phase. Design changes for operator protection are obviously less costly and easier to install than the same changes would be after the device is in production. Such an analysis technique is the hazard effects and control analysis.

The System

To develop an accurate analysis, the sheet metal feeding system components must be identified:

1. *The equipment:* The feeder, the sheet metal, the device receiving the sheet metal (punch press), and the plant utilities necessary to operate the device (electricity and pressurized air).
2. *The persons:* The operators, setup personnel, the supervisor, and repair persons. In this case, the supervisor and repair person(s) were the same.
3. *The environment:* This busy fabrication shop (typical environment for this feeder) was located in a 35-ft-by-100-ft metal building containing punch presses, press brakes, metal lathes, milling machines, and other miscellaneous metalworking machines. The interior was moderately well lighted (at or close to code) and noisy when in full operation (ambient noise approximately 87 dBa, above the action level where hearing protection is required).

The HECA for this case, shown in Table 6-2, will address the main issues presented by the lawsuit. The sample format is located in Table 6-1. Remember that HECA is a prior-analysis technique, and this illustration is intended to show what could have been done to avoid the problems that caused the litigation.

Analysis Using HECA

Column 1, Identify the Hazard

Probably the most difficult part of the analysis is to determine what hazards and components of the system to review. An actual analysis of the sheet metal feeding system in Case Study 6-1 will certainly cover more than Table 6-2, but most if not all other hazards would have received low danger level (D1) and so are not shown. The feeder is a relatively safe machine except when it is shut down, the guard removed to gain access to the jammed sheet metal, and with residual air pressure remaining in the reservoir. It then becomes a hidden trap for the unwary.

Table 6-2 Hazard Effects and Control Analysis: Sheet Metal Feeder

Identify Hazard	Hazard Source	Effects on Other Components	Hazard Class (Fig. 5-3)	Probability (Table 5-1)	Danger Level (Fig. 5-4)	Correction
1. Traveling gripper slams forward unintentionally	Powered by residual air in reservoir	Strikes operator with gripper itself or with gripper adjusting screw	3 Critical	B High	D3 Extremely dangerous	Prevent occurrence or protect operator and warn of danger
2. Operator at point of operation when traveling gripper moves unintentionally	Handling sheet metal to remedy jam	Operator struck by traveling gripper	3 Critical	B High	D3 Extremely dangerous	Prevent occurrence or protect operator and warn of danger
3. Failures 1 and 2 occur with electrical and air power shut down	Traveling gripper slams forward unintentionally	Operator struck by traveling gripper	3 Critical	B High	D3 Extremely dangerous	Prevent occurrence or protect operator and warn of danger

Specific corrective action: 1. Install automatic pressure reservoir solenoid-operated dump valve so that when feeder is shut down electrically the reservoir will automatically release stored air pressure. 2. Connect a lamp and a pressure-operated switch on air reservoir so that when there is pressure in reservoir the lamp will light. Conversely lamp will extinguish when pressure is dumped. 3. Place a test switch in lamp circuit mentioned in 2. to test for lamp burnout. 4. Place a verbal warning on machine explaining danger and meaning of lamp. See Figure 6-6 for illustration of these corrections.

Many hazards and system component failures occur when nonstandard activity is going on, such as unclogging a jam, adjusting the device after a production problem, or other nonroutine maintenance. The analyst must consider nonroutine activity such as unjamming the machine, since it would be expected that the sheet metal would jam at random times in the life of the machine.

However, the best routine for selecting possible hazards and system-component failures is to consider a much larger spectrum of possibilities. The following is a fairly complete but by no means perfect listing of what to look for when determining hazards and system-component failures. The purpose of this list is to expand understanding of what to consider when faced with complex systems. The list therefore contains references to different types of cases.

It would be impractical to list all possible types of components in the millions of existing systems, but I have included a meaningful sampling that will enable the reader to understand the idea of hazard effects and control analysis and how this effective tool can prevent litigation when it is used for prior analysis. Each listing is accompanied by a typical example taken from an actual case. Some have illustrations.

1. Access to the hazard point.

The most effective accident- and litigation-prevention method is to deny or severely limit operator access to the place on a machine where the work is being performed (point of operation). On many machines this can be at multiple locations.

Example: The operator of a table saw would fail if he did not use a push stick or hold-downs while performing a dado cut (¼-in.-to-¾-in.-wide channel in wood) with an unguarded blade. The hazard class would be critical (3), the probability of occurrence would be low (B), and the danger level, extremely dangerous (D3). This failure would injure not only the human component of the system but would also ruin the workpiece. Specific corrective action deals with using pushsticks, hold-downs, or guards.

Facilities and tasks that do not involve machinery, such as prevention of access to dangerous areas such as tanks and pits, high work station drop-off points, places of high noise, vibration areas, chemical exposure, trip and fall hazards, the back of electrical power panels, and others depending on type of task or facility, are important considerations. However, the preceding hazard types could also apply to machinery.

Example: A walking surface such as a 40-ft-high catwalk would cause system components to fail if not appropriately protected by standard guardrails. The effect on other system components would be that persons using such a catwalk would most likely fall to their deaths. Since the catwalk is 40 feet above a concrete floor, the hazard classification is catastrophic, the probability of occurrence of a death would be high (C), and the danger level is extremely dangerous (D3). Standard guardrails would correct this problem if the hazard could not be eliminated.

2. Routine system operation including adjustments.

Such operation would include mechanical power transmission, ergonomic factors (e.g., can the operator reach the shutdown switch or emergency shutoff if caught in the machine? Or, is the operator subject to repetitive motion trauma?), operator position and access to control stations, loading and unloading of raw materials and parts, adequacy of existing guarding and safeguarding devices, ambient and local noise, use of coolants, and any system component involved with a release of energy.

Example: A bandsaw sold for home or industrial use* has a table tilt adjustment knob located under the table and only three-fourths of an inch from the blade (see Fig. 6-2). This is a design failure if the operator attempts to tilt the table while the blade is still in motion, since the fingers will most likely come in contact with it. (Hazard class 2, marginal, because the blade is somewhat protected at this point and would not be capable of an amputation or other severe injury.) Even with a nonrunning blade an operator could still lacerate her hands (hazard class 2) while making this adjustment. Probability of occurrence would be low (B), and the danger level D2 (considered dangerous, but at the first level of dangerous). Moving the tilt adjustment knob to at least 3 inches from the blade would correct this problem. This could be easily and inexpensively accomplished by elongating the knob shaft.

3. Routine system maintenance.

Such maintenance includes lubrication, while operating or not, scheduled parts replacement, overhaul, and replenishment of raw materials, depending on product or facility type.

Example: A huge computer-operated milling machine, two and one-half stories high, must receive lubrication on the second level once each week while in operation. The maintenance person needs to climb a 3-ft uncaged ladder to gain access to the lubrication point. Below the ladder are numerous steel projections such as valves, fittings, and corners of the steel base of the machine. If someone should fall from even the first rung of the ladder, they could be pierced by one of these projections. The ladder is the identified component, and would fail by being slippery, thus permitting the climber to fall into the deadly area below. This component would be classified catastrophic, with a probability level of high (C), producing a danger level of D3. This danger level requires immediate correction by either remoting the method of lubrication or by the construction of a cage around the 3-ft fixed ladder. Such action would protect the maintenance person from severe injury, and the manufacturer from a lawsuit.

Hardesty v. *Grizzley.* See Appendix.

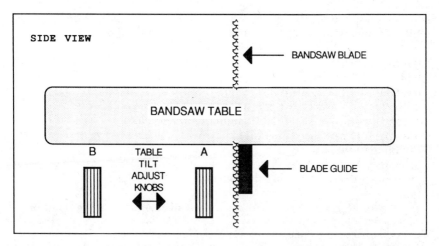

Figure 6-2. Bandsaw accident. When the table tilt adjustment knob is in position A, a hazard class 2 (marginal) exists. The operator's fingers and hands are subject to laceration by either the moving or nonmoving blade. Moving the knob to position B would correct this hazard. Such a correction should be accomplished in the design phase and could be identified through a hazard effects and control analysis.

4. Nonroutine maintenance or adjustments.

These adjustments might include a part of the product that is loose or too tight, or becomes disassembled.

Example: An accident occurred that was completely unexpected by anyone: a bridge crane motor fell into a nitric acid tank. The motor mounting bolts had corroded and failed after the crane performed for 23 years over the acid tank. Such a failure of huge, high-stress-rated bolts was unheard of, until after the fact. Had the crane been thought of as part of a parts-handling system operating in a nitric acid mist environment, and where a hazard effects and control analysis had been performed, these bolts would have been monitored and changed periodically. Hazard classification: critical. Probability of occurrence: A. Danger level: D2. Corrective action: monitor mounting bolts semi-annually, replace every five years.

5. Restoration of system operation after a malfunction while operating or not.

This is a very important area to examine for possible system-component failures. Persons responsible for restoration of product operation after a problem occurs are at times working blind without prior knowledge or experience because of the variety of things that can go wrong. It is up to the product designer and manufacturer to anticipate possible malfunctions, which would include but not be limited to:

- jamming
- leaks
- misalignment of raw material, dies, etc.
- unexplained loss of power (electrical, air, hydraulic, gas, etc.)
- correction of production of mismanufactured parts
- unexpected product movement such as the ram of a punch press double tripping
- unexpected stopping of raw material feed
- ejecting of product or machine parts

Example: Punch press accidents frequently happen during some out-of-sequence operation, as when a part hangs up in the die. In one case the press, with a seated operator, was engaged in making license plate frames. To keep the operator's hands out of the point of operation the press relied on two-hand palm buttons so that the operator had to keep both hands on the buttons until the ram started moving to its highest position. Raw material to the press was hand-fed and finished frames hand-removed.

On the day of the injury the press tripped unintentionally (double tripped) while the operator was removing a finished license plate frame. Her left hand and wrist were amputated.

Hazard classification: critical. Probability of occurrence: B. Danger level: D3. This level of danger demands that anti–double tripping devices be installed and that the operator use tongs for loading and unloading until this correction is made. The HECA also indicates that the original design that omitted the anti–double tripping circuitry is defective and the manufacturer and designer would be vulnerable in a personal injury lawsuit.

6. Possible user modifications.

Is it foreseeable that a user may modify a device or facility to make it produce faster or make it easier to operate, load, or unload? This is an important consideration because many machines are sold and resold many times in their lifetime.

Example: A manufacturer produced a wood processing machine that performed six operations for the user.* The machine would only accept blanks of a certain size that seemed to be an industry standard.

One customer bought five machines but found that they needed to change the feed mechanism to accommodate a larger blank. The change involved altering a guard that protected the infeed conveyor. Several years later, because of greater access to the point of operation, an employee was caught in the conveyor, dragged to where he could not shut the machine down, and then suffered the amputation of his right hand.

A HECA would have given the altered guard a hazard classification of critical. The probability of occurrence is B. At the developed danger level of

---

Weiss v. *Challoner Machinery*. See Appendix.

D3 the correction should be a redesign of the infeed system that would allow for the introduction of a variety of blanks with safeguards that would positively deny an operator access to the moving conveyor.

7. Problems of set-up, initial and operational.

When a user is uncrating, assembling, and operating a machine for the first time it can be a confusing and frustrating period. If initial setup is further hampered by insufficient, poorly written, poorly printed, or incorrect setup instructions, there may be possible legal consequences generated by personal injury.

Example: A truck driver delivered empty cans to a bottling plant. Each time he brought in a load he had to set up the conveyor system to bring pallets of cans to the appropriate filling stations. To access the setup position, he had to walk over the conveyor, which was on legs and approximately 24 inches from the ground. One day he slipped off the irregular walking surface of the conveyor and severely injured his knee, requiring surgery.

While other types of analysis would be as effective, a prior HECA would have shown the conveyor to be an improper walking surface that provided hazardous access to a workstation. The hazard classification is critical, the probability of occurrence would have been C, and the danger level is D3, demanding immediate provision of an appropriate walking surface for delivery drivers. Such a correction made at the initial construction of the conveyor system would have saved pain for the driver and a substantial loss for this self-insured bottling company.

8. Devices with more than one control station.

These require added scrutiny for effects on multiple operators. If a machine is normally operated or even if it can be anticipated that it will be operated by more than one operator, it is very important that each operator be given an opportunity to shut the machine down in an emergency through easy access to a shutoff switch. If this is overlooked and you expect to be in business for a substantial time, your liability insurance should be kept current.

Example: Considering the accident illustrated in Figure 4-1, HECA would have revealed the danger of overlooking an emergency shutdown device in a machine workstation that contained a hydraulic clamp and a traveling circular saw. The danger level here is clearly D3, which reads (see Fig. 5-4): "The operation of this system in its present condition is extremely dangerous to the living or inanimate system components; correction must be accomplished immediately and the process shut down or safeguarded until corrected." Again, a prior analysis would have prevented litigation and an amputation.

9. Efficacy of warnings.

The place that warnings have in the hierarchy of accident prevention was discussed earlier in this book. It should be remembered that although warnings have an important place as an accident/injury-prevention tool, their use as the sole means of accident prevention should be avoided. Unfortunately, warning labels are usually the only means of hazard notification for chemicals that are marketed in small quantities to the general public. Shippers of bulk chemicals, however, are turning to more sophisticated means of notification such as video-tapes and classroom sessions delivered by manufacturer's representa-tives. It is astounding to me how often *failure to warn* is invoked as a reason for a personal injury lawsuit. Also astounding is how often the most elementary principles of effective warnings are violated or ignored when the same amount of effort could produce a satisfactory result. Often when a plaintiff cannot find substantive negligence in design or manufacture, *failure to warn* is cited as the sole basis for a lawsuit. In his article entitled "Psychologically Effective Warnings," Dr. Robert J. Cunitz, Ph.D., discusses these well-known but infrequently practiced principles.

1. *Present when needed.* "Hey John stay out of that pit, there may not be enough air in there," would be a much more effective warning if given just before John is about to enter the pit, than given in a classroom or on the factory floor two months earlier. This issue is also important if the designer and manufacturer of a machine are relying exclusively on warnings contained in a manual. Such written warnings cannot be relied upon to be present when needed because, generally, the manual has light readership, is kept at some distance from the machine it describes, and may be permanently misplaced.

2. *Present where needed.* A woman shopper enters a supermarket after midnight intent on buying a candy bar. She is in the back main aisle about to enter the side aisle where she thinks the candy is located when she encounters a sign stating "Floor Maintenance—Floor is Slippery." She looks down the aisle and sees no activity and perceives no wetness on the floor and so proceeds 70 feet down the side aisle until she reaches the front main aisle. After taking one step onto the front main aisle she slips on wet wax stripper and breaks her hip. The stripper is so slippery that the paramedics cannot approach her without slipping and have to go around back to reach her.

   To be effective the sign needed to be adjacent to the wax stripping operation, not 70 feet away. Dr. Cunitz states that warnings buried in owner's manuals or stored in file cabinets have low effectiveness compared to warnings placed on operating controls or at danger points on machines and facilities. Dr. Cunitz also suggests that warnings be placed within a 15-degree cone, projected from the eye as the apex of the cone.

3. *Attract attention.* Persons must be able to distinguish between the warning and other visual and auditory stimuli. To be noticed and motivate response the warning needs to be brighter, flashier, more colorful, and dynamic than other stimuli. Learned sensitivity to certain colors (e.g., red, yellow), shapes (e.g., oval, triangle), signal

words (e.g., Danger, Warning), and sounds (e.g., siren, bell) can result in greater attention-getting ability than other colors, shapes, words, and sounds.

4. *Motivate behavioral change.* Weak warnings are not effective. "To Avoid Amputation" is much more effective than "To Avoid Personal Injury," which is in turn a better warning than "To Avoid the Possibility of Personal Injury," which is better than "Do Not Touch." The more motivational the content, the more effective the warning. Consequences of continuing the forbidden activity must be clear, not remote or hidden. The persons being warned must be told "what happens if," or the reason "why."

5. *Tell how to avoid harm.* The warning often used on paint spray cans, "Use Only with Adequate Ventilation," does not define "adequate" nor does it inform how to achieve adequacy. While it is difficult to correctly inform and motivate a consumer of a paint spray product, it would be more effective to advise "If Used Indoors Wear an Approved Respirator Purchased from a Safety Products Outlet." This warning may not achieve the desired result, but at least the purchaser is told how to avoid harm in the most appropriate and practical way. A safety products outlet is usually available to most persons, and these establishments can advise and provide the correct respiratory protection.

6. *Conflicting motivation.* Though the sign on a table saw warns "Do Not Remove Guard," the manufacturer has to know that the guard must be removed to perform a dado cut (except on one special brand of saw using a specific type of guard). This conflict reduces the impact and reliability of the warning, and the user will not heed it. Warnings must be practical and cannot ignore the intended function of the product or facility.

7. *Provide first-aid information.* If first-aid treatment will be effective, this type of information should be included.

8. *Other considerations*
   • Durability
   • Appropriate size
   • Sufficient contrast
   • Use simple, blunt language
   • Illumination of the warning may be necessary
   • Audible signals should be considered
   • Chronic "false alarms" should be avoided
   • Test efficacy of warnings
   • Standardize where possible
   • Use of pictorials may be appropriate

Example: An articulated manlift using a fiberglass bucket was specifically designed for work around power lines.* Thus, if a worker in the bucket were

*Stone v. Asplundh. See Appendix.

to touch a power line, he would be protected by a nonconductive path to ground. A key safety link was the nonconductive hydraulic hoses that stretched from the metal valves in the bucket to other similar fittings on the metal base of the lift.

One day, after the lift had been in service for over 5 years and was in the hands of its third owner, a worker in the bucket contacted a 112,000-volt power line with his neck. Apparently at the time of contact there was a conductive path to ground because he received a severe shock.

It was found that at some time in its maintenance history someone had replaced the nonconductive hydraulic lines with lines that were conductive! The fittings at both ends of both types of hoses were the same and there was no warning on the lift or in the manual that only orange-colored nonconductive hoses should be used.

Had a hazard effects and control analysis or a fault tree analysis been performed (see Chapter 8), the hoses would have been identified as a hazardous component of the system. One of the failure modes would be the substitution of conductive hoses. Hazard classification: catastrophic. Probability of occurrence: C. Danger level: D3. This danger level, considering that it is at the fifth or highest place in the extremely dangerous classification, demands urgent and positive correction. Durable, explicit warnings must be placed at hose fitting locations, at the bucket control station where the operator stands, and in the owner's manual. This hazard is so severe it cries out for the redesign of the fittings, so that only nonconductive hoses can be used. Even if the redesign were to take place, the warnings would still be necessary.

The warning should read:

Warning!!
REPLACEMENT OF THIS HOSE WITH
CONDUCTIVE (BLACK COLOR) HOSES WILL CAUSE
ELECTROCUTION OF USERS OF THIS MANLIFT.

This would be far preferable to: Caution—Use Only Nonconductive Hoses.

10. Hidden sources of energy.

Devices containing springs, pressure tanks, capacitors, or any component capable of storing and discharging energy unexpectedly should be classified as a hidden hazard. Such sources of injury usually require elimination or safeguarding, and at a minimum, explicit warnings.

Example: Capacitors are devices that are capable of storing electricity even after power to the circuitry that contains the capacitors is shut off. Computers, for example, contain capacitors that operate at over 2000 volts. If a seller of random-access memory (RAM) boards were to omit warnings of this hidden energy source in the installation instructions, the door could be open for a personal injury lawsuit.

The stored energy could be lethal to certain susceptible individuals and secondary motion caused by the initial shock could result in broken limbs.

Through HECA the seller could, for the "component" column, identify capacitors in the charged condition and within reach of the installer of the memory chips. The hazard classification would be critical and the probability of occurrence would be low (B), producing a danger level of extremely dangerous (D3). Effective warnings would be the absolute minimum corrective action that would be appropriate for this situation.

11. Training failures.

Training failures are often seen in rental companies where rentals of heavy equipment, particularly construction equipment, are available. The rental establishment relies upon the owner's manual, the warnings that are placed on the device by the manufacturer, and on the experience and knowledge of the customer. These are generally insufficient to ensure that the customer understands the complex nature of operating equipment that sometimes requires a year of training for professional operators. Often there are OSHA standards that control particularly deadly hazards associated with the operation of this equipment. The following example describes a particularly tragic use of rental equipment.

Example: A farmer rented a boom truck with a large flatbed that he used to carry grain elevator "legs," large steel structures, which in this case were over 25 feet long. The boom was to be used to lift the legs for installation on the grain elevators.

As the truck moved slowly over a dirt road, the boom was at a 70-degree angle with the ground, and the legs were steadied on the flat bed by means of chains held by farm laborers who were walking beside the truck. Twelve-thousand-volt power lines ran parallel to the road. As the truck approached the grain elevators it made a right turn onto the access road and the boom came in contact with the power lines. Fortunately for one of the laborers, he had, for some unknown reason, dropped his chain; the other three laborers were electrocuted.

The failure to appropriately train renters of heavy equipment in this case is classified as catastrophic, probability of occurrence is low (B), and the danger level is extremely dangerous (D3). This severe hazard associated with the use of boom trucks would require the rental company to ensure that their customers are fully aware of the requirement of law that booms are not permitted within 10 feet of 12,000-volt power lines, with a larger distance requirement for voltages over 50,000. Before leaving the rental establishment the customer must understand that traveling over roads with the boom in the raised position should never be considered.

12. Efficacy of owner's manuals.

Owner's manuals have windows of use. Two of these are when a device is first set up, and when the first users are learning the operation of a machine, tool, facility, etc. Subsequent owners usually also have an interest in the owner's manual for the same reasons. The owner's manual can make a significant contribution to the training and safety of an operator by being carefully written and by giving emphasis to operations and cautions important to the operator's safety and health. Because of the frequency with which failure to warn is used in litigation where plaintiffs are catastrophically injured, it is justified to give a general rating of extremely dangerous (D3) to this type of failure.

Example:

THE PNEUMATIC SYSTEM

The pneumatic system is composed of an internal air reservoir that is fed by plant air through a quick release fitting. The system is the sole source of power to the traveling and stationary gripper, operating both the jaws and lateral movement of the rear gripper.

A pressure dump valve, actuated by a handle located on the rear of the feeder base, will void all air pressure from the reservoir. If the reservoir is to remain unpressurized, the plant air must be shut down. Also, it is important to realize that the internal pressure facility will operate the feeder from stored air even after electrical and air sources have been shut down. The internal reservoir is a Model A-657-8UV Vickers rated at 1000 PSI working pressure, with a volume of 3000 cu. in. The reservoir is. . . .

More often than not the example above is typical of an owner's manual entry containing vital safety information for users of potentially harmful equipment. Examining this entry carefully (which is hard to do) you should be able to find much the same information that is displayed with emphasis below. The top entry violates most of the principles for effective warnings, while the entry below is more likely to be read and affect the behavior of the reader.

WARNING
FEEDER WILL OPERATE UNDER STORED AIR
PRESSURE EVEN IF ELECTRICAL POWER AND PLANT
AIR PRESSURE ARE SHUT DOWN

---

13. Devices with more than one place of access to dangerous moving parts.

Many industries use large machines that have access to multiple points of operation. These are inherently more dangerous than devices with single points of operation because persons can become trapped in danger areas without the knowledge of the operator. Often these machines are so large that individual room-size components are entered by persons for maintenance, set up, cleaning, or observation. If this is done while the device is operating, a severe injury or death could occur.

Such a machine opens a large number of possibilities for serious injury. If there is a miscommunication between workers where worker B understands worker A to say that the machine should be turned on just as worker A enters the machine to clean it, the consequences of this seemingly simple act can be disastrous.

Example: Just such a miscommunication occurred between workers in a mushroom farm compost preparation area. This area had an ambient noise level of over 100 dBa, which would make voice communication extremely difficult.

In this actual case,* a mushroom worker told a fellow employee that he was going into the composting machine to clean it. The second worker thought that he said to start it up to lubricate the drive chain (which was a normal thing for him to do). Worker number one, because he was in a hurry to get to the market that day and wanted to get the job done quickly, squeezed into the out-feed hatch of the machine instead of entering through the rear access hatch, a violation of company rules. Had he opened the rear access hatch and left it open, he would have been in full view of worker two, who was standing at the machine control station. The injury was catastrophic and permanently disabling.

This is an interesting case because it not only illustrates multiple-access problems, but also covers failure to lockout, insufficient training, and, more importantly, the interaction between the safety responsibilities of the employer, employee, and the manufacturer. The question is whether or not the employee acted so outrageously that he was the sole cause of his injury. This is not just a philosophical issue, since there was a personal injury lawsuit against the machine manufacturer and an OSHA citation, which the employer contested.

There is no question that had the injured party acted prudently in several areas there would have been no injury. This fact must be weighed against how dependent both the employer and manufacturer were on the safe practice of workers. Was there any safe design activity on the part of the manufacturer or actions on the part of the employer, which could have been easily included in the design of the machine and operation of the company, that could have mitigated this accident in spite of what the worker did or did not do? In other words, should both the manufacturer and employer have conducted a hazard effects and control analysis to determine whether the composting operation could have been made safer by compensating for possible unsafe practices by employees? Did they go as far as they could go considering the state of the safety art, so that problems such as these could be prevented?

If the manufacturer and employer wanted to avoid litigation, then some type of analysis—HECA for the manufacturer and job safety analysis (see Chapter 5) for the employer—would have had to have been made. Since we are concerned with HECA in this chapter, let us examine what the manufacturer would have discovered.

The composting device is known as the *green machine* and is widely used on mushroom farms. It must be regularly cleaned because the beaters get contaminated with string and other materials that reduce the effectiveness of

Roses-Montes v. Petaluma Mushroom Farm. See Appendix.

the beater action. The danger here is immediately apparent. When cleaning this machine, a person must come in intimate contact with a potentially lethal point of operation composed of two contrarotating shafts, each with over a hundred projections (beaters) that intermesh. Access to the beaters are from either the in-feed or out-feed side, with the most popular cleaning position on the out-feed side (see Fig. 6-3).

The device must be cleaned every day that it is in operation, and the danger level for the cleaning operation is extremely dangerous (D3). This means that in addition to a lockout system, which is subject to failure, additional means of shutdown should be included. Shutdown switches should be provided at the recommended cleaning positions so that if the green machine is inadvertently started while it is being cleaned, an opportunity is given for emergency shutdown.

Explicit warnings such as, "Warning! This Machine Must Be Electrically Locked Out Before Cleaning," must also be provided. Since the green machine is primarily used on mushroom farms that employ Latino labor, the signs must be in English and Spanish. Other warnings that deal with the correct cleaning position must also be mounted on the machine in plain view.

All of this does not necessarily mean that there can never be a repeat of this accident, but it does skew the odds in favor of prevention. If the employer also applies some of the other analysis methods suggested in this book, such as management oversite and risk tree (MORT), the chances of injury are greatly reduced.

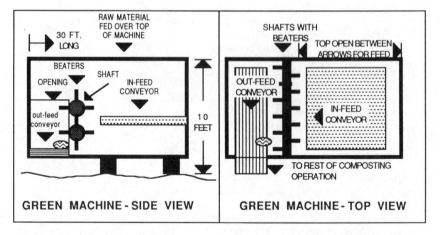

Figure 6-3. The green machine, part of a larger compost system. The injured worker climbed into the machine through the opening shown in the side view. The position of his head is illustrated with the oval symbol ☜. The basic question that is discussed in the text is, "Is it reasonable to anticipate that a person will permit his desire to leave a workplace quickly at the end of a workshift to overcome good sense in the protection of his life, especially when in his mind the operation seems perfectly safe?"

14. Machinery overrun.

Overrun is the time it takes for a machine to stop its motion after the off switch has been thrown. When persons try to gain access to the point of operation while overrun is taking place, they can be hurt by the dangerous parts of machinery.

Persons who are already caught in the point of operation, and who manage to shut the machine off, are also victims of overrun.

To protect machinery operators and maintenance persons it is necessary to limit, eliminate, or safeguard overrun. Electrical, mechanical, or electromechanical brakes can limit and sometimes eliminate overrun, while safeguarding requires preventing access to the point of operation until motion stops. In the following example a 24-second overrun is safeguarded.

Example: This actual accident and injury* took place on a cattle feed lot where grain was ground into cattle feed by a rotary feed mill (see Fig. 6-4). The raw grain is introduced into the milling machine through a hopper at the top and is immediately engaged by the feed rolls. Frequently, the raw grain contains detritus such as rocks and paper, which eventually slow or even halt the feed to the main rolls.

When this occurs the machine is shut down by the operator. An access hatch directly in front of the feed rolls is opened and the operator clears the debris from the rolls with a piece of steel re-bar. On many occasions before this accident the operator was in the habit of not stopping the mill when performing this operation, since he found it easier to clear the rolls while they were under power. For some reason not known to him he decided to kill the electrical power before this accident occurred.

As stated earlier the rolls took 24 seconds to stop, and in that time the operator's right hand became caught in the feed rolls. Had the power been on, this could easily have been a fatal accident.

A hazard effects and control analysis points to a catastrophic hazard (4), with high probability of occurrence (C), and a danger level of extremely dangerous (D3). This result demands that this hazardous situation be corrected at the design stage by employing the safeguards described in Figure 6-4.

Two last but important issues: first, the manufacturer knows that the machine must be cleaned often and provides an easily opened hatch for this purpose. However, the operator's access to the hatch, which is the outlet pipe that makes a 45-degree angle with the ground, is totally inappropriate. A stable platform must be provided.

Second, referring to the hierarchy of prevention in Chapter 2, the best that the designer of this mill could have done would have been to design a method of cleaning the feed rolls without having the operator get into the point of operation. One way this could be accomplished would be to provide a method of separating the feed rolls so the debris would fall by gravity and be filtered out by a screen.

*Case did not reach trial level.

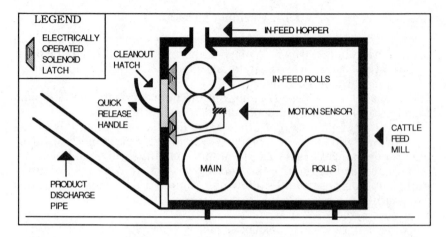

Figure 6-4. Overrun illustration on a cattle feed mill. In this accident the mill operator was required to periodically gain access to the in-feed rolls to clean out foreign matter such as rocks. The rolls would continue to turn for 24 seconds after power was shut down. During this time the operator removed the access door and became caught in the in-feed, which cut off most of his right hand. Note that the operator was required to stand on the product discharge pipe to gain access to the cleanout hatch. Correction of this problem involves a motion sensor that detects roll movement attached to a pair of electrically operated solenoid latches mounted on the cleanout hatch. With this arrangement the access hatch cannot be removed until roll movement has ceased. Further, a stable platform must be provided for the operator and the access hatch must be electrically interlocked with the roll motor so that the rolls will not operate with the access hatch removed.

15. Failure of protective equipment.

Most manufacturers of protective equipment understand the importance of good equipment performance, even under such adverse conditions as high noise and vibration, impact, and high environmental heat and cold, as well as exposure to hot and cold materials, toxics, ionizing and nonionizing radiation, and falls. If the equipment fails to perform as designed, serious injuries are bound to occur, generally followed by litigation.

Failures of quality protective equipment usually occur when the user is provided the wrong type of equipment, or when misuse of the equipment is a factor. To guard against these problems manufacturers need to stress the readability, understandability, durability, and the other important features of effective warnings (see number 9 earlier in this chapter).

*Johnson v. Bausch & Lombe et al. See Appendix.

Example: An operator of a direct chill casting machine in an aluminum smelter was severely injured* when he was provided the wrong protection for a job that required him to lean over a mold containing molten aluminum. The hardened outer surface of the mold is routinely sprayed with water while the billet is formed. Sometimes, particularly at the start of the casting process (a drop), a misalignment occurs and molten aluminum can contact the water spray.

When this occurs a violent spray of molten metal can ensue, sometimes minor, sometimes soaring as high as 50 feet into the air. The operator of the casting machine stands over the mold at the beginning of the drop to make sure such a misalignment does not occur, by manually adjusting the flow of molten me͞   ͞to the mold. Sometimes this is not successful and a splash occurs.

One d   ⅂y violent surge of molten aluminum occurred and the operat   ⅃iquid metal. His face shield disintegrated, leaving him ͭ   ͞inum in his nose, mouth, and eyes. It was later shͨ   ͭ rated for exposure to molten metal.

͞ad complied with all applicable standards
y engraved in the upper left-hand corner. In
sufficient to warn the employer or employee of
͟uct for molten metal protection.

ssified catastrophic (4), probability was high (3),
͟emely dangerous (D3), as one might expect expo-
͟e. Under these conditions the manufacturer needs to
͟ warning users of the limitations of his product.

16. Failure to lockout.

Of all po͟͟ ͭ͟͟e hazards, failure to lockout is among the highest for lethal potential. Lockout of available energy sources is generally required for entry into tanks, voids, and food and product mixing facilities; maintenance, repair, or dismantling of machinery; and work on any task where an unexpected release of energy will hazard the components of a system. Possible energy sources are electrical (requires lockout of switches, switchboxes, breakers, etc.), mechanical (requires lockout of spring-loaded levers, mixing paddles, gravity-actuated equipment, and the like), chemical [requires lockout and blankout (*blankout* is a procedure where a steel plate is inserted in a chemical line, usually at a flange, that positively interrupts the flow of the chemical) of chemical lines, valves, retorts, tanks, etc.], gas (requires lockout of gas valves and lines), radiation both ionizing and nonionizing (requires prevention of entry into radiation areas), and pressurized air (requires lockout of lines and valves).

Almost every, if not all, lockout situations are extremely dangerous (D3) and require immediate corrective action composed of establishing physical provisions for locks and blanks, and the administrative and procedural systems for assuring the installation of lockout equipment.

Example: In Example 13 the injured worker failed to install a lock on the switch that controlled the composting machine on the mushroom farm. The switch was of the service entrance type that would accept a lock. At first glance it is easy to condemn the worker for the oversight, but if the machine had the appropriate configuration, such as an interlocked entry door where the machine would not operate as long as the door remained open, the possibility of this injury would have been reduced to a minimum.

In this case, the desire of the worker to get to a store before it closed superseded good sense. In most cases, including lockout situations, manufacturers must create their designs on the principle that workers will not follow safe practice at all times, and that feasible protective measures will sometimes be ignored, eventually leading to severe injury or death. Litigation follows.

17. Fall protection.

Another area where careful attention to the protection of the human component of any system is mandatory, is where a fall can occur. Falls are prevalent in all walks of life, and are responsible for a broad spectrum of serious injuries, including death. In the construction industry falls account for 30 percent of fatalities and often result in personal injury lawsuits against general contractors. Because the construction site is so dynamic, unless there is strict attention to fall-protection preplanning involving general and subcontractor employees, a serious or fatal fall is inevitable on jobs where construction superintendents ignore this essential task.

Example: A warehouse was almost completed except for the roof, which was in the process of being mopped with hot tar.* The roof had large quantities of combination skylight–heat vents already installed. Each vent–skylight was 2-by-4 feet, and had aircraft cable attached diagonally across each vent (see Fig. 6-5) to prevent the wind from lifting the plastic dome. Even with the cable in place there was ample room for a person to fall through the skylight opening if the plastic dome were penetrated.

One of the roofers was very experienced and had been with the same company for over ten years. As is typical in the trade, he was backing up while mopping the hot tar. He apparently did not see the skylight because he tripped over it, penetrated the thin plastic dome, and fell between the cables 26 feet to his death on the concrete below.

As the story unfolded it seems that the heat vent manufacturer was advertising that the skylight was approved by OSHA because of the aircraft cables. The fact is that OSHA does not approve products, and the skylights did not come close to meeting the standard, which requires a 42-in.-high rail with a midrail or a fastened-down and marked cover. The mesh created by the cables also was not close to the OSHA requirement of a 6-in.-maximum mesh if the cables were intended to act as a net.

The unfortunate part of this story is that the misinformation that the skylight was OHSA-approved was passed from the marketing department of the manufacturer, to the representative, to the purchasing agent of the general contractor, to the project superintendent, and finally to the foreman

*Caraveau v. SDL. See Appendix.

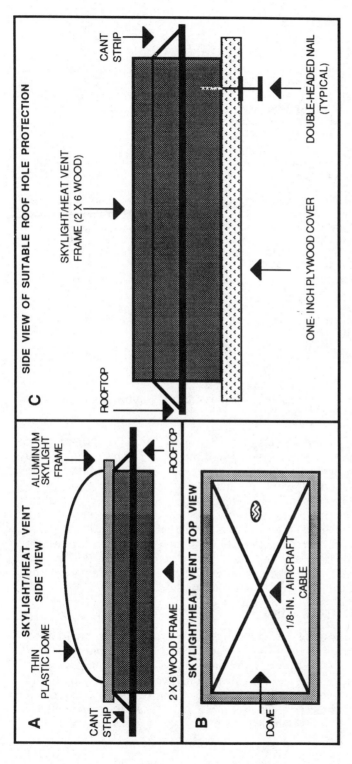

Figure 6-5. Three views of skylight–heat vent problem. *View A* shows the skylight–heat vent in a side view. The plastic dome is made of very thin material so that in case of fire, the heat and flame will cause the dome to disintegrate and vent the heat. *View B* shows the positioning of the aircraft cables that the manufacturer was relying upon to meet OSHA standards (of course, this does not meet standards). The symbol 〰 shows where the roofer penetrated the skylight when he fell on it. *View C* shows what should have been done to protect the roof hole according to OSHA standards. The double-headed nails make removal easier and provide sufficient strength to prevent penetration of the cover. This type of cover permits the roofers to bring the roofing paper over the cant strips and over the 2 × 6 wood frame without interference from the skylight.

81

on the job. They all believed it and a man died. The jury awarded one million dollars to the widow, who needed the money but really wanted her husband.

If HECA had been performed by the manufacturer and a task hazard analysis (THA) been done by the general contractor, the following litigation-avoidance steps would most probably have taken place.

1. The skylight/heat vents would not have been advertised as meeting OSHA standards. On the contrary, the manufacturer would have included warnings as to the danger of using his product as a roof hole cover for fall protection.
2. Instead of installing the skylights, the general contractor would have provided plywood covers nailed to the skylight frames from underneath. This type of installation has many advantages: it is secure fall protection, it permits the roofers to work on the skylight frames without interference, it catches any debris that falls into the skylight holes, it is inexpensive, and is easy to install and remove.
3. The general contractor would have accomplished the necessary preplanning such as:

   • Measuring and cutting plywood covers and supplying them at the right place at the right time.
   • Installing and removing the covers at a preplanned time.
   • Notifying the roofers that they were not to work until covers were in place.

If these steps had been taken, this danger level D3 hazard would have been safeguarded effectively and litigation avoided.

Manufacturers need to consider the possibilities for danger to all system components when a system malfunction occurs, such as the one described in the accident where the sheet metal jammed in the feeder. The HECA method, if used as suggested in this chapter, leads to appropriate corrective action, as described in Figure 6-6. Some of the other analysis techniques would also lead to suitable corrective action, but the HECA is a good choice for this particular problem.

Figure 6-6 shows the corrections to the feeder that will safeguard the system and would have avoided the litigation that followed the accident.

At the end of this part we have included a matrix that shows the best uses for each of the six types of analysis methods presented.

TASK HAZARD ANALYSIS

Task hazard analysis (THA) is a quick and relatively easy method for examining a series of step-by-step activities to determine how each activity or their interactions affect health and safety. The simple act of entering a place of business involves consideration of fall potential, including walking surfaces that have a low coefficient of friction, obstructions that can interrupt stride, as well as broken surfaces such as a tear in a carpet. In a task hazard analysis entering a business establish-

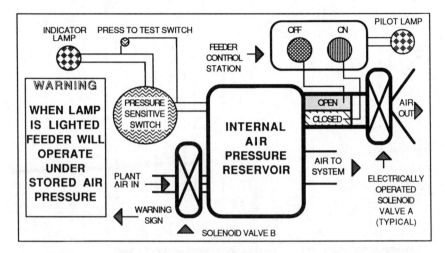

Figure 6-6. HECA-derived corrections to sheet metal feeder. Using the system shown in the diagram, when the on switch is pressed a pilot lamp lights, solenoid valve A closes and solenoid valve B opens. The internal reservoir becomes pressurized and the indicator lamp lights, signaling that there is stored air pressure. At the end of shift or if the machine becomes jammed, the off button is pressed. This opens the solenoid dump valve A and closes valve B, permitting the reservoir to void its pressure. The indicator lamp goes off, and the machine is now safe to repair. The warning sign explicitly informs workers of the hidden danger, but the dump valve essentially eliminates the hazard when the feeder is shut off electrically. The *press to test* switch assures against giving a false signal because of indicator lamp burnout.

ment is treated as one of the activities required to complete the job of engaging in the business to be transacted in the establishment.

Example: If an optometrist (or any other business owner) invites custom-ers into his or her establishment to be fitted for glasses and would like to avoid litigation generated by an unsafe premises, a task hazard analysis will highlight areas that require attention. For example, if there were parking berms placed in front of each parking stall, the analysis should consider if they are properly fastened to the asphalt. Figure 6-7 shows the layout of the optometrist's office, and from this layout we should be able to complete a task hazard analysis that deals with customer entry from the front road.

The type of customers who patronize optometrists' offices range from mothers with children to ambulatory elders who are driven to the premises in a specially equipped van. This is important to the development of the "person" component in the system concept. The inclusion of elders should prompt careful consideration of access and egress to the facility, since the walking surfaces that would be satisfactory for the general population may be more hazardous for the ambulatory elderly.

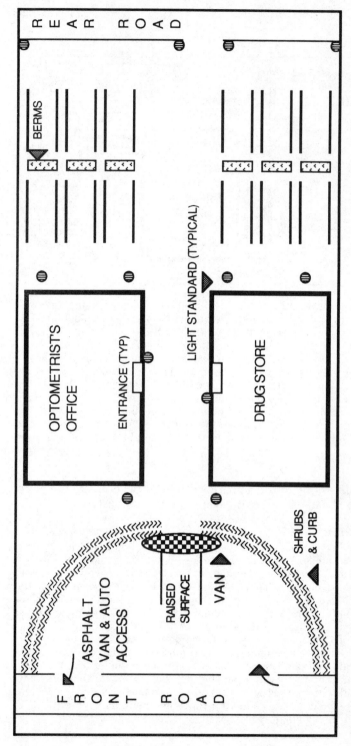

Figure 6-7. Entrance layout of an optometrist's place of business. The optometrist's office receives many elderly patrons who are usually driven in a van that pulls up so that van egress will permit access to the raised surface. Patrons can then walk to the office entrance without encountering the curb and the shrubbery. Notice that the van has pulled up to the raised area, which is rather narrow compared to the length of the van. This difference makes it probable that at some time the van will be misaligned with the raised surface and passengers will be forced to exit onto the asphalt surface and therefore may unexpectedly encounter the curb and the shrubbery. With normal robust persons this would probably not be a problem, but with the elderly such a change in egress could prove to be a serious problem. See task analysis in Table 6-3.

The format for task hazard analysis is shown in Table 6-3. The analysis technique is straightforward, requiring a knowledge of the task steps and a familiarity, but not a professional familiarity, with hazard control. The illustrated analysis will cover only the access to the optometrist's office from a van entering from the front road.

After examining the problems of the front road entrance the analyst can go on to look at the parking area, the optometrist's office itself—even the eye examination procedure can be reviewed in this way for possible safety problems. Table 6-3 reveals several easily corrected van egress hazards that normally would not be considered until an injury occurred.

After performing this analysis and making the required corrections it is of course still possible that an accident, injury, and subsequent lawsuit will occur. The difference is that the business owner or manager can be identified in court as being reasonably prudent in the conduct of his or her business, particularly in protecting the elderly customers. It is doubtful if such a case would come to court after depositions reveal a complete record of the analysis and the follow-up corrections.

To illustrate a different but common use of task hazard analysis, Table 6-4 describes how a manufacturer or user of radial arm saws can determine whether their customers or employees are as well protected from injury as the state of the art will allow. Lawsuits involving radial

Table 6-3 Task Hazard Analysis of a Business Entrance

Step	Hazard	Correction/Protection
1. Van pulls into front vehicle entrance 2. Passengers exit from van	1. Driver misaligns the passenger door with the raised surface 2. Passengers exit on asphalt close to curb. Curb is then out of vision range and presents tripping hazard	• Widen raised surface to same length as van • Place an alignment post to assist driver in achieving correct alignment • Driver assists older, more infirm passengers • Raised surface is painted (crosshatched)

Note: This technique enables the owner/operator of an optometrist's office that services elderly patrons to quickly determine the safety of the drive-up entrance. In this case, litigation would have been avoided if a task hazard analysis and appropriate corrections had been made prior to a serious fall. Total analysis time: 30 minutes. Total cost of corrections: $375. Cost of litigation: $28,000. Time cost: 18 hours.

Table 6-4 Task Hazard Analysis of Ripping on a Radial Arm Saw

Step	Hazard	Correction/Protection
1. Raise saw blade 1/4 in. from table 2. Loosen carriage swivel lever 3. Rotate saw head to the *rip* position and tighten swivel lever 4. Set blade width 5. Lock carriage 6. Lower blade to table 7. Set upper guard to 1/8 in. over stock to be ripped 8. Start saw 9. Push stock through saw 10. Retrieve finished piece and waste	1. Saw may start while being adjusted 2. Operator may rip from wrong end of saw 3. Operator may stand behind blade while cutting 4. Operator may not adjust upper blade guard 5. Operator's hand may contact rotating blade while ripping. Wood may strike face or eyes 6. Operator may not use push stick or other wood-handling device 7. Operator may panic if saw jams while running 8. Operator may reach through point of operation to retrieve wood or push wood off saw table	• Provide key lock for start switch • Provide warning for proper rip position Same for eye and face protection • Provide warning for correct operator position when ripping • Include adjustment of upper blade guard in manual as a safety procedure (with emphasis) • Provide self-adjusting lower blade guard with saw • Emphasize in manual the importance of lower blade guard and push sticks • Strongly advise in manual (with emphasis), the purchase and use of hold-down devices in conjunction with push sticks when ripping

Note: The radial arm saw is probably the most dangerous woodworking machine, with the possible exception of some multistation, multioperation devices. In the ripping mode the radial arm saw is in its most dangerous position. Touching the blade at any place on the in-running periphery will most likely whip the hand through the point of operation resulting in an amputation. Because radial arm saws are sold for home use and many novices and even experienced users may not be aware of the dangers of this machine, it is imperative that the machine be guarded to the extent that the state of the art will allow. Appropriate warnings on the machine and in the manual are mandatory. Safety elements of training with recommendations that the owner take a formal training course should be included in the manual. This task hazard analysis points out many of the salient safety issues when using this saw in the rip mode, and the correction/protection column illustrates how such an analysis can be used to avoid future litigation.

arm saws are ubiquitous and many times involve grim injuries such as whole-hand amputations. Judgments can range from one-half million to over two million dollars.

Other types of analysis, for example fault tree analysis, can be used to protect saw operators when a much more comprehensive (but more time-consuming) examination of saw operation is required. The table at the end of this part defines the attributes of each analysis type, and it is recommended that the analyst consult this information when attempting to determine the best method of analysis.

Other examples of situations where the use of task hazard analysis would be appropriate are:

1. Determining whether or not business invitees could safely negotiate the distance from the parking lot to the business entrance.
2. Determining the hazards of a punch press during operations with sheet metal, such as punching, bending, shaping, and cutting.
3. Determining if a baby's crib would injure the child in some way.
4. Determining if a ski lift operation is hazardous at entry, egress, and during emergency situations (e.g., lift stops, lift runs backwards, skier falls from chair at entry or while enroute, or high wind conditions).
5. Will a can opener present unnecessary hazards to users?
6. Will the use of an exercise machine hazard its user?
7. Will a door designed for handicapped entry and egress on a bus injure a passenger as he or she leaves the bus? Such a door, moved from its fully open position by the wind, once broke the elbow of a passenger in a wheelchair.
8. Will the removal of a blade in a woodworking plane injure the woodworker?
9. Is the use of a recreational vehicle, such as a powered water ski, unnecessarily hazardous?
10. Will the operational change from attendant-to-customer-pumped gasoline be hazardous to customers?

Chapter 7

Management Decision Point Analysis

In this part two methods of analysis comprehensively deal with the duty of management to consider the health and safety of users of their products, employees (including subcontractors), and the community. One of these methods is management decision point analysis (MDPA) and the other, covered in Chapter 8, is management oversight and risk tree (MORT). MDPA is predicated on the idea that during the conception, initial planning, testing, material procurement, production, and marketing of a product or service, there are numerous opportunities for management to consider and resolve inherent hazard potential.

The use of MDPA is an indicator that management is interested in avoiding litigation arising from defects in their products, planning, or production and marketing techniques. MDPA is described in six sections covered in three flow diagrams beginning with Figure 7-1. An explanation of each figure is provided. The chapter ends with the use of MDPA in a study of an actual case.

It is important to note that MDPA is designed to cover both physical and health hazards. This makes MDPA useful to companies producing or marketing chemicals or chemical processes, as well as companies marketing consumer products other than chemicals, such as appliances, scaffolds, and baby carriages.

Before attempting the analysis the analyst must focus on a chemical, product, or process that may be hazardous in the planning, production, or consumer-use phase. For example, if a company planned to produce a new biological pesticide, they should be concerned about the safety of the production process as well as the safety of the product in the field. The best time to develop an MDPA is always at the concept and early testing stage. The analysis process itself will automatically address the subsequent production and consumer stages.

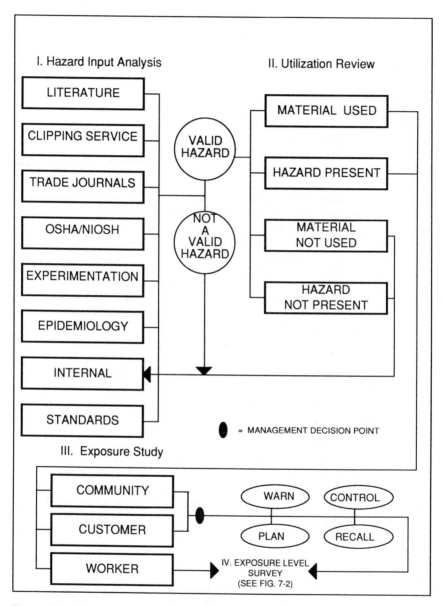

Figure 7-1. Management decision point analysis (MDPA).

Except in sections I and II of the MDPA, the management decision point symbol will be shown as ●. When this symbol occurs it indicates that this is a time for management to consider the safety and health consequences of their activities. If, for example, the production process results in community exposure through contaminated soil or air, then management is obliged to assess the danger, and if there is a danger to the community, decide between eliminating the exposure or safeguarding the community by reducing the danger, and whether or not to continue the production process.

MDPA SECTION I: HAZARD INPUT ANALYSIS

The purpose of this section of the MDPA is to determine if a valid hazard exists. For example, the Johns Manville Company knew early on that asbestos was dangerous to the health of its production workers and to its customers. Had they used an MDPA, Section I would have revealed that asbestos was a valid hazard.

To establish the validity (or nonvalidity) of a hazard the analyst should consult available literature, regulatory agencies and other sources of standards, accumulated internal information on the material or product, as well as any epidemiological data relating to all injuries associated with the analyzed or similar products.

Other sources of information should also be consulted, such as experimental information obtained from company or independent laboratories, clipping services (services that provide newspaper and magazine accounts dealing with a requested subject), and trade publication and trade association material.

A situation where the establishment of a nonvalid hazard should be mandatory would be the development and production of a food, food additive, or a child protective device. In the first case, some companies are developing a noncaloric fat substitute for foods. Imagine noncaloric french fries! To consider any product in this category (food) rigorous experimentation and literature searches must be accomplished to the satisfaction of the Food and Drug Administration that the product is nonhazardous to health.

In another, actual case,* a company that produced an automobile child restraint failed to conduct an adequate analysis of its product, indicating that validity of the hazard was not specifically ruled out. As a result some children who were using the product in the way recommended by the manufacturer were killed or catastrophically injured while they were passengers in cars that crashed. How this company could have avoided the costly litigation that followed through the use of an MDPA is discussed in the final paragraphs of this chapter.

*Caption may not be released (by court order).

If, after the Hazard Input Analysis, the hazard proves to be nonvalid, this information and how it was derived returns to the bank of internal information. This information will be valuable at a later date if the product is involved with injury or if changes in the product are made.

Assuming that there is a valid hazard, the analysis format moves forward to the next section, Utilization Review.

MDPA SECTION II: UTILIZATION REVIEW

This section requires the determination of whether the hazard is present (or if the hazardous material is used) in the workplace, in the community, or if the hazard affects the customer. Admittedly this intermediate section represents slow progress toward a solution, but this methodical approach is necessary to produce appropriate evidence that the analyst (company) was sincerely interested in preventing injury.

If, for example, a product is hazardous, but the utilization review reveals that it will always be used in a closed system where no routine exposure is expected, then later planning needs to include the warnings and procedures associated with the prevention and treatment of emergencies. However, if the hazardous material, process, or hardware is used or present ubiquitously, then the analysis proceeds on to the exposure study.

The determination of data for this section will require a survey of possible uses and misuses of the product throughout the plant, local community, and at the customer level.

The notations of *present* and *used* refer to physical hazards (present) and chemicals (used), respectively. Again, if the chemical is not used or the hazard not present, this information returns to the bank of internal information for possible use at a later time.

MDPA SECTION III: EXPOSURE STUDY

The purpose of this section is to determine who is exposed—workers, customers, or the community. If workers are exposed, the study proceeds to Section IV: Exposure Level Survey, where the extent of the exposure is determined. If the customer and/or community are exposed or can be exposed through accident, then the analysis shifts to a path where management must decide how to manage the exposure.

There are many options open to management, but at a minimum they must consider the following.

1. *To warn the customer and/or the community.* If a product can be hazardous under certain conditions or an emergency can cause harmful exposure, then the company may be obligated to warn their customers or the community of the type and extent of the danger. Warnings should follow the principles of good warning practice described in the Hierarchy of Prevention in Part I.

2. *To control the danger at the source.* The company should take meaningful action to control the danger through product design changes, containment techniques (such as providing a catch basin under acid tanks that may leak), pressure relief valves, contaminant sensors, or training of employees.

3. *To recall the product for retrofit of redesigned parts of other changes.* A recall is usually expensive, but if the classification of the hazard is critical or catastrophic, it should be given very serious consideration (see description of hazard effects and control analysis for the meanings of the critical and catastrophic classifications). Sometimes, as with food or toys, it is necessary to request that the product be destroyed rather than recalled. Again, if the hazard classification warrants, this action should not be delayed.

4. *To develop a disaster plan to mitigate emergencies.* The Bhopal disaster in India was an example of a catastrophic emergency where the lack of disaster planning resulted in thousands of deaths and injuries. Disaster planning requires serious and dedicated attention by experienced planners; therefore, such action must be authorized and funded.

The above actions on behalf of customers and the community are results of the Exposure Study's management decision point (see Fig. 7-1). Without such an analysis many companies may never consider the dangers associated with their product or service until it is too late. Or, they may consider the dangers in a piecemeal fashion, which would be almost as bad.

The study now proceeds to Figure 7-2.

MDPA SECTION IV: EXPOSURE LEVEL SURVEY

In the Exposure Level Survey we are concerned with the danger level of the hazard, either physical or chemical. Chemical hazards, usually measured by a trained industrial hygienist, are defined by threshold limit values (TLV) and action levels, which are usually one-half the TLV. To determine TLVs, industrial hygiene measurements are made with charcoal tubes or impingers and the obtained air samples are quantified in an analytical laboratory. Direct reading instruments such as a portable chromatograph or H-Nu, are also used to determine the concentration of an air contaminant at the source. Other instruments measure noise, vibration, temperature, and ionizing and nonionizing radiation.

For example, toluene (a common ingredient in paints) has a TLV of 100 ppm (100 parts of toluene to one million parts of air by volume) for an 8-hour exposure (time weighted average [TWA]). If an air sample reveals that 75 ppm of toluene is in the breathing zone of workers, it would be above the action level and would require the analysis to proceed to Section V. Noise exposure has a TLV of 90 dBA (decibels, A

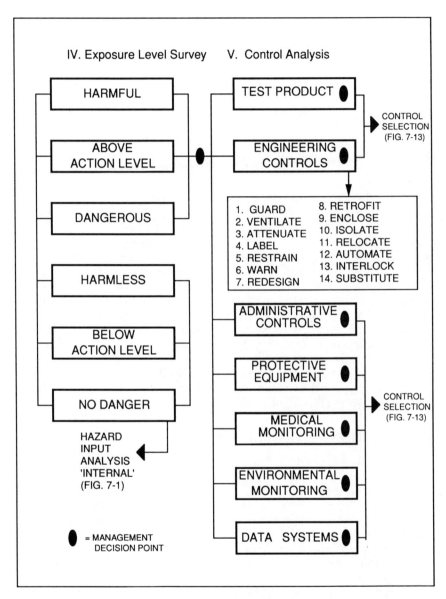

Figure 7-2. Management decision point analysis (MDPA) (continued).

scale) for an 8-hour exposure with an action level of 85 dBA. If the measured exposure was 75 dBA, then this level would be considered harmless. This information, as well as overexposure exposure data, would return to the internal information bank for future reference. It is important to note here that to accurately measure the contaminants just referenced, the services of a trained industrial hygienist would be required because of the complexity of sampling and quantifying them.

It would be necessary to continue the analysis where chemical or other industrial exposure is concerned when a measurement is equal to or above the action level. Where there is no specified action level, one-half of the TLV should be the criterion.

The Exposure Level Survey includes physical hazards that can be measured by the hazard danger level chart (see Fig. 5-4) used in the hazard effects and control analysis (HECA). If a hazard meets the criteria for danger level D2 or D3, the analysis proceeds. For example, a worker using a press brake is bending small sheet metal parts using a foot switch. The job requires that the operator bring her hands within 1.5 inches of the closing die and then press the foot-actuated switch. This is an extremely dangerous operation, classification D3, and should be stopped until appropriate safeguards are installed or alternative means of fabrication are found. This requires continuation of the management decision point analysis to Section V, entitled Control Analysis. The words "Dangerous" and "No Danger" are the operative terms for physical hazards.

The denial of danger or harm must be well thought out, preferably after a quantitative determination that there is a reasonable probability that danger level D2, D3, or an action level does not exist.

MDPA SECTION V: CONTROL ANALYSIS

If you reach the Control Analysis point in the MDPA, it has been determined that persons are exposed to a harmful chemical or physical agent or a dangerous physical safety hazard. The Control Analysis section offers alternatives that address the mitigation of this problem as well as the retention of problem-related data. Continuous monitoring of exposed workers and the work environment are also necessary. The alternatives presented in Figure 7-2 may not be the only available options, and some of the choices, such as medical and environmental monitoring and the establishment of data systems, must be employed concurrently with the selected method(s) of hazard control. It is impor-tant to remember that the control selections listed in Section V are alternative methods, and therefore only a few or only one may apply to a given problem.

The objective of Section V is not only to determine what engineering controls will mitigate a problem but also to help determine if the cost of correction is equal to, less than, or more than the benefit derived from the application of the control. For example, if it is established that in an industrial setting where there is a noise pressure of 107 dBA, a large expenditure will achieve a reduction of 3 dBA, such a reduction would still expose workers to noise far beyond the permissible exposure limit (PEL) of 90 dBA for an 8-hour period. Therefore the noise attenuation attempt, even though it would result in noise reduction, would be ineffectual.

Another important aspect of the Control Analysis section is the need for the organization of formal and documented consideration of controls. Deliberations on the choice of controls should involve safety, technical, and management personnel who are high enough in the organization hierarchy to authorize and fund the chosen remedy. When a management decision point is reached, it is a signal for these deliberations to take place.

A last important consideration before making a control analysis is the use of the hierarchy of accident prevention. It is always wise to prioritize according to hierarchy principles and to use the secondary methods (where applicable) of warning, training, and protective equipment along with the primary techniques of hazard elimination and safeguarding.

The following paragraphs discuss the attributes of Part V, Control Analysis. Some of the information will be in the form of questions that are intended to make the reader aware of an action that may be necessary to avoid a litigation-producing event. For example, if, when using a hand-held power grinder, it is possible for the grinding wheel to shatter if the wheel being used is underrated for speed, then a question related to warnings on the tool itself and in the owner's manual would be appropriate. In just such a case, the tool manufacturer neglected to use warnings on the product or in the related literature. As a result, the operator, with very unsatisfactory results, used a grinding wheel rated at 7000 rpm on a hand grinder that turned at 12,000 rpm. This case settled out of court. The manufacturer neglected to consider the propriety of effectively written warnings that would have prevented litigation in this case.

Product Testing

If a defendant has done insufficient or has completely neglected to do product testing, he or she has little chance of prevailing in a lawsuit. The product designer and manufacturer must examine the need for testing the product from several angles. The first consideration is the official government criteria for the class of product. For example, the Food and Drug Administration requires extensive testing of foodstuffs, cosmetics, and over-the-counter and prescription drugs. If these criteria are met, then the national consensus standards (e.g., ANSI, ASTM) as well as industry or trade standards should be consulted to determine if the product meets all these criteria. And last and probably most important, because this type of testing is most often omitted, is "foreseeable use" testing.

Foreseeable use testing requires that the product not only be tested as it would be assembled and used in the manufacturer's instructions, but tested in a foreseeably altered configuration that a customer may consider to be advantageous to production, accuracy, or ease of use. If during this process a hazard or hazards are uncovered, then appropriate warnings and modifications should be made.

If, for example, a machine can only process raw material of certain dimensions, it is foreseeable that a user would modify the device to accommodate larger size material. In performing this modification barrier guards have to be removed and the operator is brought closer to an exposed point of operation. The manufacturer should warn against this modification and interlock the guard so that removal would render the machine inoperative. Another solution would be to redesign the machine to accommodate the larger size raw material with effective point of operation guarding.

This latter solution is the more appropriate one, especially if the larger size material is often or even sometimes used in the industry. This means that the designer/manufacturer must do competent research into the needs of the industries that are being serviced to determine standard operating procedures, as well as future and nonstandard requirements.

Mechanical Controls

The controls described here give a representative sampling of the type of controls that will eliminate or reduce the number and seriousness of hazards, or otherwise reduce exposure to litigation. None of them are mutually exclusive in the sense that it may take more than one type of control to realize the desired effect.

Guards

The guarding of machinery is a voluminous subject, and can fill a book in itself. However, because guarding is so often required to protect product users, it is necessary to include here a substantial, but not a complete treatment of this subject. For more detailed information on guarding it would be wise to consult a dedicated book on machine guarding. Since new titles appear often, the National Safety Council, The National Institute for Occupational Safety and Health (NIOSH), and the reading lists contained in *Professional Safety*, the journal of the American Society of Safety Engineers (ASSE), are good sources for titles of these books.

The basic principle of guarding deals with exposure to the point of operation (PO), or the place on the machine where work is accomplished. If the operator of a machine requires access to the point of operation in order to accomplish a task such as sawing wood, forming sheet metal, or milling wood or metal, then some method must be considered that will deny operator access to the PO, or in the least make access very difficult.

As a technique for litigation prevention, the consideration of appropriate guarding is mandatory. OSHA law requires it, elimination or safeguarding against hazards (see accident prevention hierarchy) requires it, and juries will generally find for the plaintiff in cases where appropriate guards or even appropriate application of guards have been omitted.

As an example of inappropriate application, if an in-place guard is easy to remove or it is advantageous to the machine operator to remove the guard for cleaning or to expedite machine operation, then the guard should be designed to prevent removal or the necessity for removal should be eliminated. Interlocking the guard with the electrical power and making the guard more convenient for routine use are methods for preventing or mitigating the need for removal.

Methods of guarding are many, but they fall into a number of broad categories. These are fixed guards, self-adjusting guards, trip devices, control guards, interlocking guards, distance guards, two-hand controls, overrun devices, and barriers. Following are descriptions and illustrations of these types of guards.

Fixed guards are usually used to prevent access to machinery drives such as belts, shafts, pulleys, and conveyor rolls. They should be constructed of sturdy material similar to the construction of the machine on which they are used. Fixed guards should be designed to be difficult to remove but still enable access to the dangerous nip and shear points of drive trains by trained maintenance personnel who have a need to repair, lubricate, or adjust these machine areas.

Example: In one case,* the omission of a fixed guard resulted in the violent removal of a worker's leg, when the mere compliance with the elementary principle of guarding a conveyor transmission point would have prevented the catastrophic injury (See Fig. 7-3.) The huge conveyor involved was used to carry wood chips to the sixth-floor storage area in the digester building of a pulp mill. At a point where the conveyor belt at ground level ran around a 2-foot-diameter pulley, wood chips fell from the belt and had to be periodically shoveled from the area. The area was surrounded on three sides by a 3-foot-high cement wall.

One day after he had finished shoveling chips, a worker boosted himself up to the top of the cement wall by placing his right foot onto the bed of the moving conveyor belt. His foot was drawn into the in-running nip of the pulley. He was unable to extricate himself, and his leg was taken off by this powerful machine.

Taylor v. Atlas Systems. See Appendix.

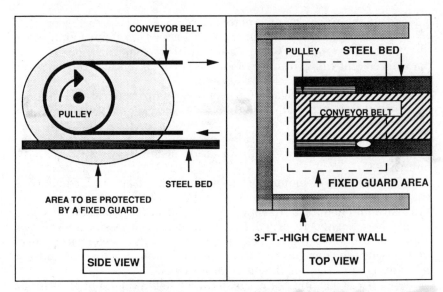

Figure 7-3. Conveyor belt accident. The text describes a catastrophic injury to a worker who boosted himself up on top of the cement enclosure by placing his foot in the area marked with this symbol ○. The object of the fixed guard is to deny access to the nip point of the conveyor transmission. This is yet another illustration of the futility of depending on safe practice. The designer must foresee that a worker may come into contact with this unguarded nip point. The reason for contact may not be supportable from a safety point of view, but the unsafe practice of the worker is not justification for the unguarded area. The case settled out of court.

Had one of the suggested analyses been performed before the conveyor was placed into service, a simple but effective fixed guard would have been installed by the conveyor installer (designer) that would have effectively prevented access to this conveyor danger point.

Self-adjusting guards are used to accommodate the varying shape of the workpiece as it passes through the PO. This type of guard is used on table saws, jointers, and radial arm saws. On the radial arm saw a self-adjusting lower blade guard is used in combination with an adjustable upper blade guard.

Self-adjusting guards do *not* prevent access to the point of operation if the part of the body approaches it in the same plane as the workpiece. For example, on a radial arm saw if a part of the body is in the path of the blade as the carriage is pulled, the saw will remove that body part even though a lower blade guard is in use. This is because just as the saw would process the workpiece, it would also "process" any part of the body in its path. The lower blade guard will protect only against side access to the point of operation.

> *Example:*   In one case,* a worker was using a cutoff saw, which has guarding similar to a radial arm saw. Since the worker was producing several thousand wood parts of the same dimensions, he used the expected operational cadence. It was a cold day, there was no heat in the factory building, and the worker wore gloves to keep his hands warm. This greatly reduced his awareness of the location of his fingers. As a result, the fingers of his right hand were eventually placed in the cutting plane of the saw and were amputated. In this case, the guard operated as expected and simply treated the worker's fingers as a workpiece. The allegation by the injured of improper guard design could not be supported in this case (see Fig. 7-4).

Trip devices describe a large class of guards that are used to shut down machinery when the trip device detects that the possibility of a danger-ous worker–machine interface exists. This would mean that a worker who gets his or her hand too close to the in-running nip of a rubber mill would first contact a lever or a taut cable that would trip the power switch that controls the mill. The lever and the taught line mechanically senses the presence of the worker's hand, and the motion of the hand becomes linked to the power shutoff by means of the lever or taught line.

As is the case with most trip devices, it is important that the dangerous machinery stop immediately, that is, with little or no overrun. In an actual incident the rolls of a feed mill continued to turn for 24 seconds after the power was shut down. During the overrun period the worker was caught in the nip and seriously injured. Overrun devices are a class of guard discussed later in this section.

Other types of trip devices are:

- *light curtains*—beams of light that are broken as a worker passes into the danger zone at the wrong time (for example, when the ram of a punch press is in the down stroke), thus shutting down the machine.
- *pressure-sensitive mats*—sense that a worker has stepped too close to the point of operation and electrically interrupt the circuit so that the machine shuts down.
- *strip switches*—can be 100 feet or more in length, and if touched with light pressure at any point over their full length, will shut down the machine electrically. These devices are often used to protect people who work around motorized conveyors, or are used where a worksta-tion size varies over distance. See Figure 7-5 for illustrations of trip devices.

Control guards (Fig. 7-6) use the shutoff mechanism of the machine to prevent access to a dangerous point of operation or to the machine itself

---

*Case not filed.

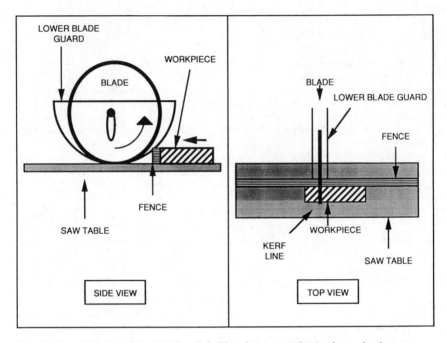

Figure 7-4. The self-adjusting guard. The diagrams depict how the lower blade guard on a radial arm saw will swivel upward to accommodate the thickness of the workpiece. As the saw blade cuts the wood, the kerf line is produced, which is of course the same width as the thickness of the blade (including the set of the teeth). It is important to note that the lower blade guard will not protect the operator if his hands are in the kerf line as the saw is pulled. The lower guard will protect against side entry into the point of operation.

while it is in operation. For example, if a belt-driven compressor is contained in a cabinet and it must be serviced periodically, it may be dangerous for the maintenance person to lubricate the machine while it is running. To assure that this does not happen, the control switch is so placed that the cabinet door will not open unless the switch is in the off position. Here again, overrun is an important consideration.

Overrun devices prevent or minimize the continued operation, due to momentum, of machines after the shutdown switch has been activated. The most common overrun device is a mechanical or electrical brake. Mechanical brakes use the same principle of automobile braking systems where the moving surface is slowed by frictional forces. There are a variety of electrically operated brakes that use capacitors, motor reversing, or direct current injection to accomplish braking.

A third class of overrun device uses a mechanical or electronic time

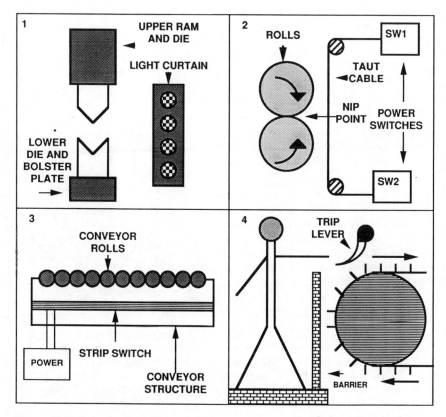

Figure 7-5. Trip devices. This illustration shows four applications of trip devices. In the first box a light curtain protects the point of operation on a press brake. If any of the four light beams are interrupted while the upper ram is in the downstroke, the brake will shut down. In the second box, the taut cable, if pushed or pulled, will actuate the shutoff switches SW1 and SW2. The third box shows a motorized conveyor where some roller pairs have the capability of pulling in hair, clothing, or a body part. In the event a person becomes caught in the in-running nip, all that person need do is to lean against the strip switch to shut the belt down. The fourth box shows a worker who has access to a dangerous point of operation. If the worker's hand gets too close to the point of operation, the trip lever actuates a switch that effects machine shutdown. In all cases machine overrun is a consideration and must be minimized or eliminated.

delay at the point of operation to prevent the machine from operating until it has had sufficient time to stop its motion. Figure 7-7 illustrates these devices.

Interlocking guards are used to prevent or discourage guard removal by making the presence of the guard necessary to machine operation.

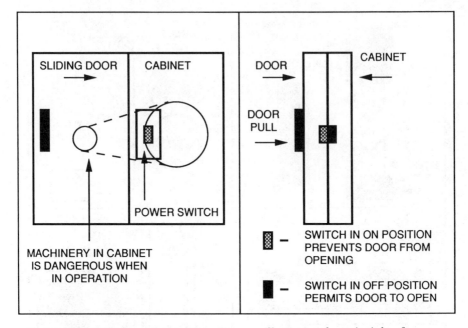

Figure 7-6. Control guarding. This diagram illustrates the principle of control guarding, where to gain access to dangerous machinery while it is in operation requires that the power be shut down. In this case, a problem may be machinery overrun. If the motor continues to turn for a period of time after the power is shut off, there may be enough time for a person to access the machine while it is in the dangerous mode. See the section on overrun control devices for more information.

This can be accomplished by interlocking the guard with the electrical, pneumatic, or hydraulic power, or by mechanical means, as illustrated in Figure 7-8.

> **Example:** The operator of an electronic riveting machine removed the guard to the power supply because he needed to periodically gain access to the power supply circuitry to make minor adjustments.* During one of these adjustments his elbow contacted a large capacitor and he was electrocuted. The argument raised by the plaintiff in the subsequent litigation was that the power supply guard should have been interlocked so that removal would shut off the power. The warnings on the guard explaining the danger of removal were considered insufficient because of the need to gain access to the power supply circuitry in order to keep the device operating.

*Author did not participate in this case; cited for example only.

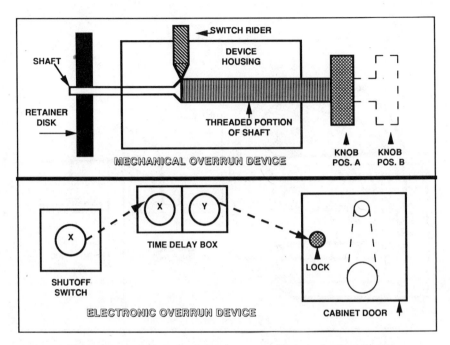

Figure 7-7. Mechanical and electronic overrun devices. In the *upper diagram* when the knob is in position A, the motor is running and the shaft is in the hole in the retainer disk. When the shaft is in this position the door to the dangerous machinery cannot be opened. When the knob is turned counterclockwise the switch rider drops down to the level of the reduced-diameter shaft and the power to the motor is shut off. However, because the motor overruns, this design requires the operator to continue turning the shaft until the knob is in position B and the shaft has cleared the retainer disk. The time that this takes allows the motor to come to a complete stop. In the *lower diagram* two keys (key X and key Y) are used. Only key Y will open the cabinet door for access to the dangerous machinery. Key X can be removed from the shutoff switch only if the switch is in the off position. To gain access to the cabinet interior the operator shuts off the power and transfers key X to its noted position in the time delay box. This actuates the time delay mechanism, which releases key Y after the motor completes its overrun. Key Y is now available to safely open the cabinet door. The machine may not be started again until the cabinet door is locked and all keys are in their original positions. The concepts used in these examples can have many applications.

Interlocks can be electrical or mechanical, should be difficult if not impossible to defeat, and in most cases should be considered as required unless it can be shown that the dangerous parts of machines or devices are out of reach of the operator.

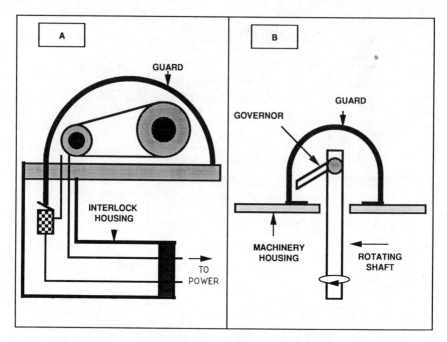

Figure 7-8. Electrical and mechanical interlocks. In diagram A the power to the dangerous machinery depends upon proper guard installation. If the guard is removed, the switch, represented by the symbol ▨ is actuated in the open position, thus shutting down the power to the motor. When the guard is reinstalled power becomes available. It is important to the design of this interlocked guard that the controlling switch be difficult to access by the operator, making the interlock difficult to defeat. In diagram B, when the shaft is rotating, the lever (governor) swivels outward due to centrifugal force, thus preventing removal of the guard. When the shaft ceases rotation, the lever recesses and permits guard removal. In both of these cases overrun is a consideration.

The theory of the popular *two-hand control* operation is that the operator's hands are occupied with the two-hand control buttons while the machine is performing its work and therefore cannot come in contact with the dangerous parts of the machine. One of the major shortcomings of this type of guarding is that the operator is not protected during the loading and unloading of the machine.

Unless proper design principles are carefully followed, the advantages of two-hand control can be, and have been, defeated in actual use. These principles are:

1. The distance between the controls must be such that the operator cannot actuate them with a hand and an elbow of the same arm, thus leaving the other hand free.

2. If the operator removes his or her hands from the buttons while the machine is in the danger mode, such as a punch press with the ram in downstroke, then the machine must stop as quickly as possible.
3. The circuitry has to be designed so that the buttons must be actuated within microseconds of each other. This will prevent the operator from defeating their purpose by permanently wedging down one of the buttons.
4. The design of the two-hand control system must prevent double tripping. Double tripping means that the machine could operate unexpectedly when the operator's hands are in the point of operation, and is a source of many disastrous injuries.
5. The buttons on punch presses must be designed so that they can be moved a greater distance from the point of operation to compensate for brake wear. As breaks wear the press takes longer to stop, providing the operator with more time to bring his or her hands into the point of operation. A formula in the punch press section of OSHA law prescribes the appropriate distance to account for brake wear.

Stroke-limiting and *mute-point guarding* are used with punch presses and press brakes, and rely on the principle of limiting the upward travel of the upper die. In stroke limiting the upper die never ascends high enough so that fingers can be inserted between the dies (this is known as the mute point). Since these machines are often used on sheet metal, there is still enough room for the work to be inserted between the dies for processing. Figure 7-9 illustrates stroke limiting.

Another, similar type of guarding, used mostly on press brakes, is *mute-point guarding.* With this type of guarding the upper ram is raised to its uppermost position. The ram (upper die) is then brought to the mute point by means of two-hand control. With the upper die at the mute point, the work is inserted between the dies, and the operation is completed by using a foot switch. After the part is formed the upper die again ascends to its uppermost position.

Distance guards are devices that keep the operator a sufficient distance from the point of operation so that he or she cannot reach into the danger area before the machine completes the dangerous phases of its motion. This can be accomplished by hard wiring a foot switch to an appropriate distance instead of wiring the switch with flexible cable. Another method is to surround the machine with a pressure-sensitive mat so that the machine shuts down if the operator gets too close. See Figure 7-10 for an illustration of a distance guard.

This figure also contains a distance table published in the OSHA machine guarding standards that relates the operator's distance from the point of operation to the size of the opening in a guard that provides operator access to the PO. In other words, the larger the opening in the guard, the greater the operator's distance must be from the point of operation.

Distance guards are not popular because they may restrict the

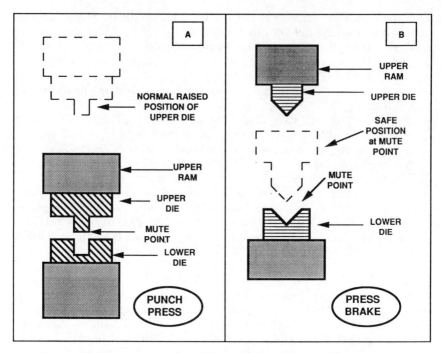

Figure 7-9. Stroke-limiting and mute-point guarding. In stroke limiting, illustrated in diagram A, the upper ram and upper die are never raised above the mute point. In this way the operator's hands can never fit between the dies, but the sheet metal that is being processed can. In mute point guarding, shown in diagram B, the upper ram is permitted to ascend to its uppermost position, but when it is brought down by actuating two-palm buttons, the upper ram stops at the mute point (safe position). The sheet metal work is then inserted, and the fabrication is finished by actuating a foot switch that brings the dies together. See text for mute-point definition.

number and type of operations that a machine can perform. This is because an operator who is not using a distance guard will have greater access to the point of operation and a wider variety of parts, both in size and type, can be processed and more accurate control can be exerted.

Barriers will usually prevent all access to the PO, except where the opening exists to admit the work. The size of this opening and its distance from the point of operation are regulated by the OSHA table shown on Figure 7-10. Barriers are particularly useful on automatic machinery where the only necessary human contact is not for production, but for set up, repair, and maintenance. This greatly reduces worker exposure to danger.

DISTANCE OF OPENING FROM POINT OF OPERATION HAZARD (INCHES)	MAXIMUM WIDTH OF OPENING (INCHES)
1/4 TO 1 1/2	1/4
1 1/2 TO 2 1/2	3/8
2 1/2 TO 3 1/2	1/2
3 1/2 TO 5 1/2	5/8
5 1/2 TO 6 1/2	3/4
6 1/2 TO 7 1/2	7/8
7 1/2 TO 12 1/2	1 1/4
12 1/2 TO 15 1/2	1 1/2
15 1/2 TO 17 1/2	1 7/8
17 1/2 TO 31 1/2	2 1/8

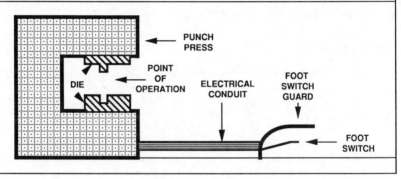

Figure 7-10. Distance guard. The table in the upper diagram shows the distance that guards shall be positioned from the danger line (point of operation). The various openings are such that for average-size hands an operator's fingers won't reach the point of operation. This table is part of OSHA law. The distance guard illustrated in the lower diagram depicts a foot switch that is "hard-wired," meaning that the switch is wired with steel walled electrical conduit that prevents the switch from being moved closer to the punch press. In the switch's present location the punch press operator cannot reach the point of operation while the upper die is moving toward the lower die. The operator's distance from the point of operation accomplishes this requirement.

Ventilation

Producers or users of chemicals; paint booths; paints; protective equipment such as respirators; confined spaces such as tanks, pits, and vats; aerosols or related equipment; fiber products such as asbestos, rock wool, or fiberglass; and other materials and devices that can asphyxiate and poison, need to consider the need for correct ventilation for customers, incidentally involved persons, and workers. The following questions should be addressed on behalf of persons who may use or purchase this type of material or equipment:

1. Are there appropriate warnings in the owner's manual, on the product, and at the dangerous facility?
2. Do the warnings meet the effectiveness criteria in Chapter 6 of this book?
3. Do the instructions give explicit advice as to what constitutes adequate ventilation?
4. In cases where premature death or serious injury may be the outcome of an adverse exposure, is this possibility explained?
5. Where included ventilation devices will reasonably reduce or eliminate serious exposure, has such equipment been integrated into the product or facility?
6. Are properly filled out material safety data sheets provided?

Attenuation

If your product is a machine or equipment that generates a noise pressure level to the operator or persons nearby that can cause TTS (temporary threshold shift), and there are relatively simple means to attenuate (reduce) the noise, then you are a potential defendant in a lawsuit. Temporary threshold shift refers to the loss of hearing acuity that occurs after exposure to noise pressure levels above 85 dBA. Although it is really not temporary in the sense that hearing acuity never completely returns to its former level after exposure ceases, a slight, unnoticeable amount of hearing ability is lost each day of exposure until constant exposure over the years results in significant hearing loss. Manufacturers, designers, and users of such machines or devices should ask the following questions.

1. Are there appropriate warnings in the owner's manual, on the product itself, or in the noisy facility?
2. Are the warnings effective? (see Chapter 6).
3. Do the warnings deal explicitly with the danger and the type of hearing protection required?
4. Is it feasible to use noise attenuation devices such as mufflers, sound absorbant materials, or enclosures to attenuate the noise?
5. Can the high noise be eliminated or safeguarded against by the use of a different means of power (internal combustion to electric), changing the location of workstations, or changing fastening methodology, for example, from riveting to the use of bolts or squeeze fasteners?
6. If any of the actions in 5 are options, is their availability made clearly known to the machine/device purchasers?

Labeling

Manufacturers, importers, and distributors of chemicals must not only label their products in accordance with federal, state, and local regulations but must also comply with federal and state right-to-know legislation. This requires that a material safety data sheet (MSDS) accompany the product at the time of purchase. If an MSDS is already in the hands of the customer, then it must be updated when applicable.

To avoid possible litigation MSDSs need to be completely filled out with meaningful, truthful information so that users are aware of potential dangers from handling the material and how these dangers are to be treated in the event the users are exposed.

Some questions related to labeling are:

1. Are users of the material at risk of injury?
2. Are appropriate labels affixed?
3. Do the labels meet the criteria discussed in Chapter 6?
4. Is there a program in place for developing and updating MSDSs?

Restraints

> **Example:** A woman hired herself out as an independent contractor to service an atrium in an office building. Her job was to water houseplants on four levels in the inner court of the building. To gain access to the plants she had to step out onto a walkway composed of 2 × 10-in. boards. The plants were in planter boxes located outboard of the walkway. On the other side of the planter boxes was a dropoff that became 10 feet higher with each level.
>
> Fall protection was provided in the form of an outboard rail, but for aesthetic reasons the configuration of the railing did not meet regulations. The midrail was missing and there was no toeboard. See Figure 7-11.
>
> The second reason for not providing adequate fall protection was low exposure. Because only one person was required to use the catwalk each week, it was felt that the chances of a problem were minimized. However, the danger level from a 35-foot fall is at the high end of D3 (extremely dangerous) and positive fall protection must be provided in this case either through a standard rail or through the use of belts, lanyards, and adequate tieoff provision.
>
> In this case, the improper fall protection resulted in a 35-foot fall to a brick floor that caused catastrophic and permanently disabling injuries.

Warnings

Warnings are covered in detail in Chapter 6, and little more need be added here except for some questions that will enable the analyst to discover oversights.

1. In the case of dangerous machinery, are warnings considered each time a user may be in danger? For example, a radial arm saw can

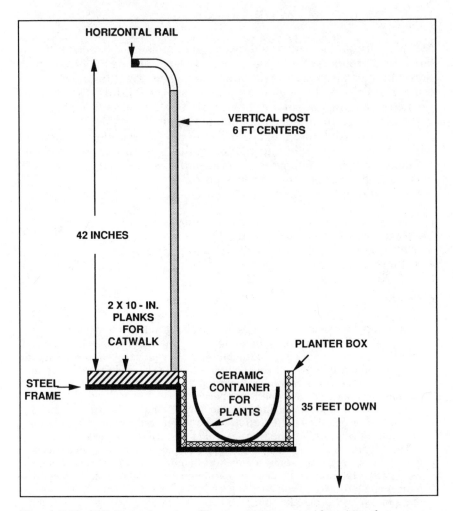

Figure 7-11. Fall from elevation. There were two considerations that resulted in inadequate fall protection for persons who watered the plants contained in the planter boxes. They were the aesthetic design of the rail that resulted in the omitted midrail and toeboard, and the fact that only one person would be required to be on the catwalk per week (low exposure). Both of these considerations must be discarded in favor of appropriate restraints, either in the form of a standard rail or in the form of a belt and lanyard with adequate tieoff provision.

crosscut, rip, sand, route, mitre, and perform numerous other functions. Each of these functions may have significant hazards to the operator. Therefore each hazard must be highlighted in the most appropriate place, for example, in the owner's manual and/or on the saw itself.
2. Are warnings in the owner's manual, on the instruction sheets, and on the device itself?
3. Are the warnings durable, explicit, and placed where needed on the equipment?
4. Are audible or visual signal types of warnings appropriate?
5. Is color coding a good option?
6. Are warnings sufficiently highlighted in the owner's manual so that they are in marked contrast to the textual materials?

Redesign

There may be hundreds of reasons for redesigning equipment. For litigation-prevention purposes the most compelling (other than the discovery that the device is unreasonably hazardous for use as the designer intended) is foreseeable use. If it can be foreseen that a machine will be used or modified for use in any way that is different from that which the designer intended, and that that usage is clearly hazardous, the device should be redesigned to enhance safety. Before the device is marketed the designer and manufacturer should ask themselves the following questions:

1. Is it probable or desirable that the machine or device will be used without existing guards? If this is anticipated, then existing guarding should be interlocked or existing interlocks made more difficult to defeat.
2. Is it probable or desirable that raw material that is beyond the capacity of the machine or device will be processed? If such misuse will bring the operator in closer contact with the point of operation, a redesign should be considered that will enable the machine to process material that meets the needs of the industry.
3. Is it probable or desirable that the machine or device will be operated at a dangerous feed or speed? Appropriately placed warnings may be the answer to this problem.
4. Is it probable or desirable that the machine or device will be used with underrated accessories such as a grinding wheel rated at too low a speed? Warnings on the device are a way of protecting the operator and avoiding litigation from this source.
5. Is it probable or desirable that a user will misapply a fastening or restraining device with the result that the user will be at risk? Some type of fail-safe design may be required to prevent possible misuse.

6. Is it probable that a failure to lubricate or otherwise service a machine or device will cause a catastrophic failure that could place the user at risk for personal injury? Redesign of the bearing surfaces may be necessary, along with appropriate warnings.
7. Is it probable that replacement of certain critical parts with interchangeable parts of the wrong type may create a lethal hazard? The user must be warned against this wrongful act, and whenever possible the design should be configured so that the installation of the dangerous parts is impossible or very difficult.
8. Is it probable or desirable that the user of a machine or device would use it beyond its capability, and thereby create a personal injury hazard?

These questions can by no means cover all foreseeable misuse conditions. The designer and manufacturer must devote time and effort to anticipate how operators of their equipment can misapply the intentions of their design.

Retrofitting

There are many machines still in operation in this country and abroad that are primitively fitted for operator safety. The press brake usually requires the operator to hold the raw material within inches or even fractions of an inch from the descending ram, which has been set in motion by a foot treadle. This hand to foot to eye coordination is easily interrupted with a traumatic amputation as the consequence.

Example: In a recent case an operator, his right foot poised on the foot pedal, was holding sheet metal between the dies on a press brake when he lost his balance. Instinctively he placed both hands in front of him between the dies to prevent a fall. At the same time his forward motion placed all of his weight on the foot control. Both hands were amputated. With some small variations this incident is classic in the sense that through the years operators have been suffering the same type of traumatic amputations on press brakes, even though there are devices and techniques that can greatly reduce the probability of these injuries.

Designers and manufacturers that produce dangerous equipment, if they wish to avoid litigation, should retrofit their machines to conform to the advances in the state of the safety art. At the minimum they should supply users with detailed information on protective devices, schematics, and promotional literature in order to improve safety to operators. It may cost five to fifteen thousand dollars to retrofit a press brake, but this is a small price to pay to avoid traumatic amputations and litigation that has already cost businesses many millions of dollars.

Enclosure

There are some exposures that require complete enclosure of the operator for adequate protection. Examples are crane operators who work over fume-producing operations such as metal smelting, and paper machine operators exposed to high noise. The equipment designer and manufacturer must determine if in the course of using the equipment an operator will be exposed to harmful radiation or to physical, chemical, or biological hazards. If the answer is yes, then enclosing the operator may eliminate this problem.

Isolation

Some exposures, such as ionizing and nonionizing radiation, by their nature must be isolated from workers and the general public. Plastic fabrication and pesticide manufacture are other operations that fit this category. Here the operation rather than the operator is enclosed. The question for the designer and manufacturer is the same, "If there is harmful exposure, will isolating the operation protect from harm?"

Relocation

Sometimes the simple act of changing the position of part of an operation or facility will reduce the level of exposure or eliminate the problem entirely. A chip-collection device for a wood shop was first located inside the shop, where the noise of 87 dBA was extremely annoying and considered harmful by the employees. The manufacturer failed to say in the owner's manual that the optimum location for the vacuum device was outside the building. When the device was finally moved outside, the problem went with it. Here again the manufacturer and designer cannot rely upon the safe practice of their customers, and must be forthcoming with the correct safety and health advice.

Automation

Elimination of the man–machine interface many times will eliminate the hazard. Care must be taken not to create a new, possibly more dangerous situation such as personnel put at risk from unguarded or malfunctioning robot arms. In one case where many operator-controlled punch presses were making chainsaw blades, the operators were at continued risk when loading and unloading the presses. By automating the procedure (see Fig. 7-12) not only was the hazard eliminated but the number of presses was reduced from eight to two.

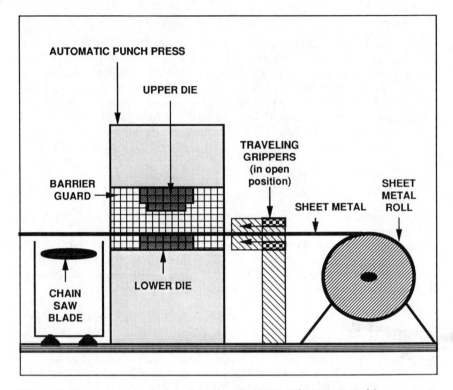

Figure 7-12. An automatic punch press eliminates the man–machine interface. In the diagram, when the upper die is ascending, the traveling grippers grip the sheet metal and move a fresh surface onto the lower die. The upper die then descends and stamps out a chainsaw blade blank. As the upper die begins to raise, the grippers open and an air blast pushes the blank out of the press into the storage bin, and the whole process starts over again. The die area is completely enclosed, preventing operator access to the point of operation.

Interlocking

Guarding is a very effective way to prevent operator access to the point of operation, but guarding has foreseeable limitations. Guards are often of flimsy construction and will self-destruct over time. Many times they will be removed because the machine must be cleaned or repaired or otherwise serviced, and sometimes they will not be replaced. Guards also will be removed because the operator does not like the inconvenience, or because using the guard reduces accuracy.

Whatever the reason for operating a device without a guard, the prudent designer will interlock the guard with machine power so that the machine will not operate with the guard removed. Further, the interlock should be designed so that it is very difficult to defeat. Because the machine will not operate without it, the guard should be as heavily built as the machine itself.

Substitution

During the major part of the twentieth century farmers found that crop production was proportional to the amount and effectiveness of pesticides they used; now, many of these farm chemicals, identified as carcinogens, are being replaced with biological agents and insect predators that are considered benign to humans . . . Some hardeners in two-part epoxy compounds have serious sensitization problems; other polymer systems using hardeners with less sensitization potential can be substituted successfully . . . As a solvent, the leukemia-generating benzene is almost gone from paint and other product formulations, and other solvents with far less illness-producing potential have been substituted. These are three examples of chemical substitutions that have eliminated or reduced a serious exposure hazard.

Two examples of substitution in machine operations are (1) a normally hazardous radial arm saw operation may instead be accomplished on a swing arm router using a fixture that keeps the operator away from the point of operation, and (2) since hand deburring operations produce a parade of minor injuries that can become infected or result in scarring over long periods of exposure, it is frequently possible to accomplish deburring in a punch press, for example, if the die is correctly designed. A consideration in all cases of substitution is that the substituted chemical, process, or machine should not be as hazardous as or more hazardous than the original.

Administrative Controls

In some instances exposures to harmful substances or forms of radiation, such as noise and microwaves, cannot be controlled by traditional means. If the exposures are not excessive and production penalties are not prohibitive, worker exposures can be adjusted administratively over time. This means that if a group of workers exposed to a noise pressure level of 95 dBA for 8 hours can be moved to a low-noise area (below 80 dBA) for 4 of the 8 hours, then the letter of the law is met. However, the question still remains as to what to do with these employees for the 4 hours they are not at their regular workstation.

In theory the same system would work for chemical exposures, where limiting the time an employee works in a contaminated environment could reduce the time-weighted average to below the action level. However, because of their action on the body, certain chemicals have additional exposure limitations other than the permissible exposure limit (PEL). That is why it is necessary to obtain the advice of a trained industrial hygienist before attempting administrative controls for any exposure, including noise.

Protective Equipment

This section on protective equipment is concerned with the need for providing information on the limitations of protective equipment to the end user. Other than defective design and manufacture, which is heavily covered in other sections of this book, when the user does not understand the limitations of the protective equipment he or she is using, the manufacturer and distributor are at their most vulnerable for a lawsuit.

Case Study 7-1

Few clearly thinking persons will use a plastic crucible to hold molten aluminum, yet there have been molten-metal splash injuries where workers were protected by only a 0.040-in.-thick plastic faceshield. In one (previously cited) case* a worker, whose job it was to tend a direct chill casting machine in an aluminum smelter, was leaning over the machine during the start of a cast (called a *drop*). In the course of operating the machine over the years, the worker had found that small to large explosions of molten aluminum would occur randomly, especially at the start of a drop. Sometimes the force of a particularly violent explosion would carry molten metal to the ceiling, 60 feet above.

As the start of the drop proceeded the worker, who wore an aluminized coat and a faceshield with prescription safety glasses underneath, noticed that the casting was not proceeding normally. He attempted, as he had done many times in the past, to adjust the flow of aluminum to correct the problem. At that moment an exceptionally violent explosion of molten aluminum occurred, penetrating the face shield, and resulting in permanent blindness in both eyes.

In the subsequent lawsuit the manufacturer of the faceshield was faulted for not warning, in a clear manner, of this limitation in the use of his product. The case against the manufacturers and designers of both the casting machine and the faceshield was settled out of court.

There is no assurance that an appropriately designed and distributed warning would have prevented this injury, but the issues are (1) did the manufacturer use all open avenues to inform users, their supervisors, and safety professionals of this limitation on the use of their product? and (2) was there a consideration that by emphasizing limitations, the

---

Johnson v. *Bausch & Lombe*. See Appendix.

manufacturer would lose a percentage of market share? If the latter occurred, it constitutes imprudent marketing of a product that is used for personal protection against highly dangerous industrial exposures.

Table 7-1 contains a list of protective equipment and its limitations that can serve as a guide for appropriate warnings. The list serves as a model, and therefore is not a complete listing of all protective equipment. It is assumed that manufacturers and their distributors are knowledgeable of their own product's limitations and would be able to develop and satisfactorily locate explicit warnings to their customers.

A manufacturer intent on avoiding litigation would use this list to develop a warning strategy for their users by (1) developing explicit warning copy; (2) placing warnings on the product, if possible, but also on the box, on an insert in the box, and, if practical, on a tag attached to the product; and (3) transmitting the explicit warning information to distributors and other suppliers, to users and their supervisors, and to health and safety professionals. This can be done through flyers, seminars, videotapes, slides, and other media.

Table 7-1 Protective Equipment and Its Limitations

Product	Limitations
Eye protection	Chemical exposures
	Molten metal
	Peripheral penetration
	Type and fit
	Frontal penetration
	Radiation protection
Hearing protection	Expected attenuation
	Type and fit
	Use with radios
Respiratory protection	Correct type for exposure
	Contaminant concentration
	Fit and fit testing
	Correct type for rescue
	Correct type for escape
	Correct cartridge/cannister
	Selection of demand, pressure, pressure/demand
	Correct for hot exposure
Body protection	Fit
	Type
	Spark and flame protection
	Penetration resistance
	Breakthrough of solvents
	Electrical resistance
	Rated loading (shoes and hard hats)

In one example of a use of Table 7-1, a manufacturer and/or distributor of hard hats could mount a highlighted explicit warning label on the inside of the hat that would be clearly visible to a person who was adjusting the hat. The label should address the maximum utility of the hat in terms of penetration resistance as well as its resistance to the flow of electricity. It should also mention the importance of using the hat suspension system correctly. The same information could be conveyed by other means and to persons other than the user, as mentioned in the text earlier in this section.

The education of supervisors and other professionals is necessary so that appropriate decisions can be made when purchasing equipment for a particular exposure. For example, if a hard hat had low resistance to the flow of electricity because of the material used in the hat's fittings, this fact would have an influence on its use for personnel engaged in work that would bring them into possible contact with a source of electrical energy.

Medical and Environmental Monitoring

Whether a material is a confirmed, suspected, or an experimental substance that is a carcinogen, there is need to determine community and/or worker exposure to the substance. Even when controls are installed, the need for monitoring the degree of exposure (environmental monitoring) and the degree of illness (medical monitoring) is mandatory. In the case of large populations an epidemiological study may be indicated.

The purpose of the management decision point analysis is to avoid exposure to contaminants and to avoid illness caused by the exposure. Therefore instituting controls will not in itself be sufficient to rule out harm. We must be quantitatively and qualitatively sure that harm does not exist. The cost of monitoring both medical and environmental aspects becomes a constant and must be added to the cost of whatever controls are contemplated.

Data Systems

Similarly, the data collected from monitoring must be cataloged, interpreted, and retained. The data system is another fixed cost that must be added to the cost of controls.

An important consideration is the establishment of a program for the collection of product injury data. This program can be instituted by subscribing to a clipping service, which will collect and forward newspaper, magazine, and journal articles published anywhere in the nation. Other sources of data are trade associations, product distributors, users, governmental agencies, and a company's sales force and those of its competitors. The consequences of ignoring product-failure information are tort proliferation and the inability to defend well in court.

This concludes MDPA Section V, Control Analysis. The reader will have noticed a number of management decision points in this section; these indicate that deciding whether or how to control a hazard is a logical and necessary task for management. When good ethical sense is employed at this point, management will be able to show that it looked for the existence of a problem and, when one was discovered, that it acted in good faith and judgment to resolve it. The final result of a diligently prosecuted MDPA is either avoidance of litigation or the ability to muster an effective defense in court.

The MDPA now proceeds to the final section, Problem Resolution (see Fig. 7-13).

MDPA SECTION VI: PROBLEM RESOLUTION

By the time Section VI of an MDPA is reached, the problem and alternative hazard controls will have been thoroughly analyzed. The question that needs asking at that point is, Do I want a plaintiff's expert to make this analysis and tell a jury what I should have done, or should I make the analysis, correct the problem(s), and avoid the probability of a lawsuit? As we proceed through this section we will encounter important management decision points that deal with ethical dilemmas such as whether a process or product line should be continued when it is shown to be hazardous and to be causing serious injury to customers or employees. Even if the ethics of continuance under the latter circumstances could be discounted, it is easy to define the devastating impact of such an action on a defendant's argument in court.

Although Section VI is self-explanatory, Table 7-2 describes the consequences of each decision point so that there may be little doubt of the intent of the flow diagram.

While Table 7-2 may seem repetitive, it is fraught with meaning. From this table and the information prepared in other MDPA sections, either a course of action can be charted that will preserve the company's reputation as an ethical corporate entity, or an expert can be permitted to tell a jury (1) what was known about the hazardous nature of the product/process, (2) what was done with this knowledge, and (3) what should have been done.

Let us consider the manufacturer of a chemical used in agriculture to prevent potatoes from sprouting while in storage. The material is applied at a temperature that is above autoignition, and the company knows that if the material burns one of the products is an isocyanate, a highly toxic substance. Subsequently, there are a few reports of fires and some illness and sensitivity among workers and others in the farm community.

This information places the company's situation in line 7 in Table 7-2, where it is faced with discontinuing production, continuing production with mitigation (changing the formula, warning effectively, reducing application temperatures, etc.), or just continuing as it has in the past.

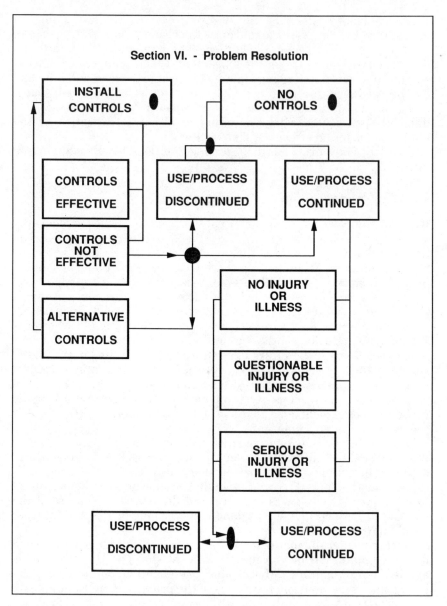

Figure 7-13. Management decision point analysis (MDPA) (continued).

Table 7-2 Consequences of Decision Points

Decision/Condition	Options/Results
1. Do not install controls	1a. Use/process discontinued
	1b. Use/process continued (see number 5)
2. Install controls	2a. Controls ineffective
	2b. Controls effective
3. Controls effective	3a. Product/process continued
	3b. Monitoring and data collection continued
4. Controls not effective	4a. Use/process continued
	4b. Use/process discontinued
	4c. Alternative controls selected
5. Use/process continued	5a. No injury/illness
	5b. Questionable injury/illness
	5c. Serious injury/illness
6. No injury/illness	6a. Use/process continued
	6b. Use/process discontinued
7. Questionable injury/illness	7a. Use/process discontinued
	7b. Use/process continued
8. Serious injury/illness	8a. Use/process discontinued
	8b. Use/process continued

Should a serious injury or death occur, and if the company has decided to continue as before, it would be faced with a lawsuit that would be very difficult to defend. The object of the MDPA is to not let the problem progress until the company is faced with the injury or death of its customers and the likelihood of an indefensible lawsuit.

Case Study 7-2: Model XXX Child Restraint

The Accident and Injury

In a case* where a company produced a unique automobile child restraint that the plaintiff claimed to be defectively designed, the company felt obliged to settle the case during trial. Conclusions drawn from a management decision point analysis were presented at trial to inform the jury where and how company management could have prevented catastrophic injuries to users of its product.

The child restraint was unique in the sense that it was designed to have a useful life for a 2½-year period, while the child was of ages approximately six months to three years. It accomplished this by

---

*Caption withheld by court order.

providing a standard five-point harness for use until the child reached 17 pounds (the transition weight), at which time the instructions included with the package advised the parents to discard the harness and instead use an attached hinged barrier to restrain the child and prevent ejection during a crash.

Although the device was extensively tested with the harness and with the barrier using 30-lb dummies, it was never tested with a transition-weight (17-lb) dummy. The result was that the company was recommending that parents discard the traditional and effective harness in favor of an untested barrier. Since this was a highly touted feature of the restraint, most parents followed this advice. However, during the first year of use the company received numerous letters from parents complaining that their child was uncomfortable using the barrier, as well as some letters stating that while using the barrier their 17-lb (transition weight) child had come out of the seat during a violent maneuver of the car. The company ignored these letters.

The consequence was that at least three transition-weight children were ejected from their seats during a crash—one died, and the others became paraplegics. There was also evidence that other children had been ejected but not as seriously injured.

As part of trial preparation approximately 1000 memoranda that had been circulated between members of management were examined. These memoranda dealt primarily with the design, testing, manufacture, and marketing of the new-model child restraint. From the information contained in the memoranda an MDPA was developed.

Trial Conclusion

The corporation embarked on a project to produce a state-of-the-art automobile child restraint in order to greatly increase their market share for this high-demand product.

In spite of the fact that the design of the model XXX would affect transition-size children involved in life-threatening situations (car crashes), the company made an initial decision not to exhaustively test the product for the transition-size child before marketing it nationally and internationally.

The net effect of this and subsequent company management decisions to ignore product deficiency warnings by their own chief designer and product failures during tests and in the field was that the company conducted human experimentation with thousands of transition-size infants and their unknowing parents as the human subjects.

The results were disasterous, and ultimately the company stopped manufacturing the model XXX. Unfortunately, the damage had been done.

The management decision point analysis shows that the company was aware of the model XXX safety shortcomings, but did nothing substantive to correct the situation despite the fact that the opportunity presented itself many times (see MDP symbols).

It is clear that the company was highly motivated by money and was even unwilling at times to spend relatively small amounts on product testing. There appeared to be no management plan of action to bring the model XXX to a safe configuration, since funds for testing and redesign were requested on a piecemeal basis. No clear record exists of funding being allocated to redesign and retrofit for safety purposes.

Since the model XXX was a new concept in child restraint, untested under actual crash conditions as well as untested in the laboratory with transition-weight dummies, the company reasonably and responsibly should have informed their model XXX customers of the substantial risk they were taking. Given the knowledge that the company had prior to production, it was imprudent to market the model XXX without arranging for the informed consent of their customers.

The severity of injuries that could occur to transition-weight children involved catastrophic injury and death; therefore, the actions of the company were clearly unreasonable and irresponsible.

Analysis

Had the company performed a management decision point analysis before marketing their new product, they would have determined the following:

I. *Hazard Input Analysis* reveals that there is a valid hazard to children using the restraint if the device fails during a crash.

II. *Utilization Review* shows that this hazard is present while the restraint is in use.

III. *The Exposure Study* reveals that there is customer and community (parents of users) exposure.

IV. *The Exposure-Level Survey* describes a danger level of D3, which includes death and serious disability as consequences [see hazard effects and control analysis (HECA), also Fig. 5-4, which describes the derivation and meaning of danger level].

V. *Control Analysis* provides for exhaustive testing of the product, from the point of view of the official governmental requirement, from that of the manufacturer's instructions, and from that of foreseeable use. Tests of the ability of the product to contain a 17-lb child during a car crash, and while restrained only by the barrier arrangement, would be mandatory.

The transition-weight testing described in the previous paragraph, had these tests been performed, would have revealed that the child restraint as designed would not restrain a transition-weight child with the seat held upside down, let alone during a crash!

Before examining Section VI, Problem Resolution, it will be helpful to list the actual management decision points derived from this analysis so far (see Table 7-3). By doing this the reader will be able to observe how

Table 7-3 Management Decision Points Derived

Analysis Section	Management Decision Point	Options Open To Company
I. Hazard Input Analysis	None	
II. Utilization Review	None	
III. Exposure Study	Shall the company deal with the serious injury potential to users of the child restraint?	1. Warn parents of danger of the untested transition weight position 2. Plan the control of the danger 3. Recall sold restraints if necessary
IV. Exposure Level Survey	Shall the company control the recognized serious hazard to transition-weight children?	Proceed to Section V, Control Analysis, and take the necessary action
V. Control Analysis	Shall the company invest time and money to produce a product that will protect all restraint users from serious injury or death?	1. Exhaustive testing in all weight categories 2. Redesign if necessary 3. Warn of danger 4. Retrofit sold product 5. Collect appropriate injury data

prior MDP analysis would have prompted management to consider injury- and litigation-prevention actions in this case.

Analyzing the actions of this restraint manufacturer from the standpoint of Section VI, Problem Resolution (see Fig. 7-13), we can trace their actions starting at the position of No Controls through Use/Process Continued to Serious Injury or Illness to Use/Process Continued. Obviously, this is an indefensible pathway that cannot help but eventually result in serious harm to product users and disaster for the company in the courts. The obvious answer is to install effective controls, as described in Section V.

Tables 7-4 and the Trial Conclusion section show a summary and conclusions from the management decision point analysis of the restraint manufacturer. The basis for these is the deposition testimony of company management and the various communications contained in

Table 7-4 Management Decision Point Analysis for Model XXX Child
Restraint: Summary

What did the manufacturer know?	1. The model XXX restraint was designed for a transition-weight child (17 to 20 lb) for use without a harness	MDP
	2. A 20-lb child had been killed in an actual crash	MDP
	3. The restraint was untested for use with a transition-weight child	MDP
	4. Sales of the model XXX was in the hundreds of thousands	
	5. Other 20-lb children had come out of position in the model XXX	MDP
	6. Neck loading was 50 percent or more higher in the model XXX than competitive restraints, and experimental animals had been killed under high neck loads	MDP
What did the manufacturer do?	1. Ignored the fact that transition-weight children could get out of position in the model XXX	
	2. Ignored product failure in the field	
	3. Performed inadequate testing of the model XXX	
	4. Allowed marketing to override safety recommendations	
	5. Ignored warnings of their own chief designer	
What should the manufacturer have done?	1. Conducted exhaustive tests (before marketing) on the crashworthiness of the model XXX restraint with transition-size anthropometric dummys	
	2. Heeded numerous complaints that the model XXX was not functioning as advertised	
	3. Cataloged complaints for possible serious safety problems	
	4. Redesigned the restraint system for transition-size children, retrofitted already purchased restraints, or provided customers with a safe alternative restraint. If the latter was too expensive, they should have discontinued production of the model XXX	

Note: MDP = Management Decision Point. A point in the history of product design, manufacture, and sales where management must assess known adverse product safety information and make the decisions necessary to correct the product safety deficiencies, or to not proceed with the marketing of the product.

the memoranda. The implication is clear that if the company had acted ethically and judiciously by developing an MDPA or facsimile while the product was in the conceptual and planning stages, and then followed the advice offered by the analysis as described in Table 7-4 and the Trial Conclusion section (p. 122), all the participants would probably be fully functional today.

A last significant comment: The company tested their product in accordance with the existing federal standards for child restraints. What the company and their customers found out to both their disadvantage was that the existing standard was insufficient to cover unique designs such as the subject of this example. This means that a prudent designer must go beyond existing standards into the realm of all foreseeable uses. In this case, the testing did not even cover recommended use, which placed the manufacturer in an indefensible position.

Chapter 8

Hazard Control Analysis, Fault Tree Analysis, and Management Oversight and Risk Tree Analysis

HAZARD CONTROL ANALYSIS

Figures 8-1 through 8-3 contain the format for hazard control analysis (HCA) that is used to derive hazard control procedures for a discrete operation in any type of business including construction. The advantages of using HCA are that it is quick, self-contained, and available for use on the job by foremen or others charged with accident/injury prevention.

This type of analysis has obvious litigation-prevention qualities for both general and subcontractors. It establishes a meaningful accident-prevention program for a specific operation and thereby creates a large measure of good faith effort that will reduce accident experience. If such an analysis is made and, most importantly, reasonably applied, it will be very difficult for a plaintiff to prove negligence.

In the following sample problem, a hazard control analysis is employed to generate accident-prevention activity for an operation where construction workers are exposed to toxic materials and falls from elevation.

PROBLEM

Eliot Meres, supervisor of a work crew (12 persons) for the New Face Company, is assigned the job of sandblasting the old Pioneer Building, which was the highest structure in town until 1954. The building is 18 stories tall and is located in the busiest area of downtown Metropole, Indiana. Meres's crew is composed of 50 percent new people of varying experience and 50 percent old-timers. Meres himself, although experienced in this type of work, was hired only the week before by the New Face Company, so this is his first job for them. Still, Meres knows that he had better do some safety program preplanning for this extensive job.

The purpose of Section 1, shown in Figure 8-1, is to identify the type of project that is to be analyzed. Notice that Number 10, Field Operations, is printed in italics. In an actual analysis Number 10 would be circled to indicate that the operation under analysis is a field operation.

The next step, shown in Figure 8-2, is a narrative description of the operation to enable the analyst to understand the operation.

The analyst is now in position to determine the type of accident and injury to which each worker would be exposed and propose methods of avoidance. The remainder of the HCA is devoted to these objectives. Figure 8-3 describes the type of accident that may occur, especially if little or no prevention is planned.

Once the type of accident that may occur is identified, the next logical step is to determine what could cause the accident and any subsequent injury. This step is accomplished by using the format in Figure 8-4 (Section 4). Again the analyst only need circle the number next to each appropriate cause.

Figure 8-4 identifies 16 potential accident causes that must be mitigated through some type of corrective action such as training, protective equipment, warnings, and barriers. This brings the analysis to Sections 5 and 6, which deal with corrective action.

Section 5 (Fig. 8-5) outlines the necessary corrective procedures much in the same way that the previous sections have done. Section 6 (Fig. 8-6), however, is a narrative that is very specific, detailing the specific actions that must be taken to avoid the problems identified in the prior analysis sections.

This particular job requires work at heights, use of hazardous equipment, such as sandblasters and power washers, and use of hazardous materials, such as silica sand, so the analysis proceeds in a structured manner. The foreman analyst is channeled to the establishment of a safety program that will handle the identified safety and health problems. To show how this analysis method accomplishes its objective, let us examine four potential accident causes shown in Figure 8-4 and follow them through to where specific corrective measures are identified.

Example 1: Numbers 1 and 7 in Figure 8-4 are Unauthorized Use of Equipment and Using Tools/Equipment Unsafely. This refers to the unauthorized use of the sandblasters and power washers by the public as well as the improper use of the same equipment by the workers, such as in horseplay. Another consideration is using tools in such a manner

SECTION 1	**PROGRAM PHASE**

1. DESIGN

2. FACILITIES PLANNING

3. TEST OPERATIONS

4. TOOL DESIGN AND FABRICATION

5. EQUIPMENT PROCUREMENT,
    STORAGE, AND HANDLING

6. RAW MATERIAL PROCUREMENT,
   STORAGE, AND HANDLING

7. FABRICATION

8. TRANSPORTATION AND STORAGE
   OF PARTS AND ASSEMBLIES

9. MINOR AND MAJOR ASSEMBLY

10. FIELD OPERATIONS

11. FINAL ASSEMBLY

12. PLANT MAINTENANCE

13. OTHER (identify)_____

Figure 8-1. Hazard control analysis, Section 1: program phase.

SECTION 2	SPECIFIC OPERATION
A crew of twelve workers plus foreman will sandblast the old Pioneer building in downtown Metropole, Indiana. A safeway scaffold will be erected on the three exposed sides of the building. Workers equipped with air-operated wrenches will erect the scaffolding. One-half of the crew are long-time employees of the company, while the other half, including Elliot Meres the foreman, are local hires. Meres, however, is experienced in this type of work. After scaffold erection the three exposed sides of the building will be sandblasted from the eighteenth floor down to the ground level using standard sandblasting equipment and silica sand. Following the sandblast operation the building will be power washed. The scaffold will then be dismantled and returned to the rental agency. All of the preceding to be accomplished expediciously and without accident.	

Figure 8-2. Hazard control analysis, Section 2: specific operation.

SECTION 3	ACCIDENT TYPE
1. *LIFTING* 2. PUSHING - PULLING 3. *FALL* 4. *FALLING OBJECT* 5. FLYING OBJECT 6. *INHALATION OF DUST, VAPORS, FUMES, and GASES* 7. CONTACT WITH HARMFUL CHEMICALS and SUBSTANCES 8. HOT OR COLD OBJECTS 9. EXPOSURE TO RADIANT ENERGY 10. ELECTRIC SHOCK 11. *SLIP - TRIP* 12. LASER EXPOSURE 13. ULTRASOUND EXPOSURE 14. *NOISE EXPOSURE* 15. SQUEEZE 16. *OTHER (identify) HAZARD TO THE PUBLIC, WATER JET, MATERIALS HANDLING*	

Figure 8-3. Hazard control analysis, Section 3: accident type.

SECTION 4	POTENTIAL CAUSE

1. UNAUTHORIZED USE OF EQUIPMENT
2. FAILURE TO SECURE
3. OPERATING AT UNSAFE SPEED
4. FAILURE TO WARN OR SIGNAL
5. REMOVING OR MAKING SAFETY DEVICES INOPERATIVE
6. DEFECTIVE TOOLS OR EQUIPMENT
7. USING TOOLS/EQUIPMENT UNSAFELY
8. STANDING IN UNSAFE PLACE OR TAKING UNSAFE POSTURE
9. SERVICING RUNNING EQUIPMENT
10. FAILURE TO WEAR OR USE PROTECTIVE EQUIPMENT OR
        DEVICES
11. WEARING HAZARDOUS ATTIRE
12. EXPOSURE TO HAZARDOUS MATERIALS OR PROCESSES
13. OTHER(identify)_____

DEFICIENT CONDITION

1. OVERLOADING
2. LACK OF ESTABLISHED SAFE WORK PRACTICES
3. INADEQUATE TOOLS, VEHICLES, OR EQUIPMENT
4. IMPROPER LAYOUT
5. INADEQUATE ILLUMINATION, VENTILATION
6. INTENSIVE NOISE
7. LACK OF GOOD ACCESS
8. LACK OF ADEQUATE GUARDS OR SAFETY DEVICES
9. OPEN-SIDED WORK PLATFORM
10. OTHER (identify)_____

Figure 8-4. Hazard control analysis, Section 4: potential cause.

that they could be dropped on other workers or the public. By providing Proper Work Procedures (item 12 in Fig. 8-5) that include the securing of equipment that is not in use, the unauthorized use will be prevented. Section 6, as in Figure 8-6, will contain a narrative description of what will be done specifically to correct potential hazards. In this case, the following notations would appear:

1. Purchase a butler building 10×10 to house sandblast and power-wash equipment when not in use. Building should be capable of being securely locked at night.
2. Horseplay is a violation of work rules. Violators will be verbally warned for the first violation, receive a written warning and two days

SECTION 5	PREVENTIVE ACTION

1. DESIGN CONTROL STATIONS TO PROVIDE MAXIMUM OPERATOR
   PROTECTION (TWO-HAND CONTROL)
2. ELIMINATE PROTRUSIONS
3. PROVIDE PINCH POINT PROTECTION
4. *PROVIDE INTEGRATED BARRIERS*
5. *PROVIDE EMERGENCY RELIEF*
6. COMPENSATE FOR OVER/UNDER PRESSURE, VOLTAGE,
   TEMPERATURE RADIATION, ILLUMINATION

PROVIDE

1. *PROTECTIVE EQUIPMENT*
2. *PROPER HANDLING EQUIPMENT*
3. *WARNING SIGNALS AND SIGNS*
4. WELDING ARC BARRIERS
5. *RAILINGS*
6. *TRAINING*
7. EMERGENCY SHOWERS
8. *REGULAR PHYSICAL INSPECTION OF WORK AREA AND
       EQUIPMENT*
9. PROPER MAINTENANCE AND/OR CLEANUP PROCEDURES
10. CHEMICAL HOODS
11. *PROPER EGRESS AND ACCESS*
12. PROPER WORK PROCEDURES
13. *PERSONNEL BARRIERS*
14. OTHER (identify) _____

REORIENT

1. *CURRENT PROCEDURES*
2. *EMPLOYEE ATTITUDE*
3. OTHER (identify)_____

ENFORCE

1. *PROTECTIVE EQUIPMENT AND DEVICE USE*
2. *COMPLIANCE WITH SAFETY PROCEDURES*
3. OTHER (identify)_____

TRAIN

1. *SPECIALIZED EQUIPMENT*
2. *SAFETY AND HEALTH PROCEDURES*
3. OTHER (identify)_____

Figure 8-5. Hazard control analysis, Section 5: preventive action.

SECTION 6	SPECIFIC CORRECTIVE ACTION

PURCHASE:
1. 168 pieces of plywood for protective tunnel for public and sufficient 2 x 4 for structure.
2. Fall protection systems for individual workers including chest - waist harnesses and double lanyards. Erect sufficient static lines.
3. Fall protection system for climbing access. Consult Rose Mfg. Co.
4. Dust respirators for silica dust.
5. Warning signs for workers and public.
6. Tool lanyards for all employees.
7. Ventilated hoods for sandblasters. Consult 3M Co.
8. Hard hats and safety glasses for workers and visitors.

TRAIN:
   All workers regardless of experience to be trained in the use of double-lanyard fall protection system, access and egress fall protection system. The following subjects will also be covered
   A. Dangers of silica dust
   B. Keeping tools from falling
   C. Noise protection
   D. Penalties for safety rule infractions
   E. Use of job status bulletin board
   F. Methods for lifting equipment to job site
   G. Dangers of sandblasting and power washing
   H. Reporting injuries and unsafe conditions

ACTION ADDRESSEE   George Johnson, Superintendent
                        Paul Michaels , Safety Manager

Figure 8-6. Hazard control analysis, Section 6: specific corrective action.

off without pay for the second violation, and will be terminated for the third violation.
3. All workers will be trained in the appropriate use and handling of sandblast and power-wash equipment. At a minimum, each worker will know how to set up the equipment, how to connect to electrical power, how to avoid injury from direct contact with the power head while operating, how to recognize malfunctions, and how to safely clean and store.

4. Fourteen tool lanyards will be purchased to be used to prevent hand tools from falling.

   Example 2: Item number 8 on Figure 8-4 reads Standing in an Unsafe Place or Taking an Unsafe Posture. This refers to bystanders and pedestrians who may stop to watch the proceedings and who must be protected from possible falling materials and airborne water and silica sand. Figure 8-5 provides for Warning Signals and Signs (number 3 under Provide) and Personnel Barriers (number 13). Section 6 (Fig. 8-6) will list the following:

1. Purchase 168 pieces of 3/4-in. plywood and appropriate 2 × 4 to build tunnel to protect public.
2. Place warning signs for public and workers to say:

WARNING
HARD HATS MUST BE WORN
WHEN ON SITE. RESPIRATORS
MUST BE WORN DURING
SANDBLASTING OPERATIONS

   Example 3: Number 10 on Section 4 (Fig. 8-4) states: Failure to Wear or Use Protective Equipment or Devices. This refers to the fall protection system used on this job, which is composed of chest–waist harnesses and double lanyards. The double lanyard makes it possible to walk the scaffold and to be tied off at all times. When a worker approaches an obstruction to the movement of the tied-off lanyard, he or she just fixes the second lanyard at a point beyond the obstruction and then unfastens the first lanyard. The worker is now free to move while still tied off. Workers must be trained in the use of this system, and because there may be some resistance to its use, the system must be enforced until all realize that they will not be permitted to work without it. Soon all workers will also realize that they can expect to go home at the end of the day in one piece because of positive fall prevention. Section 5 (Fig. 8-5) will show the need for enforcement and training in the use of the system. Section 6 will read as follows:

1. Purchase thirteen double-lanyard systems, including chest–waist harnesses. The scaffold will be so constructed that this fall protection system is accommodated, including the use of static lines where necessary.
2. Formal training sessions will cover the use and importance of the fall protection system.

   Example 4: The last example refers to line 7 under Deficient Condition in Section 4 (Fig. 8-4): Lack of Good Access. Most scaffolds have very rudimentary, marginally safe means of access and means of getting from one level to another. This scaffold will use a fall protection system so that when a worker is hooked on, it will detect a fall and prevent it before significant acceleration has taken place. The system will be designed to accommodate movement in the up or down direction. Section 5 (Fig. 8-5) will adequately channel the analyst toward the application of appropriate fall protection by the identification of numbers 5 and 11, Provide Emergency Relief, and Proper Egress and Access. Section 6 (Fig. 8-6) should identify the actual fall protection system by trade name and specify its installation. Training and enforcement must also be included as before.

There is no denying that the hazard control analysis (HCA) would be minimally time-consuming to develop (in our Problem case, about 3 hours) and would cost money and additional time to apply. On the other hand, it is a positive means of accident prevention that will insulate the user from litigation and reduce the probability of serious injury. We must also not overlook the tremendous production advantages of fewer on-the-job injuries and a workforce that is confident that they are protected from a fatal fall.

FAULT TREE ANALYSIS

Fault tree analysis (FTA) is an effective tool for analyzing complex systems such as nuclear plants or missile systems for possible malfunctions that may result in catastrophic consequences. Its basic approach is negative and backwards, that is, it begins at the unwanted event, such as the "inadvertent launch of an intercontinental missile" (the negative event) and backs up by determining the successive series of system component failures that could cause the negative or undesirable event. Remember that a system is composed of equipment, personnel who operate the equipment, and the environment where the equipment and personnel reside.

For example, if a solitary hiker is lost in the wilderness in −50°F weather, he must light a warming fire to survive. The system components are (1) the cold and shivering hiker (the person), (2) matches, paper, and wood (the equipment), and (3) the very cold climate with snow falling (the environment). The negative event would be *unable to light a fire*. Starting at this top event the question is asked, "What would cause this (unable to light fire) to occur?" The next events would contain such conditions as lack of proper size fuel, hands too cold to light matches, matches wet, and improper striking surface for matches. If the analysis had been made before the hiker left home, the conditions that would prevent a fire from being started could be determined and mitigated.

The technique for doing an FTA is structured, requiring the use of a computer on very complex issues such as those described earlier. It is advisable for those who are involved with complex systems with thousands or millions of components to seek the help of a trained systems safety engineer in performing the FTA.

The approach to FTA that will be used here is based on the danger level scale (see Fig. 5-4, danger level matrix). Since the negative event will generally always be critical or catastrophic, the danger level for an FTA for a litigation-prevention problem will probably always be D3.

The probability scale in Table 5-1 can be used to assess the probability of the events leading to the top event. We are again de-emphasizing probability in favor of revealing the path to a litigation-producing accident, so that the prudent controlling person can intervene and take preventive action. In the example below, the analyst needs only to understand the mechanism of systems failure to prevent a death. Probability cannot be proved and therefore is a relatively minor consideration.

Before the fault tree example, we need to consider the symbols illustrated in Figure 8-7, particularly the AND and OR gates. Figure 8-8 illustrates the concept of these two signs. It will become clear in Figure 8-9 how these symbols are used in a fault tree analysis diagram.

The other symbols in Figure 8-7 are fairly straightforward and deal mostly with different types of events. The rectangle describes a malfunction such as a guard on a table saw that does not protect the operator as intended or a cover on a machine that does not close all the way. The unwanted or top event of a fault tree is usually enclosed in a rectangular event box.

The circle describes a component or part failure such as a bias resistor in an electronic circuit that burns out and causes a capacitor to retain its electrical charge. Ultimately, the charged capacitor could cause a fatal electrical shock to a technician who expected the capacitor to be in a discharged condition.

The diamond describes a failure where there is no intention to deal with the causes of that failure. A power plant that fails to produce electrical power because of generator breakdown would be one example. Generally, there is no information on why the power plant failed to produce, or there is not much that can be done by a customer to mitigate such a failure. The lack of power must be dealt with at the user's facility and not at the power plant.

Fault Tree Analysis of a Product Design

In Chapter 6 we described an accident involving a tree trimmer who sustained severe electrical burns while he was operating a manlift. The design of the manlift was ultimately brought into question by the trimmer who, as plaintiff, claimed that the designer was negligent, because it was probable that nonmetallic hydraulic hoses would be replaced with metallic hoses at the time when hose replacement became necessary. The fittings on the manlift would accommodate both

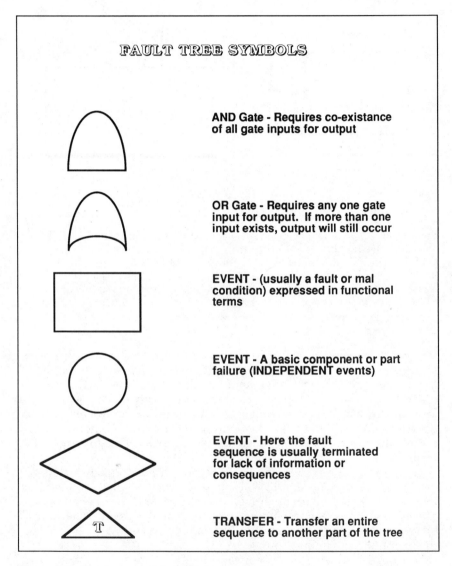

FAULT TREE SYMBOLS

AND Gate - Requires co-existance of all gate inputs for output

OR Gate - Requires any one gate input for output. If more than one input exists, output will still occur

EVENT - (usually a fault or mal condition) expressed in functional terms

EVENT - A basic component or part failure (INDEPENDENT events)

EVENT - Here the fault sequence is usually terminated for lack of information or consequences

TRANSFER - Transfer an entire sequence to another part of the tree

Figure 8-7. Symbols used in fault tree analysis.

metallic and nonmetallic hoses. The jury agreed enthusiastically with the plaintiff in this case.

If the manlift designer had performed a fault tree analysis before the device was marketed, this oversight would have been discovered and corrected. Figure 8-9 shows a simple FTA that illustrates this point.

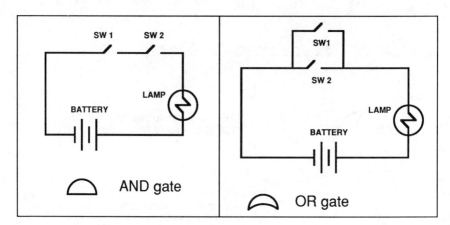

Figure 8-8. AND and OR gates. *Left diagram*: In this illustration of an AND gate, in order for the lamp to light it must have the coexistence of all inputs. Both switches 1 and 2 must be closed for the circuit to operate. If only switch 1 or only switch 2 is closed, the lamp does not light. *Right diagram*: In this illustration of an OR gate, in order for the lamp to light any one input must be present. If either switch 1 or switch 2 is closed, the lamp will light.

Figure 8-9 shows a five-tier fault tree analysis of the manlift design where the first tier, the top or undesirable event, is the electrocution of the manlift operator. The remainder of the analysis is devoted to determining how the top event could occur with the hope that the information will lead to a design that will prevent the top event from occurring. We will describe the analysis tier by tier and point out the places where correction or redesign must take place if the top event is to be prevented.

The second tier comes off an AND gate, and establishes that for electrical injury to occur the worker must touch the high-voltage line (which frequently happens in tree-trimming work) *and* be grounded. The analyst now sets out to determine what could cause the operator to be grounded despite the fact that the manlift was designed to prevent the operator from being grounded.

The third tier, also derived from an AND gate, states that when standing in the plastic manlift bucket the operator, in order to be grounded, must be touching a metal fixture (the valve handle) *and* that fixture must be grounded. The analyst continues to try to determine how the operator could become grounded despite the fact that when the manlift leaves the factory it is equipped with nonmetallic hydraulic hoses, and therefore creates a nonconductive path from the valve to ground.

The fourth tier shows that the operator would be touching the

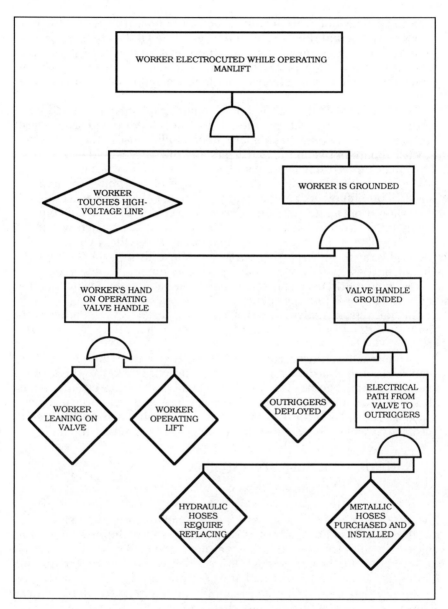

Figure 8-9. Fault tree analysis of manlift design.

operating valve if he were leaning against it *or* operating a manlift. Tier four also states that the valve would be grounded if the outriggers were deployed (touching the ground) *and* there was an electrical path from the valve to the outriggers. We must now determine if there is any way in which there could be an electrical path between the outriggers and the valve.

Tier five suggests that if the hoses require replacement, which they most certainly must during the life of the manlift, *and* they were replaced with metallic instead of nonmetallic hoses, then such an electrical path between the outriggers and the valve would be created. The top or undesirable event could now most certainly occur.

We have now discovered that the design of the manlift would be unsafe if manlift owners and operators were not effectively warned that they should not under any circumstances replace the orange-colored nonmetallic hydraulic hoses with black metallic hose. Such warnings must be placed in the owner's manual and on the manlift itself, preferably at the hose fittings. Also, the hose fittings on the manlift should be designed so that only specific nonmetallic hose from the factory would fit. These corrective actions are a direct outgrowth of the fault tree analysis just completed.

The fault tree analysis in this case was used very effectively to determine that a machine, as designed, could be harmful, even lethal, to its user.

Unquestionably, there is high probability that a tree trimmer could be electrocuted by this device in its original design. The key to the usefulness of the fault tree analysis developed in this case is the revelation that it was predictable that someone, some day would switch hose types. Once that action is accepted as inevitable, the analyst can develop a safe design that will make the hose switch impossible or very difficult.

MANAGEMENT OVERSIGHT AND RISK TREE ANALYSIS

Of the six analysis types described in this part, MORT is my favorite for two reasons. First, it can be used in the positive mode, that is, the top event is expressed as successful safety and health administration of a place of business or operation. The second reason I like MORT is that its safety management orientation allows effective preplanning of operations. The traditional "try it; if it fails, then correct it" approach is replaced by a "before the fact, identify, analyze, control" philosophy. The latter approach has the best chance of avoiding the costly retrofit, serious injury, and litigation problems associated with operations where safety is an afterthought.

There are four major sections to the MORT format: the top event, assumed risks, management systems, and rewards. Each of these sections is described, followed by a MORT analysis of a department store fall-prevention program. (A completed MORT analysis for a recreational ski facility is contained in Chapter 12.) The explanations should enable the reader to use MORT as an injury- and litigation-prevention tool.

The Top Event

In fault tree analysis the top event is expressed as the undesirable condition or event the analyst wants to avoid. In MORT analysis the *top event* is expressed as a desirable condition such as "injury-free operation of an amusement park" or "electrical-shock-free construction site management." Expressed in this way the top event establishes a positive endpoint for the analysis.

Assumed Risks

Assumed risks are the hazards of the operation to which customers, workers, equipment, etc., are exposed. For example, skiers at a ski resort are exposed, among other things, to steep hills that may be beyond their skill level, to the possibility of being run over by other, reckless skiers, and to the possibility of skiing into unfamiliar territory and getting lost. These are some of the risks that must be assumed by ski resort management when offering recreational skiing to the public.

In the top event previously mentioned, "electrical-shock-free construction site management," some of the assumed risks are damaged extension cords, working in wet environments, and ungrounded or shorted equipment. Once these risks are identified, positive steps can be taken to manage them so that injury and litigation do not materialize. This is the purpose of the management systems phase of the MORT analysis.

Management Systems

Management systems are defined as those systems that must be in place to eliminate or reduce the consequences of the assumed risks. In the ski facility example, in order to compensate for the inherent risks involved with a ski resort there must be, at a minimum, inspection, warning, training, maintenance, security, emergency, and volunteer systems. Many of these same systems would apply to the safety management of an amusement park or even to electrical safety at a construction site.

Preceding the management systems on the MORT format (see Fig. 8-10) is the systems safety analysis symbol for an AND gate (see Fig. 8-8). This means that to eliminate or mitigate the assumed risks all management systems must be applied together to achieve the desired result (top event). If an OR gate had been used (which is not proper), it would mean that any one of the suggested management systems used alone would achieve the desired result.

The number and type of management systems necessary should be appropriate for the facility or operation under analysis. In a hospital for mentally disturbed patients, for example, you would expect to have, at a minimum, patient restraint, medical emergency training, and outside volunteer and inspection systems to compensate for the risks of violent patients.

For the purposes of MORT analysis each management system must be expanded by naming the component parts. For example, at the ski facility a warning system should include the difficulty of the slopes, the boundary of the ski area, hidden obstructions, warning sign maintenance, lodge and cafeteria warnings, and a warning sign development and fabrication facility. An inspection system should include lifts, terrain, warning signs, lodge and cafeteria, parking facilities, danger areas, and hill clearance after the day's skiing is over.

Of course, after the MORT analysis is completed, all you have is a piece of paper. Each management system must now be converted to an action program. Using the ski facility as an example, if an emergency system were to be set up, the following actions would need to take place:

1. A medical station would be set up with equipment for performing first aid, including splints, bandages, compression bandages, airways, defibrillator, blankets, and beds.
2. A medical staff composed of volunteer physicians who exchange service for free use of the facility should be arranged.
3. Hill evacuation sleds purchased.
4. Chairlift evacuation devices purchased.
5. Ski patrol trained and drilled in first aid, hill and lift evacuation, avalanche recognition, and control would be formed.
6. Emergency communication devices purchased.
7. Listing of emergency assistance agencies.

What has occurred in this example is that the analyst, using MORT analysis for the ski facility, has logically included the need for an emergency management system to compensate for the known or assumed risks of skiers to incur minor and serious injuries, as well as possible heart attacks and other serious problems. Once the system is identified and its components listed in the MORT format, the required actions to place the system into active use are easily developed. The objective of eliminating or limiting the effects of the ski area risks can then be achieved.

Rewards

A list of the consequences of reducing the effects of the system's risks finishes the analysis. For example, the rewards of mitigating the risks of the ski area would be fewer accidents, less-reckless skiers on the hill, fewer court actions, faster recovery for injured skiers because of prompt professional care, generally more enjoyment for each skier, and increased patronage of the ski area.

A Sample MORT Analysis

Department stores have a greater than average exposure to customers who may fall in their premises. The reasons for this are that customers may encounter slip, trip, and fall opportunities at many of the store's entrances, and conditions of the walking surfaces are subject to constant change both outside and inside the store. A minimal or failed effort to control injuries from falls could result in increased insurance premiums and lawsuits.

PROBLEM

The Smythe Emporium is a nine-story department store that covers a city block. Through the years the Emporium has had continuing problems with customer falls from slippery floors, obstructions, and from other causes.

One day a customer falls off a storage balcony when she wanders into the area. A new loss-control manager familiar with MORT success analysis decides to apply this technique to loss prevention in this area. (The results of this application are shown in Figure 8-10.)

Customer falls due to slips and trips are the bane of any large retail establishment. Often the reason for such an incident is a loose or torn rug, a wet or oily floor, an obstruction in a walkway, a floor with a low coefficient of friction, or an unknown cause where the injured party is as bewildered as anyone else.

When people who are carrying food or packages fall, strange mechanisms start to work. For example, if a cafeteria patron who is carrying a food tray to his or her table slips on some soup spilled by another cafeteria patron, the falling party will many times hang on to the tray for dear life. The result is usually one or two broken wrists because of the leverage created by the outstretched arms. This means that a department store cafeteria is a place that requires special care for slip and fall prevention. Such care is provided under management systems in the MORT analysis shown in Figure 8-10.

Further examination of Figure 8-10 shows that when a department store starts business its managers must assume certain risks and install appropriate management systems to mitigate the hazards associated with the following risks.

1. Older patrons. Older customers present a particular problem because falls can be fatal to them. Some of the input under management systems that is intended to handle this risk are an escort service and

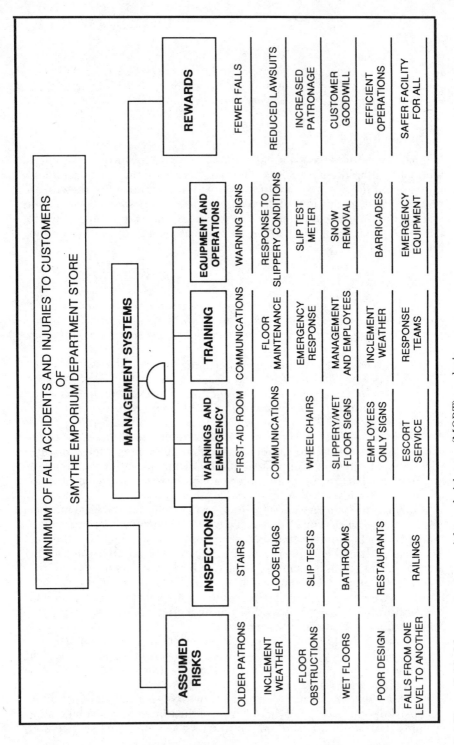

Figure 8-10. Management oversight and risk tree (MORT) analysis.

wheelchairs for particularly frail elders, specially equipped bathrooms, and response teams that will attempt to eliminate slippery floor conditions before harm is done.

2. Inclement weather. When rain and snow appear, the store can expect slippery conditions to be brought into the building. Here, the response teams, snow removal, and special gratings that provide secure footing are some of the system attributes that will reduce the risk.

3. Floor obstructions. A department store is a dynamic place with new products, floor displays, and department relocations a common characteristic. Under these conditions it is possible that obstructions may be left or placed in aisles. Inspections, trained employees and managers, and warning signs are some of the system components that must be in place to thwart these hazards.

4. Wet floors. Not only are wet floors created incidentally by the weather and inadvertent spills but ordinary maintenance may create wet, slippery conditions, especially if the store is open 24 hours a day. Here barricades and appropriately worded and placed signs are important prevention systems that must be properly deployed.

5. Poor design. Two important considerations in the design of walking surfaces are (1) Will the coefficient of friction that the surface creates with a walking shoe with leather heels and soles be greater than 0.5? and (2) Are all floor openings, regardless of depth, appropriately guarded by railings? The system components that deal with these considerations are slip (coefficient of friction) tests, slip test meter (see Fig. 8-11), railings, and barricades.

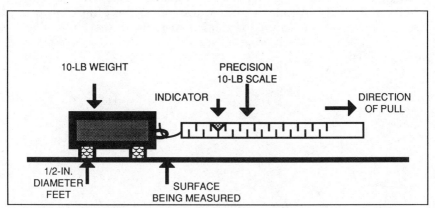

Figure 8-11. The horizontal pull slipmeter is a device that is described in American Society for Testing and Materials (ASTM) standards. The 10-lb weight is supported by three ½-in.-diameter feet that are made of (or simulate) shoe sole material. The slipmeter is pulled by hand, or by motor in some commercial models. The indicator is of the reading-retention type. If an average reading of 5 pulls is 5 lb, the coefficient of friction is 0.5. Point five is the accepted bench mark for a safe walking surface. The greater the reading below 0.5, the more slippery the floor.

6. Falls from one level to another. Falls from one level to another must be prevented at all costs because they are so devastating in their effects. Customers should be prevented from wandering into dangerous storage facilities where floor openings and open balconies may temporarily exist to accommodate a storage operation. The management systems that will help accomplish this are warning signs, railings, barricades, and management and employee training.

While there is no assurance that the development of a MORT analysis will prevent all patron falls, the development of the analysis will provide optimum fall prevention as long as the appropriate management systems are installed. Again, if there is a fall followed by litigation, the store will be able to point out the detailed preparations that were made to prevent such occurrences. It will be difficult for a plaintiff to prevail under these circumstances.

CONCLUSION

We have now covered six methods of analysis. The application of one of the six types will most certainly cover most conditions that are vulnerable to litigation. Table 8-1 has been prepared to help the analyst determine which is the best type of analysis to use in a given situation. In some cases two or more analysis types will work well, and in other cases a type of analysis that may not be the best method may be preferable because the development time may be shorter.

The matrix in Table 8-1 enables the matching of prevention requirements of individuals, industries, and disciplines with the appropriate type of analysis. This can be of major assistance to those who have a need to determine the actions necessary to avoid future injury and litigation problems.

Table 8-1 Analysis Selection Matrix

	Type of Analysis*					
Situation	1 Task Hazard	2 Hazard Effects and Control	3 Management Decision Point	4 Hazard Control	5 Fault Tree	6 Management Oversight and Risk Tree
An owner of a retail establishment wishes to assure customer safety	S	S	S	S	U	E
A manufacturer or an engineer wishes to assure that their product is safe for routine and for foreseeable use	U	S	E	U	S	S
An engineer wishes to determine if any discrete product component could hazard the whole system	U	E	U	U	E	U
A lawyer and/or expert witness prepares for trial in a personal injury case dealing with:						
1. Product liability	1. U	1. E	1. E	1. U	1. S	1. E
2. Construction injury	2. S	2. E	2. U	2. E	2. S	2. E
3. Failure to warn	3. S	3. S	3. E	3. S	3. S	3. S
4. Slip and fall	4. U	4. S	4. U	4. E	4. U	4. E
5. Unsafe premises	5. U	5. S	5. S	5. E	5. S	5. E
6. Electrocution	6. S	6. S	6. U	6. E	6. E	6. U
7. Regulatory penalties	7. S	7. U	7. S	7. S	7. U	7. S
8. Inappropriate management	8. U	8. E	8. E	8. U	8. U	8. E
9. Comparative negligence	9. S	9. S	9. S	9. S	9. U	9. E
10. Job or task design	10. E	10. S	10. U	10. E	10. U	10. U

Legend: E = excellent; S = satisfactory; U = unsatisfactory.
*See text for details on each analysis type.

Table 8-1 Analysis Selection Matrix (continued)

	Type of Analysis*					
Situation	1 Task Hazard	2 Hazard Effects and Control	3 Management Decision Point	4 Hazard Control	5 Fault Tree	6 Management Oversight and Risk Tree
An administrator of a mental hospital wishes to determine if staff is fully protected against injury from patients	S	U	S	S	U	E
An insurance company wishes to determine if they should underwrite a ski facility	S	U	S	U	S	E
A distributor of woodworking machinery wishes to know if all the machines adequately warn his customers	E	U	S	S	S	E
An owner of an appliance repair firm wants to know if her employees are adequately protected	E	S	U	S	S	U
A worker's compensation administrator wants to improve the quality of investigations of disputed claims	E	S	S	U	U	S
A large equipment rental agency wants to know if their customers are adequately protected and trained	S	E	U	E	U	E

Legend: E = excellent; S = satisfactory; U = unsatisfactory.
*See text for details on each analysis type.

Table 8-1 Analysis Selection Matrix (continued)

Situation	Type of Analysis*					
	1 Task Hazard	2 Hazard Effects and Control	3 Management Decision Point	4 Hazard Control	5 Fault Tree	6 Management Oversight and Risk Tree
An accident investigator wishes to determine the best corrective action	E	S	U	S	S	S
A general contractor or a subcontractor wants to determine if they are optimally safe for: 1. A particular job 2. The entire project	1. E 2. U	1. E 2. U	1. S 2. U	1. E 2. S	1. S 2. S	1. U 2. E
An inventor wants to know if a woodworking machine that processes wood six ways will harm its user	S	E	U	S	E	U
The principal of a high school wants to know if the school's industrial arts classes are organized for student safety	U	U	S	S	U	E
An industrial arts teacher wants to know if the practical projects are safe for students	E	S	U	E	S	E

Legend: E = excellent; S = satisfactory; U = unsatisfactory.
*See text for details on each analysis type.

PART III

Programmed Control of Safety and Health in the Private and Public Sectors

This part deals with many aspects of safety and industrial hygiene programming. To avoid repetition whenever the words "safety program" are used alone it should be understood that the industrial hygiene program is meant as well.

This part contains three chapters that deal with the organization of industrial hygiene and safety programs in public agencies, general industry, and in the construction industry.

General industry is ordinarily immune from litigation brought by an employee against the employer because worker's compensation laws in all states and for federal employment prohibit such two-party lawsuits. Often, however, there is protracted litigation within the compensation administration when there are disputes over payments, percent of disability, origin of the injury, etc.

In the state of California there is a penalty phase where an employer can be liable for an additional 50 percent of the entire cost of compensation on a particular case if it can be shown that the employer acted recklessly or willfully with respect to the cause of an employee's injury. In California and in 26 other states there have also been successful lawsuits against employers where the employee could show willful behavior on the employer's part.

In addition to this source of litigation, the OSHA law often creates disputes that are resolved in a quasi-courtroom setting where opposing attorneys, a judge, and witnesses are present. Beginning in the 1980s there has been an increasing emphasis on treating willful violations of safety laws as felonious, with the management community at risk for jail time and personal fines.

In view of these litigation opportunities the effectiveness of the safety program can play a significant role in injury and litigation prevention in the industrial or public setting. Chapter 10 therefore presents a prototype industrial safety and health program that can assist general industry and public agencies in avoiding litigation by placing them in the best possible position to prevent accidents and industrial illness.

The program prototype is preceded by a chapter that includes a discussion of staffing the safety and industrial hygiene office. While there cannot be a perfect staffing concept, it can be beneficial as a starting point to consult a reasonable guideline such as the one presented in Chapter 9.

This chapter is important because it also develops the rationale for the issues of responsibility and accountability for safety in business and the public sector. These issues are often misunderstood by juries, judges, attorneys, the management community in general, and even by some safety professionals.

In the 1970s there was a jury trial where the defendant was the safety officer of a large corporation. He was charged with criminal negligence in a situation where almost a dozen company employees were killed in an explosion in a tunnel. The prosecuting attorney claimed that the safety professional was responsible for the deaths because the safety rule violations involved should have been discovered and corrected by him. The jury agreed and found for the plaintiff. It is not my intent to argue the case, but to buttress the contention that proper assignment of responsibility and accountability are the foundation blocks of a professional safety program. Chapter 9 will build the case for this contention.

As we have discussed earlier in the book, the construction industry is faced with the constant threat of litigation because of the industry's high accident frequency rate, the severity of these accidents, and because of the ill-defined relationship between subcontractors and prime contractors as far as industrial injuries are concerned.

The third chapter (Chapter 11) in this part describes a blueprint for construction safety management. To many in the industry this scheme, because of its relative sophistication and structured requirements, may seem to ignore the realities of the construction environment. It has long been known, however, that to be successful a safety program must be integrated with the normal operating routines of the company that it serves. The construction environment is one where a prime contractor is attempting to bring together the skills of many different artisans by carefully sequencing the materials, tools, and work so that a finished product emerges with a specified cost and quality, and at a specified time. The proposed blueprint merely adds "with specified safety" to this definition. To say that this is somehow incompatible with the construction environment is to say that we must continue to accept a high level of serious injury and death as a normal part of doing business in the construction industry.

Chapter 9

A Guide to Safety and Industrial Hygiene Staffing, Responsibility, and Accountability

The size of an enterprise will usually determine the amount and depth of its professional safety staffing. As a general rule the smaller the company, the smaller the safety effort.

Exceptions to this rule are created by differences in the type of industry. Obviously, a large company producing computer software would not have the safety and industrial hygiene problems of a logging outfit one-third the size. Of the two companies the loggers would require full-time safety staffing (of course, they might not get it), the other probably not (of course, they would probably be well staffed).

If all other factors are approximately equal, size does become important when deciding on staff and funding commitments to industrial safety and health. Very little exists in the literature that can help in this determination, and since the amount of variability is infinite with regard to the size and type of industry, no inflexible rule should exist.

A GUIDE TO STAFFING

Table 9-1 provides a starting point that a person who is responsible for safety and industrial hygiene staffing can consult to determine the company's safety needs. The following are resource factors for determining required safety staffing based on company size and type.

0. Minimal or no formal on-the-job safety commitment required.

Table 9-1 Determining Resource Commitment to Safety and Health

Type of Work	Size of Company	Resource Factor*
Administrative	0–499	0
	500–4999	1
	Over 5000	2 or 3
Warehouse	0–499	1
	500–499	2
	Over 5000	3 or 4
Retail	0–49	1
	50–499	2
	500–1999	3
	2000–10,000	3 or 4
	Over 10,000	5
Outside servicing	0–49	2
	50–499	3
	500–1999	3 or 4
	2000–10,000	5
	Over 10,000	5 or 6
Light manufacturing	0–49	2
	50–499	3
	500–1999	3 or 4
	2000–4999	4
	5000–10,000	5
	Over 10,000	6
Heavy manufacturing	0–49	2
	50–99	3
	100–499	3 or 4
	500–1999	4
	2000–4999	4 or 5
	5000–10,000	5 or 6
	Over 10,000	6
Construction	0–49	3
Mining	50–99	3 or 4
Logging	100–4999	5
	Over 5000	6

*See text.

1. Safety leadership assumed by president of the company as a collateral duty. Funding required for hazard correction and internal motivation.
2. Safety leadership assigned as a part-time function to a resident manager or supervisor. Funding for supplies, equipment, hazard correction, training, and minimal travel is required. Duties may be assigned to a consultant.
3. Safety leadership is at least a half-time assignment of a supervisor or manager. Funding required for program activities, training, hazard

correction, special-emphasis programs, publicity, incentive awards, travel, and secretarial services as required.

4. Full-time safety professional required with half-time or more clerical assistance. Funding required for a moderate range of accident/illness prevention activities, including hazard corrections, line management participation, training, travel, departmental budgeting for safety activity, special-emphasis programs, supplies, and incentive awards.

5. Safety staff required at the rate of one per two thousand of moderate-risk work force; one per thousand of high-risk work force. An example of high risk would be workers involved with fabrication, assembly, processes such as plating and heat treating, plant maintenance, and over-the-road driving. Funding required for a full range of accident/illness prevention activities, including hazard corrections, management participation, training for professional staff and other program participants, travel, departmental (other than the safety department) safety activity budgets, worker's compensation administration, special-emphasis programs, incentive awards, and supplies.

6. Safety and industrial hygiene staff as described in 5, with corporate representation a strong option. Funding required for a full range of accident/illness activities as described in 5.

Starting with the first column in Table 9-1, select the type of work appropriate to the enterprise under consideration for staffing. Still using the table, match the size of the company in column 2 with the resource factor in column 3. Now match the resource factor from the table with its description in the text to arrive at an indication of the commitment required for the company.

Remember that the skill mix is not stipulated. The ratio of safety professionals to industrial hygienists will depend upon a further breakdown of the type of operation under consideration. If there is a heavy chemical orientation as opposed to a machinery and fabrication orientation, then hygienists will predominate.

RESPONSIBILITY AND ACCOUNTABILITY FOR SAFETY

No matter what the size and type of a company, practical but firm establishment of safety responsibility and safety accountability systems are the foundation of professional safety programming.

To those unfamiliar with the mechanics of occupational safety, the safety professional would seem to be the likely candidate for safety responsibility. This view is shared by many members of the management community, and even by some safety professionals, but to give this role to the safety officer is an error from which the company will suffer impaired results. A clear understanding by all concerned of where the responsibility for safety resides and how it is exercised is a necessary ingredient of a professional safety program. For this reason the major portion of this chapter is devoted to the exploration of the concepts and rationale behind safety responsibility and accountability.

A main focus of this explanation is on "deficiency and control analysis." A double fatal accident will be described and the deficiencies that precipitated the event will be analyzed. The conclusions of the analysis will logically point to a company entity that must control safety and health if future accidents of this or any type are to be controlled. The analysis will also illustrate how this entity should operate to get the job done.

Safety Responsibility

As stated earlier in this book, responsibility for safety belongs to the management hierarchy. It does not belong to the safety professional or the union, and it is not the exclusive province of the first-line supervisor.

In their article, "Factors Apparently Affecting Injury Frequency in Eleven Matched Pairs of Companies," Rolin H. Simonds and Yaghoub Shafai-Sahrai (1977) wrote in their abstract:

> Eleven matched pairs of industrial firms were selected so that two members of each pair were in the same state, in the same industry of approximately the same size, but had marked differences in work injury frequency. They were studied for the same period of time. All were visited and their records analyzed to see whether differences in management involvement in safety, promotional efforts toward safety, work force characteristics, or physical conditions were related with the better or poorer records. Factors found to be related to lower injury frequency rates were: (1) Top management involvement in safety; (2) better injury record keeping systems; (3) use of accident cost analysis; (4) smaller spans of control at the foreman level; (5) recreational programs for employees; (6) higher average age of employees; (7) higher percentage of married workers; (8) longer average length of employment in the company; (9) roomy and clean shop environment; and (10) more and better safety devices on machinery. Factors not related with injury frequency were: (1) Efforts to promote safety through workers' families, and (2) quality control and quantity of safety rules.

This study reinforces the idea that management involvement is critical to the success of the industrial safety effort. While other factors such as the age and type of work force had an influence, these are factors that are not as controllable as management control and participation in the safety program.

Why should the safety effort be controlled by the management hierarchy? Don't they have other fish to fry, and isn't a true safety professional trained to take a leadership role in the safety discipline?

When an employee fails to perform well he or she is subject to corrective action taken by his or her direct supervisor. Corrective action may be an oral or written reprimand, retraining, transfer to another department or shift, days off, or even termination. The fact remains that in any institution, public or private, employees are subject to management controls. Even a company president can be fired by the Board of Directors if the company consistently operates at a loss, or a public institution fails in its mission. In view of this, is it logical or desirable to expect a safety professional to take the same kind of supervisory action against an employee who has no reporting relationship to the safety officer?

When an employee consistently produces rejected parts, or raw material shortages prevent on-schedule production, or expensive instruments are ruined in the production process because a worker is inadequately trained, these are conditions that require correction. Since they are the only persons with the authority, the mandate, and the resources, management is expected to take firm action by correcting the work practices, conditions, procedures, and policies that led to the poor performance.

If the same employees involved in these production problems are being harmed by fumes from an improperly ventilated open-surface acid tank, or their hands are lacerated by sheet metal burrs on improperly finished parts, or serious injuries from falls from scaffolds are increasing, the same management must also address the same work practices, conditions, procedures, and policies to correct these problems.

To give these responsibilities to the safety professional would not only be inconsistent with normal operating routines, but such a role reversal often frustrates the very persons the safety officer is trying to help. Therefore, the active, organized, and structured control of safety by the management hierarchy is extremely important to successful safety and industrial hygiene programming, so much so, that failure to adopt this posture is to accept safety program mediocrity.

In his thoughtful article, "Accident Prevention as a Management Enterprise," Dr. Francis McGlade states that "a large share of the blame for inadequately represented safety programs lies with safety management (safety professionals) for its failure to establish accident prevention within the hierarchy of top management." McGlade implies that the upper management community has separated safety from the mainstream of company operations and that by doing so, has subordinated safety to the relative position of the annual bond drive.

The primary task of safety and industrial hygiene professionals is to convince top management that a safety program that involves active participation at all management levels is required, and that safety and health must be integrated into the routine operational practices of the company.

When management is convinced of its responsibility, the safety staff will structure the program, thereby guiding the management community to exercise its responsibility. The structuring medium can be the prototype safety and industrial hygiene program plan (sometimes called an accident prevention plan) contained in Chapter 10.

Once the program is established and safety is woven into the fabric of the company, the safety staff can concentrate on supporting and auditing the effectiveness of the program. When the described optimum safety and industrial hygiene organization is in place, and it does exist in companies with superior risk-management experience, the safety staff need not worry about seeking management support for every significant hazard correction. Instead, the management hierarchy will handle the problem through the line-controlled safety program, because top management is the only entity that can authorize funds and generate the correction of most problems, production or safety.

To summarize the preceding paragraphs:

1. To a great extent industrial accidents and illness result from a lack of perception at the corporate management level, at all subordinate management levels, and at the position of individual behavior.
2. Major responsibility for control of accidents is in the hands of industrial, business, political, and social institutions, as well as with the leaders of such organizations who plan and direct the complex enterprises that control the activities of the working population.
3. These leaders and the institutions they lead have done a less-than-adequate job in accomplishing professional safety programming.
4. A large share of the blame for this inadequacy lies with professional safety management for its failure to establish accident/illness-prevention activities within the management hierarchy.
5. A primary task for safety professionals is the establishment of a safety program that is integrated with existing management structures.
6. When safety program integration is complete, the safety staff is in a position to advise a participating management hierarchy as to how it should exercise its responsibilities.

Deficiency and Control Analysis

A standard accident investigation is based on the premise that future accidents can be prevented by avoiding conditions or activities revealed in the discovery phase of the investigation. The deficiency and control analysis probes in a somewhat different direction. It is a tool that can assist the safety manager with the effort to establish a professional safety program. It accomplishes this by illustrating how the participation of the management community is necessary to program success. It can therefore be used as an aid in the task of convincing management of their safety responsibility.

For example, if in a production setting products are often returned to the factory because their containers are broken and product is damaged before shipment, the ultimate responsibility for this problem belongs to the Materials Handling Manager. That manager will be expected to discover the source of the problem, correct it, and install procedures that will prevent reoccurrence. If the Materials Handling Manager cannot do this, then his or her job may be in jeopardy.

A similar situation exists when considering unsafe practices. There is a school of thought that says that if an accident occurs, then it is the worker's fault that he or she was injured. The reality of the matter is that the worker's actions must be controlled by the same management techniques that controlled the materials handling problem—actions involving rule making, violation detection, control procedures, follow-up, and sanctions, if necessary. As before, management must participate in this problem to correct it.

Following is a deficiency and control analysis of a multifaceted study problem that caused the death of two workers in a paper and pulp mill. The analysis will show that although the two workers had contributed heavily to their own demise, it was the lack of routine good management practices that was ultimately responsible. At the close of this demonstrative analysis the vital, inescapable safety program role of all levels of management will be made clear.

Case Study 9-1

The Accident and Injury

The setting for this incident* was the mill's digester building, which contained six digesters, each capable of holding 50 tons of wood chips. Digesters are huge, five-story-high pressure cookers that remove the lignin from wood to make the pulp that is ultimately converted to paper. The liquor that is introduced under high temperature and pressure during the "cooking" process is highly acidic and produces prodigious quantities of sulfur dioxide gas.

It was discovered that a drain fixture had pulled away from the interior wall of digester 4 and two maintenance men, a welder and his helper, were dispatched to reattach the fixture (see Fig. 9-1). The two men approached the bottom of digester 4, located on the first floor of the digester building, and saw that there was a lock on the acid valve. This lock belonged to the "cook," who was responsible for starting the digesting process.

Company rules required that each of the two maintenance workers place their own lock (every employee who may work in a confined space is supplied with a personal lock) on the valve, and since they were going

*Unlitigated case.

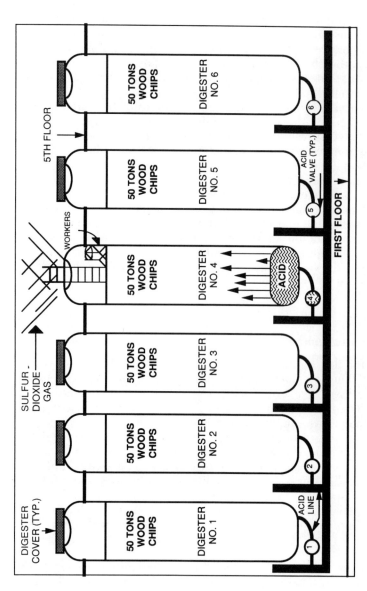

Figure 9-1. Digester building containing six digesters. When the "cook's helper" miscounted digesters he opened the acid valve to digester 4, the one where men were working. When on the first floor of the digester building a person can see the bottom of one and part of another digester, and so one does not get the panoramic view shown here. Since the numbers had long since been corroded from the wall of each digester, the counting error was almost inevitable (see text for a complete description of the incident). (Not to scale.)

to enter the digester, they were also required to blank-out the acid lines. Blanking-out is a 3-hour job that consists of placing a steel plate in the acid line at a flange. This would positively prevent the flow of acid into the digester.

The time of day was 10:30 A.M., and since to weld the drain was to be only a 40-minute job, it was surmised that the two workers neglected to both lock-out and blank-out because of the short job time and their desire to go to lunch immediately after it was finished. It they had followed lock-out procedure, they would have had to return to the valve to remove their locks instead of going directly to the lunchroom. Blanking-out probably never was a consideration.

After seeing the locked valve the two men proceeded up to the fifth floor, placed a ladder into the fill hole of digester 4, descended to the chip level, walked out to the drain, and proceeded with the repair.

Meanwhile, orders went out to "cook-off" digester 5. A worker with the title of "cook's helper" proceeded to the key shack and emerged with a key attached to a large tag with a number 5 printed on it. Upon entering the first floor of the digester building, he proceeded to what he thought was the valve to digester 5. For some reason he miscounted digesters, and since the numbers had long since been corroded off the digesters' walls, he mistakenly approached the valve on digester 4, the one in which the two maintenance men were working.

This mistake normally would not have been a problem, because another written company rule stated that no two locks that were used for lock-out purposes were to be accessible by the same key. However, as in the case of tragedies such as this, this inexorable series of events began two years earlier when the locks for digesters four and five were lost and the supervisor (at this point no longer working for the company) sent two workers to a local hardware store where they purchased two locks, both capable of being opened with the same key.

Now, using the number five key, the cook's helper opened the lock to the acid valve on digester 4, admitting the acid under high temperature and pressure. The two men in the digester were immediately blinded. One made it halfway up the ladder, but fell back and died with his partner. The fumes completely inundated the fifth floor of the digester building, sending one additional worker to the hospital for six months. The Deficiency and Control Analysis follows.

Method

To develop the analysis we will consider four of many major deficiencies. After examining each deficiency, a determination will be made as to which of three entities is ultimately responsible for the prior correction of the problem. The three entities are (1) the general work force, (2) the safety officer and staff (these persons are considered members of the management), and (3) the management hierarchy.

Each of these entities will be assigned one of three responsibility levels for each deficiency: (1) prime responsibility (P), (2) considerable responsibility (C), and (3) some responsibility (S). At the end of the analysis there will be a responsibility score based on 10 points for prime, 7 points for considerable, and 3 points for some. The major deficiencies we will consider are:

1. Improper locking and blanking of the acid lines
2. Lack of communication between departments
3. Interchangeable locks
4. Improper acid-valve location

Analysis

Deficiency Number 1. Improper locking and blanking of the acid lines.

The first reaction to this obvious and deliberate omission is that the deceased workers were grossly responsible for their own demise. If they had followed existing company policy by placing their own locks on the acid valves, and had placed a steel plate in the acid line, they would most probably be alive today. And is it not true that the decision not to lock-out, to violate written company safety rules, to choose convenience over insurance, was made by the only persons who could have taken timely action to protect themselves, the two dead men? The argument to fix responsibility with the dead workers is compelling and many in management and in professional safety who preside over this kind of disaster will feel entitled to wipe their foreheads in absolution.

This argument does not hold together under logical scrutiny. What actually occurred here is a clear failure of management. In a parallel situation that is contrary to company procedure, a valve is not locked and is subsequently opened to release the contents of a 32,000-gallon solvent tank into the river. The resultant fish kill, environmental pollution, direct cost ($12 per gallon), and production delays are unacceptable to company management.

A management investigative team would never accept the idea offered by the superintendent in charge of the solvent tank operation that it was the fault of the worker who failed to lock and opened the wrong valve. The investigation would alternatively center on what systems and procedures the superintendent had in place to prevent such an occurrence, and how these procedures were monitored to prevent the observed violations.

To reach a useful conclusion the investigation must focus on how the operation was managed, what prior planning had been performed by the superintendent and his or her subordinates, what preventive safeguards were in place, as well as whether or not the wrongful act had been a common occurrence or a one-time problem.

The fatal accident situation can be treated no differently than the production problem. The board of investigation must probe how the lock-out and blank-out systems were designed, how well they operated, and why the system failed on the day of the accident. They must reach an understanding of what procedures and controls were in place, when and how they failed, and what must be done to prevent a recurrence.

Management must not create or maintain a dichotomy in the way that it views or handles production problems as opposed to safety and health problems. They both are the product of management forces and both must be resolved by management forces.

The safety office has considerable responsibility here since they need to be a reliable source of information on how well the management-designed and -enforced procedures are performing.

Assignment of Responsibility and Control: prime responsibility to management (10 points), considerable responsibility to professional safety (7 points), considerable responsibility to workers (7 points).

Deficiency Number 2. Lack of communication between departments.

The importance of communication is obvious. Company management must use communication to attain organizational goals, and to persuade, inform, and motivate the employees who get the jobs done. Jobs are done by people, and skilled communication is an indispensable ingredient of good performance.

A well-managed company is usually blessed by a communication program that creates understanding between the many employee levels. Certainly if the acid department had informed the maintenance organization that a digester was to be cooked-off on the day of the incident, the repair most probably would have been rescheduled. At the least the maintenance workers would have been aware of this activity and would probably have been more cautious. No such communication was made, and so this avenue of prevention was lost.

It would be unfair to blame the entire management hierarchy for this single lapse in interdepartmental communication, but management would certainly be responsible for the general communications practices extant in the company at the time of the accident. If those practices were deficient—employees in one department generally not talking to employees in other departments, for example—then management is responsible for not creating or cultivating efficient information exchange. If further examination revealed that little upward or downward communication was evident, then the company should be judged seriously deficient in their communications effort, and the accident would have to be labeled a logical consequence of that deficiency.

Skilled, effective communications in a company are planned and nurtured by management. In this case, there was clear evidence that management had failed to use or encourage effective communications at almost every opportunity and therefore must be held responsible.

The safety office also has a significant communications role as a disseminator of accident prevention information to all company levels.

Assignment of Responsibility and Control: prime responsibility to management (10 points), considerable responsibility to safety (7 points), some responsibility to workers (3 points).

Deficiency Number 3. Interchangeable locks.

Two years before the accident, when the two locks from digesters 4 and 5 were found to be missing, a set of preplanned events should have occurred. These events were described in an existing company procurement procedure.

1. The supervisor of the digester operation should have been notified.
2. The supervisor would place an order for two new locks using the standard company purchase order forms.
3. Two new, differently keyed standby locks, obtained from department stores, should have been temporarily placed on the acid valves.
4. When the order reached the purchasing department the buyer would consult a list that would identify items with special ordering instructions. That list would have included locks.
5. Under locks the listing would have read, "All locks in the following departments shall be constructed of corrosion-resistant material and shall be keyed differently from any other company-owned lock: Acid Department; Maintenance Department; . . .
6. The buyer would coordinate with maintenance to determine the key sequence so that proper instructions could be relayed to the supplier.
7. Two differently keyed locks would be purchased and issued to the acid department to replace the lost acid-valve locks.

Because these (or similar) events did not occur, another prevention mode was eliminated and the accident–injury sequence was permitted to continue uninterrupted.

Close scrutiny of these events reveals a substantial degree of management responsibility and involvement. Management conceived the procedure and only timely, appropriate management controls could perpetuate its use. The list of special instructions is a management tool to assure that certain critical purchases are performed correctly. Apparently, the proper chain of events was never set in motion and an unauthorized purchase of two locks was made. Management failed to use its own system that it had designed to prevent accidents such as the one that had occurred.

Instead, the supervisor, who may not have known of the standby locks, decided that it would be expeditious, or face-saving, to purchase the new locks at a local hardware store from his discretionary funds. In two years no one checked to confirm that the locks required different keys; another management failure to monitor an important system that they had conceived.

After this accident, management discovered to their dismay that the company had many other locks in violation of company rules and that over $50,000 was required to correct the situation. Management had simply lost control of a vital company system, one that they had designed but could not maintain. This was more evidence that safety received discriminatory treatment when compared with production, a sure prescription for safety program mediocrity.

Assignment of Responsibility and Control: prime responsibility to management (10 points), considerable responsibility to safety (7 points), some responsibility to workers (3 points).

Deficiency Number 4. No acid warning system and improper acid-valve location.

When the cook's helper opened the wrong valve and pumped acid into the digester where the maintenance men were working, a relatively inexpensive alarm-delay system might have prevented the deadly consequence of his act. If such a system had been present, an alarm would sound for 50 seconds, during which time no acid would flow. Fifty seconds would give any worker in the digester time to escape before acid reached him. The cost of such a system would be approximately $7000 for all digesters.

A visit to other paper and pulp mills around the country would reveal that the acid-valve location in this plant was not optimum. If the acid valve, as was true in many other facilities, was located on the fifth floor next to each digester opening, the cook's helper would have seen an open digester with a ladder protruding from the opening. This would have made it obvious that he was at the wrong digester, and thus the accident would not have happened. The cost of relocating the acid valves was $3000 per digester, $18,000 for all six.

There are three primary considerations here. (1) Who can authorize the expenditure of $25,000 for the two preventive measures just described? (2) Who makes up the forum where such a decision can be made? (3) What is the mechanism for establishing need and bringing that information to the attention of the forum?

In most corporations no manager below the level of department head can authorize the expenditure of $25,000. A first-line supervisor who was aware of the alarm and valve problems would have to go through three or four levels of supervision before action could be taken. Without a properly organized safety program structure, the average low- or middle-level manager would recognize the futility of trying to get these corrections authorized.

Top management is the approval body for large outlays of funds, and therefore is the responsible body. The forum where approval is made must be comprised of the same top managers that approve similar expenditures for production concerns such as new tools, raw materials, and new facilities.

The safety program must be designed to expedite the transmittal of need from the factory floor to the top management safety forum. The development of need is the task of the professional safety staff. A program that includes these features is described in the prototype accident prevention plan in Chapter 10.

Assignment of Responsibility and Control: prime responsibility to management (10 points), considerable responsibility to safety (7 points), some responsibility to workers (3 points).

Summary

Totaling the score we find that of a total of 84 available points 68 points, or 80 percent, went to management (which includes safety) and 16 points, or 20 percent, went to workers. Does this mean that workers are not responsible for their own safety? No! It means that to ensure a successful safety program, management must take a controlling and participative role identical to the role they assume for production.

In the responsibility and control analysis primary responsibility for safety clearly points to the management hierarchy. Control of working conditions, procedures, and practices are the domain of company management whether these factors affect the quality and cost of a product, the safety of a product, or the safety of the workers who manufacture the product.

A manager who controls and is held accountable for a budget will initiate an exhaustive analysis when a new $40,000 hoist is proposed for the efficient handling of steel ingots. This same manager must be involved to the same degree when the hoist is proposed for the prevention of back injuries (which may be even more profitable than buying the hoist for production purposes).

The responsibility for retraining workers so that they produce fewer rejections cannot logically be separated from retraining to reduce or eliminate exposure to toxic fumes. The creation of a procedure that will produce the product at a faster rate is the domain of the same individuals who would develop a procedure to produce the same product with less hazard to workers. In all of the preceding cases the responsibility belongs to the management hierarchy.

Safety professionals must not be hired to relieve management of their role in managing accident/illness prevention. The professional's role is to convince management of their participative function and then show management how to exercise their responsibility. This is accomplished by developing a professional-quality safety and industrial hygiene program and assisting in its implementation and maintenance. The purpose of Chapter 10 is to show how this can be accomplished.

Does all this emphasis on management control of safety mean that companies that have adopted participative management schemes where all employees share in management decisions cannot benefit from this advice? On the contrary, *shared management* merely means shared control of the safety and industrial hygiene program. The prototype accident-prevention plan is based on the traditional management scheme, but the plan is flexible enough to be easily adapted to enlightened management methods.

Safety Accountability

When I am asked as a safety consultant to help install a safety program in a company or public agency, among the first questions that I ask is, "What systems are already in place to hold management accountable for their production responsibilities?" The usual system used by profit-making organizations includes measurements of standard objectives such as number of rejects, adherence to budget limitations, on-schedule production, learning curves, and cost per pound of product. For public agencies the usual measurements are the number of clients serviced, time spent per client, or total cost of service per client.

These measurements are the lifeline through which a successful company or agency remains successful. If the measurements are made ritualistically and control limits are developed for each measurement, then management can quickly assess the performance needed to control adverse situations before they are beyond redemption.

For example, if a manager is assigned to produce 1250 units of product each month for the first five months of the year, a chart can be produced biweekly (or at a different frequency) that will show the manager's production performance. A control line may be placed at 1100 units of product, meaning that if the production rate drops below the control, prompt action must be taken to restore production levels.

In all cases, the performance of the manager is judged by how well he or she manages to maintain the required production levels. Naturally, the manager, knowing that salary increases, promotions, or transfer to more satisfying jobs depends heavily on how well production goals are met, will strive to keep production at a high level.

Many companies and some agencies refine this accountability process still further by holding accountability meetings on a weekly, biweekly, or monthly basis. At these meetings a responsible manager will report in the presence of his or her contemporaries, boss, and other managers generally up to the level of the vice president.

If a production-level chart shown at such a meeting should reveal that the manager's organization has produced only 950 units of product for the reporting period, then the reporting manager must answer the following questions.

1. What has caused the problem?
2. What am I doing about the problem?

3. When do I expect the problem to be resolved and production restored to normalcy?
4. What am I doing to prevent a recurrence of this problem?

Other, specific questions may be asked by anyone in attendance at this accountability meeting. The end result is that the reporting manager knows that he or she is not only responsible for the goals and objectives adopted by the management hierarchy, but will also be held accountable at regular intervals for these targets.

There are a number of likely candidates for measurement in the safety and industrial hygiene arena. Raw injury frequency expressed as injuries per 100 employees, or as compensation claims per 100 employees, could be presented against targets set by an executive safety council (see Fig. 9-2 for an illustration). Other safety-oriented charts could deal with the results of special-emphasis programs such as repetitive-motion injury or eye-injury reduction. In all cases, the safety area is treated with the same gravity and for the same reporting period as the production arena.

When adverse safety and industrial hygiene information is shown, the responsible and accountable manager must answer the same questions that were asked for the production problems. In this way safety and industrial hygiene become woven into the company's fabric, and true integration of safety into the normal operational routines of the company or agency is achieved.

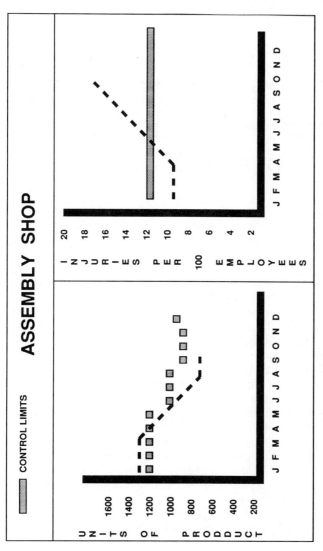

Figure 9-2. Accountability charts for the assembly shop. When these two charts are shown at the same meeting along with other production and safety measurements, it signifies an appropriate level of accountability. It means that the Assembly Shop manager is being measured on his or her ability to control accidents as well as production, and the pressures to maintain progress toward management-set goals for production and safety are approximately equal. When safety is treated in this way, it is a strong indicator that occupational safety and health are integrated into the normal operating routines of the company.

Chapter 10

Industrial Safety and Health Organization: A Prototype Safety and Industrial Hygiene Program Plan

The following prototype accident/illness prevention plan, although by no means complete enough to cover all industries, is sufficient in scope to merit its own table of contents. It is written so that this example plan could be readily adapted to almost any type or sized operation. The basic plan contains many of the features that you would expect to find in a large industry safety and industrial hygiene program. For that reason a matrix is provided at the end of the chapter that enables the reader to scale down the suggested program to a size that will fit medium and small industry.

What will this prototype do for your safety and industrial hygiene effort? The prototype plan should:

1. Form a basic safety and industrial hygiene program structure that will have longevity. That is, the program established through the use of this plan should not collapse whenever changes are made at the top level in the safety department.
2. With appropriate accountability systems the plan should integrate safety and industrial hygiene into the operational routines of the company.
3. Provide uniform guidance to everyone involved with the safety and industrial hygiene program.
4. Assist safety managers who must convince the company hierarchy of management's participative role in the safety effort.

5. Provide a medium through which official changes and improvements can be made to the safety and industrial hygiene effort.
6. Place the company in a position where it will be able to: reduce accidents, stimulate interest and participation in safety, successfully pass regulatory agency inspections, and successfully defend itself if cited or if subject to an employee action in those states where such actions are permitted.

When using this prototype it will become apparent that some customizing will be required. For example, under Policy Standards, Eye Protection, the "Ajax plan" (starting on p. 174) stipulates a 100 percent eye protection requirement: All employees will wear industrial safety glasses while on company property. If your policy is one where office areas do not require industrial safety glasses, then make an appropriate change in the Ajax prototype.

DESCRIPTION OF THREE SIGNIFICANT PLAN FEATURES

Some of the plan's features require a detailed explanation because of the particularly important or unique role that they serve. These features are: (1) the Executive Safety Council, (2) the hazard identification card system, and (3) the statistical format.

The Executive Safety Council

The Executive Safety Council, composed of top-level managers, is very important to the success of the safety effort, because council members are the persons who give the "marching orders" for the company. Without the active participation of these persons in the safety program it becomes very difficult to motivate middle and first-line management, establish a meaningful safety policy, and fund large ticket items such as ventilation systems, extensive guarding programs, or special accident/illness-reduction programs.

In order to make injury/illness prevention an integral part of company operations management must be not only responsible but also accountable for the safety of their employees. Top managers play a significant role here since they must authorize adding safety to existing accountability systems. For example, top management holds middle managers accountable for the cost of producing the product by establishing control limits for expenditures. By establishing the same type of limits for accident frequency and severity, middle management is motivated to control accidents as well as budgets in their respective organizations.

For these reasons the Executive Safety Council becomes a vital component in the safety effort. This body is therefore stipulated for programs in all sizes and types of industry.

The Hazard Identification Card System

Another program component that should be present, no matter what the size and type of company, is the hazard identification card system. This system provides all employees with an opportunity to bring hazards of all types to the attention of management with the assurance that action will be taken when justified. The employee also is allowed to follow progress toward correction. When program components such as the hazard identification card system are omitted, employees are faced with frustrations that sour their views toward cooperating with the maintenance of a safe working environment.

The Statistical Format

When the director of manufacturing wishes to monitor the quality of the product, he or she will ask for data that show product rejects on a daily, weekly, or monthly basis, depending on the gravity of the quality control problem. If rejects overrun predetermined control points, then remedial action must be taken.

In the case of quality control, the purpose of producing reports is to keep product quality within acceptable limits. Since the monitoring of product rejects is a commonly used management technique, the "reject" report can be labeled as a standard operating technique.

To be equally as effective, and this means attracting interested readership who will act accordingly based on the data presented, accident/illness reporting must answer the same type of essential questions as the "rejects" report. It is the purpose of the following paragraphs to describe the characteristics of such an accident/injury summary.

The format of an effective monthly accident summary should have the following features.

1. Familiar, Understandable Criteria.

Dr. Dan Petersen, noted safety management consultant and author, maintains that the standard criteria for accident frequency and severity measurement are not effective because of the separation of cause and effect. That is, if an organizational unit such as a machine shop has an excessive number of accidents during a reporting period, there is no assurance that the cause of the problem is what they did or did not do during that period. Similarly, what the machine shop does to correct the reported high accident frequency may have the same correlation problem. This means that if the frequency drops in the next month's report, the reduction may or may not be causally related to the increased safety activity.

To correct this problem, Petersen would eliminate frequency and severity as reporting criteria, particularly with the smaller reporting units such as the machine shop. Instead he advocates measuring acci-

dent-prevention activities, such as the number of work practice observations conducted by a supervisor. These activities, Petersen claims, are
easy to measure, are not subject to the correlation problems of standard
criteria, and are an effective indicator of accident-prevention activity
and prospective results.

Many managers, however, are results-oriented and want to measure
the fruit of their efforts with criteria that are more representative of
company objectives. A manager who is concerned about quality control
wants to see a reduction in product rejects and may not be satisfied with
being rated on how many employees were retrained to achieve that
reduction. Therefore in the proposed monthly accident summary format
we will use the more standard measurements of accident frequency and
severity: injuries/100 employees, claims/100 employees, and cost of
injuries/100 employees.

2. Be Fair.

Numbers should be reported as a rate. It would be inappropriate to
compare accidents between an organization of 200 persons with one of
500 employees if the basis were raw accidents. Injuries per 100 employees would compensate for the disparity in headcount.

Another element of fairness is headcount. If an organization—a
machine shop, for example—has a listed headcount of 274 employees, it
is very doubtful if exactly that many employees work in the shop on any
single day. The reason for this is that some employees are out sick, some
are on vacation, others are out for personal reasons. Also, overtime
would increase the accident exposure, while the aforementioned factors
would decrease the exposure to accidents.

The solution to this problem is to calculate an "exposure" headcount
by dividing the number of worker hours the entire shop actually works
in any one month by the number of hours a single employee works in one
month. If all reporting organizations are treated this same way with
regard to their headcounts, then it will be considered as fair by all. A
third element of fairness deals with "risk." In a report that requires
managers to strive for a target reduction, it certainly would not be fair to
set the same goals for an engineering organization as for the machine
shop. A solution to this problem is to set four targets, one for each
organization:

1. High-risk organizations such as machine shops, plant services, plating, and heat treating.
2. Moderate-risk organizations such as expediting, quality control, and
   warehousing.
3. Low-risk organizations such as engineering, steno pool, and personnel.
4. All-company target, which of course is the goal for the entire company organization. This is a composite of the previous three targets.

3. Be Effective.

There are four effectiveness criteria, which if followed will establish the monthly accident summary as an accountability system similar to budget and quality control reports.

1. Targets for all reporting organizations should be set by the Executive Safety Council each year. Targets should not be set by any other entity, and most particularly not by the professional safety staff. Remember that top management sets the marching orders for the company, and accident-reduction goals must certainly fall within the definition of a marching order if they are to be effective.
2. In many cases the readership of a report is inversely proportional to its anonymity. The more anonymous a report, the fewer the readers. Why should anyone care that the data show adverse results, if it is difficult to determine who is accountable for the problem? This situation can be reversed by including the appropriate manager's name in the report on the same line that displays his or her organization's data. While such a move may at first be objectionable to some, eventually it will be accepted as routine. The effect on interest and the effectiveness of the report will be gratifying.
3. Another important effectiveness technique is the use of ratings based on success in achieving the accident/illness-prevention goals set by the Executive Safety Council. If a manager is routinely judged on performance in producing a product on time, at the least cost, with maximum quality, then it is entirely justifiable to measure and rate that same manager on ability to control industrial accidents and illness. Ratings should be a simple expression with a clear relationship to the targets.
4. The last criterion for effectiveness is the distribution of the report. It is important that the report be seen by all of top management so that they may use it to hold their subordinate managers formally accountable at meetings and informally on a personal level.

If all of the preceding criteria are followed, the result will be a report that will have wide readership by those who have a great interest in the presented data.

AJAX METAL FABRICATION COMPANY
ACCIDENT/INJURY-PREVENTION PLAN

The Ajax Metal Fabrication Company has 7800 employees, most of whom are engaged in shaping, forming, cutting, heat treating, and chemically processing metals. The company also has structural steel erection and wire divisions. Figure 10-1 is a partial organization chart showing the general configuration of the company.

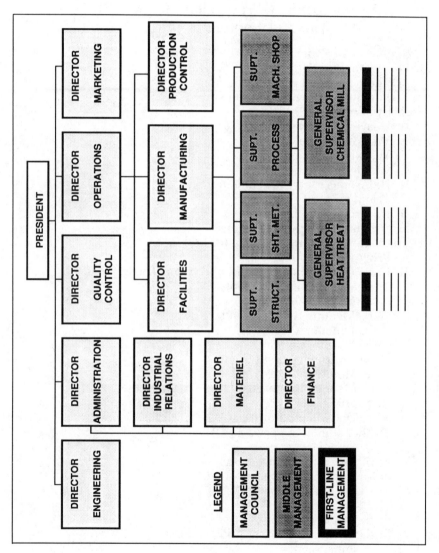

Figure 10-1. Ajax Metal Fabrication Company organization chart.

The table of contents for the following prototype accident prevention plan, using the preceding criteria, would look something like this:

Ajax Metal Fabrication Company
Accident/Injury-Prevention Plan
Table of Contents

I. Statement of Policy

The management of the Ajax Metal Fabrication Company believes that accidents result in needless losses to the company and to its employees. We believe that accidents can be prevented and that the control of accidents is a primary task for all managers.

Consistent with this philosophy the company will adopt a structured, management-controlled safety and health program where company management will be held responsible and accountable for the safety and industrial health of their employees.

II. Policy Standards

Policy standards are rules developed by the company to control recognized safety and industrial hygiene exposures.

A. The Safety and Health Program

Control of accidents will be a line management function, and therefore the company will operate a structured, line-participating safety and industrial hygiene program (see Figs. 10-1 and 10-3).

Each department will develop and implement a safety and industrial hygiene plan consistent with the company plan. The department plan should identify goals, safety requirements, procedures, responsibilities, methods, and schedules of accomplishment.

Accident prevention devices, criteria, and procedures will be incorporated into development, fabrication, and assembly at an early enough point to achieve maximum safety to company personnel in a cost-effective manner. To accomplish this objective safety and health criteria must be included for purchasing, tool design, fabrication, layout, plant maintenance, production, production planning, testing, and assembly. Safe procedure and equipment must not be overlooked or avoided in any company operation.

B. Personal Protective Equipment

Personal protective equipment is to be used only in situations where abatement of a hazard by the use of administrative or engineering controls is not feasible. With the exception of safety shoes, equipment shall be provided by the company free of charge. All personal protective equipment shall be approved by the Safety and Industrial Hygiene section. Areas where the use of personal protective equipment is required shall be posted to that effect.

C. Eye Protection

The Ajax company has adopted a 100 percent eye protection program. This means that while on company property all company employees will wear industrial safety glasses. This includes office areas. In addition to plano safety glasses the company will make prescription eyewear available on company grounds. Factory areas will be posted as follows:

> MANDATORY
> EYE PROTECTION
> AREA

D. Hearing Conservation

Any employee exposed to noise levels above 80 dBA shall be included in the company hearing conservation program. This will include at the minimum: baseline audiograms, follow-up audiograms at yearly or six-month intervals, monitoring of high-noise-level areas and high-noise-level operations, posting of high-noise areas, wearing of appropriate hearing protection devices, and noise control by engineering or administrative means.

E. Working Alone

Ajax employees will not work alone when the following conditions exist:

1. *Electrical.* Performance of work on an open, energized electrical circuit where contact with 100 or more volts is possible (unless available current is less than 2 MA).
2. *Tanks, pits, and underground voids.* Performance of work in confined

spaces where toxic, flammable chemicals have been (or are being) used, or where oxygen depletion may exist.
3. *Laboratories.* Performance of work with highly reactive chemicals or high-energy systems.

If in doubt, contact the Safety Section.

F. Working at Heights

Personnel working above ground level will comply with Table 10-1 of this document.

G. Accident Investigation

All accidents will be reported to and investigated by the injured employee's first-line supervisor. When a serious or fatal injury occurs, a formal board of investigation will convene according to the accident investigation matrix in Table 10-2. Table 10-2 also describes the investigation responsibilities of involved organizations for all other types of accidental injuries.

At the minimum, routine accident investigations should include:

1. A description of the accident
2. The names of the individuals involved
3. The date, time, and location of the accident
4. A description of the injuries or illness suffered
5. The name of the person conducting the investigation

H. Hazardous Materials Labeling

All hazardous, toxic, or potentially dangerous materials will be labeled in accordance with Part VII of this plan called Hazard Communication.

I. Training

The following safety and industrial hygiene training minimums are required to establish and maintain the safety program:

• All supervision: 2 hours
• Key management personnel (committee chairs, safety supervisors): 4 hours
• Safety monitors: 2 hours
• New hires: 2 hours

In addition, specialized training for protective equipment, safety protective devices, and specialized skills may be required from time to time. A proficiency test must be passed at the end of each training session.

Table 10-1 Protection for Employees Working at Heights

Protection	Work Station			
	Platform	Ladder	Roof	Unprotected High Surface
Chest–waist harness (to be used for restraint only)	X		X	X
Parachute-type harness	X		X	X
3-ft lanyard	X		X	X
> 3-ft lanyard with shock absorber	X		X	
42-in. rail with midrail	X		X	
Toeboard	X		X	
Warning-line system			X	
Competent person		X	X	
Tie-off, if extension-type ladder		X		
Cage, if ladder over 20 ft. and fixed		X		
Do not stand on top or next to top step of step ladders				
Fall-arrest system	X	X (fixed)		X

This table is a guide to required protection for working at heights in the Ajax Metal Fabrication Company. Considering roof work, a worker must use a warning-line system and work within the perimeter of the enclosed area. If the worker must go outside of the perimeter, then a harness and lanyard is required. If the length of the lanyard will permit a fall from the roof (over 3 ft), then a shock absorber is required. In the case of an unprotected platform (no rail), the same type of protection is necessary. An X indicates that the designated protective device is used for the indicated work station. This chart is only a guideline to fall protection. In all cases consult the OSHA standards and the safety office for the appropriate protection. Note: The requirements noted are not mutually exclusive and care must be taken that protection meets the requirements of OSHA and local statutes.

Those who fail must repeat the test. Those who fail twice must repeat the training.

J. Hazardous Testing

Hazardous tests (i.e., tests of products or materials that may pose a danger to the test conductor) shall be reviewed for pertinent hazard

Table 10-2 Ajax Metal Fabrication Company Accident Investigation Matrix

Type of Accident	Injured's Organization	Safety	Medical	Security	Executive Safety Council
First aid	Investigate	Provide statistics	Treat / Provide statistics	N/A	N/A
Reportable injury	Investigate	Provide statistics	Treat / Provide statistics	N/A	N/A
Non-losstime claim	Investigate / File claim information	Provide statistics	Treat if necessary / Provide data	N/A	N/A
Losstime claim	Investigate / File claim information	Investigate / Provide data	Treat if necessary / Provide data	N/A	N/A
Very serious noninjury	Participate on board of investigation	Investigate / Member of board	Participate on board	Participate on board	Convene board of investigation
Fatality	Participate on board of investigation	Investigate / Member of board	Participate on board	Participate on board	Convene board of investigation
Multiple fatality	Participate on board of investigation	Investigate / Member of board	Participate on board	Participate on board	Convene board of investigation
Catastrophe	Participate on board of investigation	Investigate / Member of board	Participate on board	Participate on board	Convene board of investigation

Note: This matrix provides instant instructions to the organizations that are involved with industrial injuries and industrial illnesses. Using a matrix provides the required level of uniformity to accident investigation so that hazards are routinely discovered and corrected, and that the statistical data derived from investigations are accurate and meaningful.

control criteria during the planning phase and again prior to test commencement. These reviews will be conducted by using the Test Safety Review form (see Fig. 10-2).

K. Accident Prevention Targets

Accident prevention objectives for the company shall be set by the Executive Safety Council every year. Each organization may set its own more stringent targets, but organization-set targets may not be less rigorous than those set by the council. A more in-depth discussion of safety statistics is contained in Part VI of this plan.

III. Safety Program Structure

Figure 10-3 establishes a three-tier program, with the Executive Safety Council, Safety Management Committee, and the Factory Level Committee as the three safety program controlling entities. The company's standard organization structure as exhibited in Figure 10-1 is not altered, thus ensuring that each tier or level performs duties in behalf of safety that are appropriate and similar to its normal job functions.

A. Program Components

There are seven basic components in this safety and industrial hygiene program.

1. Executive Safety Council (first tier). Chaired by the Director of Operations.
2. Functional Level Safety Committee (second tier). The official name of this committee is the Safety Management Committee. It is chaired by a superintendent-level manager.
3. Shop Safety Supervisor. Delegated first-line supervisor and chairperson of the factory-level committee.
4. Crew Supervisors (first-line supervisors).
5. Safety Monitors. Hourly or salaried employees.
6. Factory Level Committee (third tier). The official name of this committee is the Safety Monitor Committee.
7. Professional Safety Staff.

Figure 10-4 shows a more detailed illustration of the Ajax safety program. The structure maintains the standard hierarchical arrangement of the organization chart shown in Figure 10-1. On the following pages the detailed functions of each safety program entity will show how the individuals involved perform their traditional role on behalf of safety and industrial hygiene. By focusing on meaningful safety matters in a committee setting, the proper forum is established so that safety and industrial hygiene problems of any magnitude or level can be resolved.

HAZARDOUS TEST SAFETY REVIEW		
Test Title _____		
Program _____ Test Location _____		

HAZARD IDENTIFICATION AND COMPLIANCE CHECK LIST		
EXPECTED HAZARDS	**CHECK**	**CORRECTIVE ACTION**

EXPECTED HAZARDS	CHECK	CORRECTIVE ACTION	R	P
Fluids and Gasses		**R = Required** **P = Provided**		
High Pressure				
High or Low Temperature				
Toxic				
Corrosive		Fire Extinguishers		
Explosives		Personnel Egress		
Support Equipment		Protective Clothing		
Rotating or other moving parts		Eye Protection		
Controls		Hearing Protection		
Handling equipment		Pressure Relief Valves		
High work stations		Barricades		
Hazardous working surfaces		Warning Signs		
Electrical		Lighting		
Shock		Local Exhaust Ventilation		
Power Loss		Automatic Shutdown		
High Voltage		Interlocks		
Grounding		Emergency Procedures		
Combustibles		Respiratory Protection		
Fuels		"Test in Progress" Sign		
Other (specify)		Emergency Showers		
Radiation		Eyewash		
X-ray		Electrical Grounding		
Laser		Static Electricity Controls		
Microwave		Two-person Policy		
Ultraviolet		Dosimeters		
Ionizing		Emergency Alarms		
Chemicals		Communication System		
Acids		Safety Briefing		
Caustics		Test Personnel		
Mercury		Visitors		
Heavy Metals		Operator Training		
Other (specify)				

Environmental		**APPROVALS**
Noise		Test Mgr. _____ Date _____
Hot or Cold		Safety _____ Date _____
Other (specify) _____		Medical _____ Date _____

Figure 10-2. Hazardous test control form.

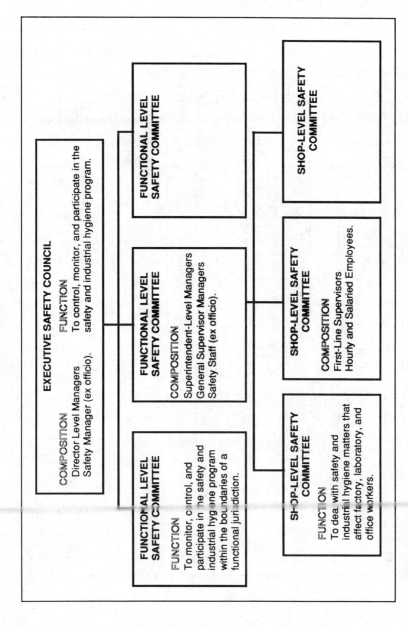

EXECUTIVE SAFETY COUNCIL

COMPOSITION
Director Level Managers
Safety Manager (ex officio).

FUNCTION
To control, monitor, and participate in the safety and industrial hygiene program.

FUNCTIONAL LEVEL SAFETY COMMITTEE

FUNCTIONAL LEVEL SAFETY COMMITTEE

COMPOSITION
Superintendent-Level Managers
General Supervisor Managers
Safety Staff (ex officio).

FUNCTIONAL LEVEL SAFETY COMMITTEE

FUNCTION
To monitor, control, and participate in the safety and industrial hygiene program within the boundaries of a functional jurisdiction.

SHOP-LEVEL SAFETY COMMITTEE

SHOP-LEVEL SAFETY COMMITTEE

COMPOSITION
First-Line Supervisors
Hourly and Salaried Employees.

SHOP-LEVEL SAFETY COMMITTEE

FUNCTION
To deal with safety and industrial hygiene matters that affect factory, laboratory, and office workers.

Figure 10-3. Ajax Metal Fabrication Company: Safety organization.

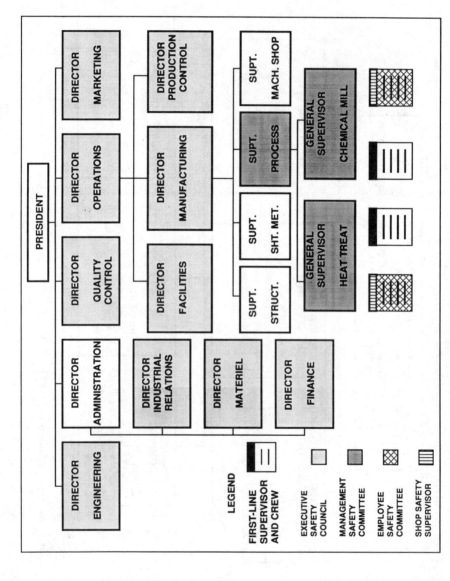

Figure 10-4. Detailed safety program structure.

B. Composition and Functions of Program Components

1. The Executive Safety Council.

1. *Membership*
   - Director of Operations—Chair
   - Director of Engineering
   - Director of Quality Control
   - Director of Marketing
   - Director of Industrial Relations
   - Director of Materiel
   - Director of Finance
   - Director of Facilities
   - Director of Production Control
   - Director of Manufacturing
   - Safety and Industrial Hygiene Manager (ex officio)
2. *Meeting requirements.* Meetings are held on the third Tuesday of each month. Delegation of attendance to subordinates should be limited. The Safety and Industrial Hygiene Manager will prepare and distribute the agenda and the minutes. The chairperson will direct the preparation of the agenda.
3. *Executive Safety Council functions*
   - Formulate company safety policy
   - Authorize the expenditure of funds to correct safety and industrial hygiene hazards
   - Authorize special-emphasis programs to reduce injuries and industrial illness; sample programs would include such topics as the reduction of back or hand injuries
   - Establish company safety objectives and goals
   - Review significant accidents and convene a board of investigation when necessary
   - Resolve safety and industrial hygiene problems forwarded to the council from the lower level committees
   - Authorize companywide safety activities such as training and award programs
   - Review and evaluate the safety performance of the company; this evaluation will include, but is not limited to, hazard control, organization and administration of the safety and industrial hygiene program, and statistical trends.
4. *Documentation.* Minutes of Executive Safety Council meetings will be taken and distributed to all managers above the level of general supervisor and to shop safety supervisors.

2. The Safety Management Committee (Functional Level).

1. *Membership.* The functional department (e.g., machine shop, stores, electrical maintenance) superintendent will chair the committee; general supervisors, who report departmentally to the chair.

2. *Meeting requirements.* Safety management committees will meet on the same day of the second week in the month. Delegation of attendance to subordinates should be limited. The chair will prepare the agenda. Minutes should be taken during the meeting, using the Safety Documentation Report illustrated in Figure 10-5.

SAFETY DOCUMENTATION REPORT

TYPE OF MEETING (if meetings are combined, check appropriate box)

☐ SAFETY MANAGEMENT   ☐ SAFETY MONITOR   ☐ COMBINED

MEETING DATE _____   **NUMBER PRESENT**_____

OLD BUSINESS

NEW BUSINESS

ITEMS DISCUSSED	COMMENTS
1. Hazard Identification Cards	
2. Monthly Accident Summary	
3. Protective Equipment	
4. Serious Injuries	
5. Injury/Illness Trends	
6. Unsafe Practices Observed	
7. Other	

ACTION ITEMS

MONTH/ITEM #	COMMENTS	ASSIGNED TO

NOTE: To identify action items use the month followed by the item number. e.g. 3-7 would be the 7th item for the March report.

ORGANIZATION_____   _____

DATE _____   SIGNATURE

Figure 10-5. Safety documentation report form.

3. *Safety Management Committee functions*
   - Appoint shop safety supervisors
   - Using the general schematic of this plan prepare a jurisdictional safety and industrial hygiene program plan
   - Under the leadership of the chairperson, maintain the level of interest in the program to ensure maximum control of hazards and maximum reduction of injuries and illness
   - Resolve safety problems referred from the lower committees
   - Refer to the Executive Safety Council those safety problems that cannot be resolved at the committee level
   - Ensure that safety criteria are included in the design of facilities, equipment, and tasks for all work performed under the committee's jurisdiction
   - Review accident trends to determine what action is necessary to reduce the rate of occurrence
   - Take immediate action to eliminate any condition or work practice obviously endangering life
   - Provide for safety program continuity during organization changes
   - Conduct a safety and industrial hygiene survey of the jurisdiction of each committee at least once every six months
4. *Documentation.* Minutes of the Safety Management Committees will be prepared and distributed within one week following each meeting.

3. Shop Safety Supervisors.

Shop safety supervisors are first-line supervisors who are selected by the functional-level committee, and who have demonstrated an interest in safety and a willingness to take a leadership role in the safety program.

1. *Functions of the shop safety supervisor*
   - Chair a Safety Monitor Committee
   - Take immediate action to eliminate any condition or work practice obviously endangering life or limb
   - Resolve safety problems referred by factory, office, or laboratory employees
   - Refer to the Safety Management Committee any safety or industrial hygiene problems that cannot be resolved
   - Review accident trends to determine the action necessary to reduce the accident/illness rate
   - Require and enforce the use of personal protective equipment and devices
   - Review hazard identification card boards (see HIC system) for timeliness and correctness of follow-up action
   - Establish a safety monitor program, and provide for the monitors' training

2. *Meeting requirements.* The Shop Safety Supervisor will attend and chair the Safety Monitor Committee meetings; these meetings will take place on a specified day of the first week of every month.
3. *Documentation.* The Shop Safety Supervisor prepares minutes for Safety Monitor Committee meetings (see Fig. 10-5), receives the minutes of the appropriate safety management committee and the Executive Safety Council. Current files of accident investigation reports and unresolved hazard identification cards are required to develop the meeting agenda.

4. *Crew Supervisor.*

The crew supervisor is a first-line supervisor who has the responsibility for directing a crew of employees. Included in the routine supervisory functions is the immediate responsibility for the safety and industrial health of crew members.

1. *Functions*
    • Select a safety monitor from among the crew
    • Provide time for the safety monitor to conduct hazard-identification surveys
    • Correct hazards identified by safety monitor or any member of crew
    • Forward corrections of safety hazards that cannot be readily resolved to higher management
    • Assure that new employees or those transferred from other areas are made familiar with the hazards of their job
    • Investigate all crew accidents (see Fig. 10-6 for sample accident investigation format).
    • Take immediate action to eliminate any condition or work practice obviously endangering life and limb
    • Correct unsafe practices that are observed among the crew as they work
    • Enforce the use of protective equipment and devices as well as other safe work rules
2. *Documentation.* After completing an accident investigation on each crew accident, forward report to the Shop Safety Supervisor for review.

5. *Safety Monitor.*

The safety monitor is an hourly, salaried, or technical employee who has been selected to perform specific safety and industrial hygiene functions. The term of office for safety monitors is six months.

1. *Functions*
    • Conduct a hazard survey of an assigned area on a schedule determined by the crew supervisor or the Shop Safety Supervisor

SUPERVISOR'S INDUSTRIAL INJURY INTERVIEW								
NAME				**DATE OF INJURY**				
ACCIDENT DESCRIPTION								
		WITNESSES						
ACCIDENT/INJURY CAUSE								
DESCRIBE CORRECTIVE ACTION								
MEDICAL RECOMMENDATION?	**Y**	**N**		**TIME LOSS?**		**Y**		**N**
RECOMMENDATION VIOLATED?	**Y**	**N**		**ALL DUE TO INJURY?**			**Y**	**N**
DATE LAST WORKED			**DATE RETURNED TO WORK**					
SUPERVISOR		**DATE**		**REMARKS**				
GENERAL SUPERVISOR				**DATE**				

Figure 10-6. Supervisor's Accident Investigation Report form. This report example is designed to record information that can be used for compensation claim purposes as well as recurrence prevention. The form would be initiated when the supervisor is notified by the medical department that an employee has sustained an accidental injury, or when a claim has been filed.

- Complete the Safety Inspection Checklist (see Fig. 10-7) as it applies to the inspected area, and originate a hazard identification card for each identified hazard
- Maintain the Hazard Identification Board (see hazard identification card system shown on Figure 10-10).
- Encourage fellow employees to use safe methods, personal protective equipment and devices, and maintain their work area in a manner that will provide maximum safety to their coworkers
- Attend Safety Monitor Committee meetings

6. *Safety Monitor Committee (Shop Level).*

The safety monitor meeting is composed of selected safety monitors from shop areas. For example, in the machine shop there will be a monitor committee for the lathe area, another for the mill area, and so on. The committee is chaired by a Shop Safety Supervisor, and the

AJAX METAL FABRICATION COMPANY SAFETY INSPECTION CHECKLIST				
SHOP_____		SUPERVISOR_____		
MONITOR_____		INSPECTION AREA_____		

LEGEND: 0 = OK X = NOT OK (HIC POSTED)		HAZARD IDENTIFICATION		
EQUIPMENT OR AREA	CHECK	DATE		
LATHES	ELECTRICAL CHUCK AND DOG STOWAGE BRUSH AVAILABLE EYE PROTECTION AIR NOZZLE OK GEARS ENCLOSED OTHER			
PRESS BRAKE	SMOOTH RAM OPERATION INCHING OK MUTE POINT GUARD TWO HAND CONTROL OTHER			
NITRIC ACID TANK	LEAKS GASSING TEMPERATURE OK VENTILATION PLACARDS OTHER			
ASSEMBLY	HANDLING EQUIPMENT RAILS HARNESSES IN USE OTHER			

Figure 10-7. Sample Safety Inspection Checklist. This is a customized safety inspection checklist for a shop that contains lathes, press brakes, a nitric acid facility, and an assembly area. Note that the shop could contain additional machines and areas, and each of the areas would have additional items to check. This checklist is for illustration purposes only.

functions of the committee, meeting frequency, and documentation are described under the Shop Safety Supervisor heading.

7. Professional Safety Staff.

The professional safety staff is composed of graduate engineers, safety consultants, education specialists, industrial hygienists, and the like. Their basic function is to convince management of their participative role in the safety program and then provide management with appropriate support and guidance when they exercise their responsibility.

1. *Functions*
   - Provide management with quantitative reports (reports that answer the question, How well am I doing?), and qualitative reports (reports that answer the question, Why are accidents occurring?)
   - Interpret accident experience
   - Counsel management on accident-prevention techniques
   - Attend and assist with safety meetings at all levels
   - Interpret and ensure compliance with the Occupational Safety and Health Act (OSHA) of 1970, as well as state and local standards and codes
   - Evaluate and approve protective equipment and devices
   - Audit the effectiveness and the effort level of the company safety and industrial hygiene program
   - Assist with the processing of worker's compensation claims
   - Provide safety training
   - Develop safety promotion and motivation programs
   - Assist management with accident investigations as required
   - Investigate complaints concerning physical hazards, toxic materials, and work practices that could lead to accident and injury
   - Provide industrial hygiene services

A more comprehensive description of the services offered by professional safety and industrial hygiene staff is contained in the plan section entitled Safety and Industrial Hygiene Services.

IV. Hazard Identification Card System

The hazard identification card system (HICS) provides for the systematic identification and correction of industrial safety and health hazards. Through the use of a three-by-five-inch hazard identification card inserted into a prominently posted hazard identification card board, the hazard description and the action taken to correct it are constantly in view. This avoids the problem of lost, mislaid, or forgotten safety problems.

Many hazard corrections require correction by Plant Services. The use of the HIC system permits the grouping of such hazards so that they can be corrected conveniently on the computerized system used by Plant Services personnel.

A significant feature of the system is the feedback provided to the originator of the card. Because the card is always displayed on the board until well past the time that the hazard is corrected, the card originator can observe the progress of corrective action. If the card originator is not satisfied with progress, the item can be taken up with the responsible supervisor or placed on the agenda of one of the scheduled safety meetings.

A. System Components

- Hazard identification cards (Fig. 10-8)
- Hazard identification boards (Fig.10-9)
- Safety inspection checklists
- Hazard correction flow

B. Hazard Identification Card System Operation

The complete flow from hazard discovery to hazard correction is illustrated on a flow chart shown in Figure 10-10. The next paragraphs follow the Figure 10-10 flow chart.

When a safety monitor or any employee discovers a hazard, either during a scheduled inspection or at any other time, the problem is

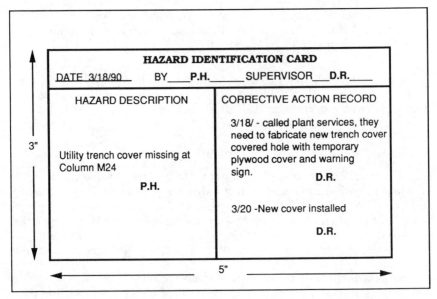

Figure 10-8. Sample hazard identification card. In the example hazard identification card the hazard can be identified by any employee or a safety monitor. Corrective action is always taken by the area first-line supervisor. The card is not considered completed and is not placed on the completed side of the hazard identification card board until actual remediation of the problem takes place.

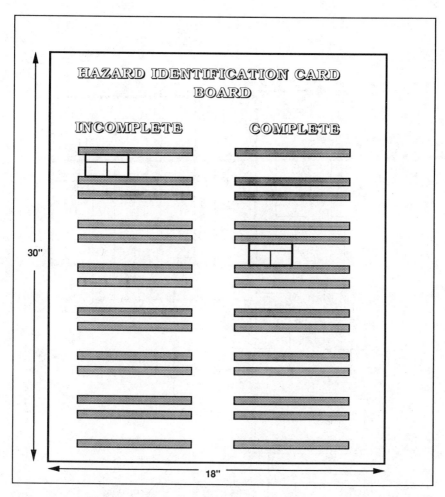

Figure 10-9. Hazard identification card board. The HIC system board is posted conspicuously in the shop where most employees can see it. Cards are moved to the completed side only after work is completed and the hazard eliminated. Completed cards are left on the board until the completed side is full, then they are taken off the bottom and filled in from the top.

written on the left side of a hazard identication card (HIC) (see Fig. 10-8). The area first-line (crew) supervisor is notified of the hazard and the card is placed on the incomplete side of the hazard identification card board (see Fig. 10-9).

The crew supervisor now has the responsibility for correcting or

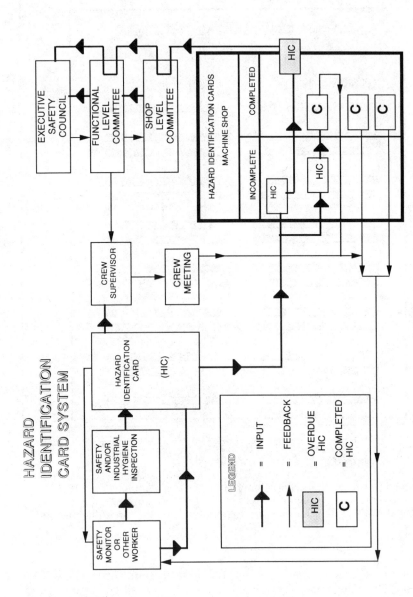

Figure 10-10. Hazard identification card system.

mitigating the hazard. This is usually done by contacting plant services who will schedule the correction according to an agreed upon priority based on degree of hazard. The supervisor has the additional requirement of discussing the hazard at crew meetings to make the crew aware of existing or newly identified hazards.

When the hazard is corrected a note to that effect is made on the right side of the HIC. Progress and actions taken toward completion are also noted on the right side of the card. However, only when hazard correction is completed is the card moved to the completed side of the board. It should remain there so the board can inform all concerned workers of ongoing and completed hazard correction activity. The usual practice is to let the completed side fill up and then drop off the oldest card and fill from the top.

Some hazards cannot be easily resolved (referred to as an "overdue HIC" on Fig. 10-10). Corrections to these problems usually require the approval of higher management because the funding and complexity of the remedy is beyond the discretion of the first-line supervisor. When this is the case the matter is forwarded to higher management either informally at a face-to-face meeting, or the hazard and its correction may be brought up at either the Safety Management Committee or the Executive Safety Council.

Before problems that originate on the factory floor are brought up at the Executive Safety Council, safety staff will research the problem correction so that the council is presented with completed staff work.

V. Safety Services

The Safety and Industrial Hygiene Department provides a complete spectrum of support services, all of which are described in this section of the plan.

A. Protective Eyewear

The safety office is the approval source for the protective eyewear worn by company employees and visitors. Information on when safety glasses or goggles are required and how to obtain them is available from the safety office. Refractions for prescription-ground safety glasses are available in the safety office every Thursday.

B. Safety Shoes

Safety shoes will be offered on payroll deduction and sold through a private outlet on company property. The contract is negotiated through the corporate office. The safety shoe van is available on Mondays and Fridays from noon until 8 P.M. Shoes are sold at industrial price, which is approximately 50 percent of retail.

C. Safety Suggestions

Safety suggestions will be submitted to the company suggestion unit in the same way that all other suggestions are submitted. Safety suggestions will be reviewed by the safety office for relevance and advantage to the safety and industrial hygiene program. Awards will be calculated by the suggestion unit.

D. Worker's Compensation

The safety office administers the company's worker's compensation program. This includes the following services:

1. Assistance with claims investigation is limited to situations where there is a question relating to whether or not the injury/illness was job related, or to very serious injuries involving amputations, fractures, unconsciousness, etc.
2. Monitoring claim activities such as time loss and medical payment amounts, claim closures, disability awards, medical treatment, and return to work
3. Providing assistance to employees who have problems receiving compensation, returning to work, or who have questions regarding medical treatment availability
4. Maintenance of compensation claim records on all employees who have filed for compensation, including logging in, payments, closures, court actions, medical examinations, return to work, and claim reopenings.

E. Protective Equipment

The safety office is the sole approval entity for protective equipment used by company employees. The safety office will also establish minimum stock lists for protective equipment distribution areas, and will train toolroom attendants in the use and limitations of the protective equipment that they dispense.

F. Facility Requests

Facility requests that deal with safety or industrial hygiene hazard corrections will first be approved by the safety office before they are performed. The following stamp should appear on all safety-approved facility requests:

```
SAFETY HAZARD
IF CANCELED FOR
ANY REASON
CALL
THE UNDERSIGNED
ON 6-8886
```

G. Program Materials

The safety office will provide materials to aid in the promotion, operation, and identification of the safety program. These include, but are not limited to, posters, pins, hazard identification cards and boards, machine inspection decals, films and program forms.

H. Training

In cooperation with the training section, the safety office will provide the following types of training.

1. General Safety Management.

This is an overview of the complete safety and industrial hygiene program for all levels of management presented in one-half-, one-, and two-day formats.

2. New Hire.

This orientation session includes the most serious hazards to which our employees are exposed and how our safety program, with the employee's assistance, helps avoid accident and injury. One day.

3. Key Safety Program Personnel.

For superintendents, Executive Safety Council members, shop safety supervisors, and safety monitors, this training program explores significant safety program features and the required participation of key personnel. One day.

4. Specific Hazard Avoidance.

Given on request, this course will address the mitigation of specific hazards such as working with solvents, two-part epoxy systems, working at heights, and electrical safety. The length of the course varies according to subject.

5. Accident Investigation.

This is an important method for achieving companywide uniformity in accident investigation. This course is primarily for first-line and general supervisors. One day.

6. Respirator Use.

This training is required by law. All employees who use respirators in the course of their employment must receive initial and yearly update respiratory training. Crew supervisors will be automatically notified when their people are scheduled. One day.

7. Working at Heights.

Working at heights is very hazardous, and this company requires that all persons who routinely work more than 4 feet from the floor receive training in the use of restraint systems and fall-prevention devices. One day.

8. Electrical Safety.

For maintenance electricians and electronics technicians, this course explores the actions of electrical current on the body and techniques for avoiding electrical shock. CPR is included. One and one-half days.

9. Hazard Communication.

This company has, in accordance with OSHA law, established a hazard-communication program. Employees and supervisors who work with hazardous materials, regardless of location, should attend this course. One day.

10. Hazard Recognition, Physical and Chemical.

This course is for safety monitors and first-line supervisors who are involved with hazard discovery and correction. One day.

In addition the safety office will upon request provide safety materials, guest lectures, and other input to courses not exclusively devoted to safety subjects.

I. Technical Support

Safety will provide technical support to include (but not limited to) the following subjects.

1. *Facility and engineering drawing review.* Aspects of design drawings that affect workers' safety and health should be reviewed by the safety office for compliance with existing regulations and for conformance with safe design principles. Designs of high work stations such as scaffolds and platforms, X-ray and other inspection facilities, fixed ladders, lifting tools, and any other device that may affect worker safety should be submitted for review.
2. *Test procedure review.* Tests that may hazard those involved with their conduct should be reviewed by the safety office for the inclusion of protective devices and procedures (see Fig. 10-2 for a hazardous test control format).
3. *Hazardous test surveillance.* The safety office can provide technical safety surveillance during the operation of a hazardous test to assess the performance of personnel, the usefulness of safety devices, and the test plan.
4. *Protective equipment requirements.* Newly formed or operating organizations can verify the quality and suitability of their protective equipment program by requesting a protective equipment audit from the safety office.
5. *Employee certification criteria (crane operators, forklift operators, scooter drivers, etc.).* Company policy requires certification of

certain job titles. Questions relating to certification can be addressed to the safety office.

6. *Proof load test requirements.* All overhead handling equipment requires proof load testing at certain periods in their working life. Test and record requirements may be obtained from the safety office.

7. *Equipment and machinery checkout.* Before new or repaired machines are placed in service they must receive a safety and industrial hygiene checkout. The safety office will perform and develop criteria for equipment and machinery checkouts.

8. *Safety audits.* A complete spectrum of physical safety audits are available from the safety office. These would include:
   • Quality of safety inspections
   • Quality of accident investigation
   • Work practice observation
   • Need for and usefulness of protective equipment
   • Machine guarding
   • Fall protection
   • Quality and quantity of safety program meetings
   • Hazard-correction practices
   • Safety supervision
   • Compensation claim management
   • Accident experience review
   • Hazard identification card system review.

9. *Preconstruction conferences.* All outside construction contracts require preconstruction planning for safety and health hazard mitigation, to protect company and contractor employees. The safety office will provide appropriately trained persons to attend planning meetings.

10. *Railing dynamometer tests.* The top rail of all railing systems including removeable rails must be able to withstand a 200-lb pull in any direction. The safety office is equipped to perform the appropriate tests for this requirement.

J. Industrial Hygiene

The following industrial hygiene services are available from the safety and industrial hygiene office:

1. *Noise surveys and dosimetry.* Using direct-reading instruments, areas or equipment of suspected or confirmed high noise can be assessed for noise pressure levels and attenuation possibilities.

2. *Radiation surveys and dosimetry.* Both ionizing and nonionizing radiation can be measured and recommendations for appropriate employee protection can be made. Materials for measuring day-to-day cumulative radiation exposure can be provided.

3. *Illumination measurement.* Precision light meters are used to deter-

mine if lighting meets the American National Standards Institute (ANSI) requirements for industry.

4. *Toxic material criteria.* A complete library and computerized network of information on the toxic effects and control measures of hazardous materials is available to all employees. Full information is available upon request; summaries are obtainable at toxic hazard control stations.

5. *Ventilation measurement, review, and guidance.* Complete ventilation audits can be performed for organizations with airborne particles, fumes, dusts, and gasses. Existing ventilation will be measured compared to optimum requirements, and recommendations made for improvement. The audit will be written in a form suitable for presentation to the Executive Safety Council.

6. *Industrial hygiene audits.* Complete industrial hygiene assessments of hazardous material handling, vibration and heat stressors, noise, dusts, human factors, including repetitive motion disorders, and radiation, can be provided on request.

7. *Hazardous material bulletins.* A complete package of internal bulletins dealing with the handling, effects, storage requirements, emergency and first-aid treatment, labeling, trade names, and uses of hazardous materials currently in use is located in the Industrial Hygiene Office and at toxic hazard control stations.

8. *Air sampling for toxics and particulates.* The Industrial Hygiene Office is capable of direct or laboratory sampling of suspected or confirmed toxic atmospheres involving all the chemicals currently in use in this company. Sampling activity is available upon request or a regular sampling schedule can be (or may have already been) initiated.

9. *Waste disposal criteria.* Water, food, and air quality will be measured and assessed on request.

10. *Protective equipment criteria.* If you require a better understanding of how to protect your employees from the effects of toxic materials through the use of protective equipment, this information is available from the Industrial Hygiene Office.

11. *Hazard communication program information and supplies.* The company's hazard communication program has been developed and is operated by the Industrial Hygiene Office. All inquiries dealing with the purpose, uses, training requirements, and written program description should be channeled to this office.

12. *Heat stress analysis.* A body at rest loses one liter of water per day. At hard work, especially in hot environments, the body loses over 4 liters of water and as much as 12 grams of salt. Unless these electrolytes are replaced, injury—and even death—can occur. An analysis of your working environment is available on request.

13. *Repetitive motion and ergonomic analyses.* A relatively new and effective injury-reduction field is that of human factors or ergonom-

ics. The placement of raw material, the use of handling equipment, the redesign of a power tool trigger switch, or the raising or lowering of a chair can have a marked effect on a worker's health. If some of your employees are complaining of body aches and strains or they are experiencing actual injuries, an ergonomic analysis may help.

14. *Limited laboratory analysis (In Plant).* The Industrial Hygiene Office is equipped with a rudimentary laboratory capable of analyzing most samples taken in our working environment. More sophisticated laboratories are also available to us, if further testing is required.

K. Statistical Support

The safety office shall prepare the Monthly Accident Summary, OSHA reports and forms, and will provide special statistical data in support of special-emphasis programs, Executive Safety Council presentations, etc. Statistical charts for posting in each shop area will be provided, but posting will be a shop responsibility.

L. Accident Investigation

Professional safety staff will assist with the investigation of serious accidents (where serious injuries [fractures, amputations, etc.] have or could have occurred) and with boards of investigation. Routine accident investigations are the responsibility of first-line supervisors.

VI. Safety Statistics

A. Purpose

It is the objective of the safety and industrial hygiene program to eliminate as many injuries and illnesses as possible, to control the number of serious injuries, and to reduce accident costs. To achieve these ends the Executive Safety Council sets accident-reduction goals and objectives for all company organizations. The purpose of accident statistics is to keep all managers and employees informed of their progress toward achieving these goals and objectives.

B. The Accident Summary

A monthly accident summary will be published in which reporting organizations will be measured on the raw injuries/illness frequency (injuries/100 employees), the number of worker's compensation claims (claims/100 employees) and an indicator of serious injuries (cost/100 employees). The report will contain a number of unusual elements that are described in the following paragraphs (see Table 10-3 for an illustration of the summary format).

Table 10-3 Monthly Accident Summary

March 19____

Organization	Organization Manager	Hazard Class	Number of Employees	Total Injuries	Injuries 100 Employees	Total Claims	Claims 100 Employees	Cost	Cost 100 Employees	Rating
745 assembly shop	Paul Ord	1	264	34	12.9	9	3.4	$345	$131	Poor

Goals	All Company	Hazard Class 1 High	Hazard Class 2 Moderate	Hazard Class 3 Low	Rating Scale	
Injuries 100 Employees	8.4	10.3	7.5	2.2	Make 3 goals	Excellent
Claims 100 Employees	3.8	4.6	2.5	0.9	Make 2 goals	Good
Cost 100 Employees	$54	$73	$44	$8	Less than 2	Poor

Note: Monthly accident summary format showing the assembly shop. Paul Ord is the shop superintendent. See text for a complete explanation.

C. Elements of the Accident Summary

1. *Headcount.* It is essential that statistical computations be based on an exposure headcount rather than the official organization population listing. This is because on any one day some workers are off the job for reasons such as vacations, sickness, or personal considerations. Since accident rates are inversely proportional to headcount, the use of actual exposure is a reasonable way to achieve fairness. The exposure headcount is achieved by dividing the actual number of hours worked by all employees in a shop by 155.5 (the average number of hours one employee works in a month). This procedure compensates for vacations, sick leave, personal days off, and overtime. Employees on loan to another shop will be counted in the headcount of the receiving shop.

2. *Hazard classification.* It is impractical to try to determine the exact degree of hazard for every type of work that is performed—the list would be huge. Yet, it is not fair to expect persons working in particularly hazardous factory jobs to meet the same injury targets as those set for lower risk groups such as office workers and draftsmen. To compensate for these risk differences, three hazard classifications have been established:
   • High risk
   • Moderate risk
   • Low risk

   To determine the hazard classification of a shop a variety of factors are considered, such as working at heights, with dangerous machinery, in high noise areas, with electricity, with chemicals, in confined spaces, in an office environment, and with transportation equipment, to name a few. An analysis of the risk classification of each company organization will be made by the safety office.

   In general, most factory production and maintenance work will be considered high risk; stores, toolroom, and expediting will be moderate risk; and office, engineering, and support organizations will be low risk. Changes in class can be negotiated yearly. Each risk classification will be assigned its own set of targets, as will the entire company (see Table 10-3). The first year's targets are derived from an average of the previous three years. Subsequent year's targets are set by the Executive Safety Council, based on a reduction of the prior year's results.

3. *Names and ratings.* In addition to the reporting organization's name, the name of the organization manager will also appear in the summary on the same line as the manager's organization. Organization managers will also be rated on their ability to control injuries and industrial illness. Ratings will be based on the three measures in the accident summary section. If the month's scores result in meeting all three targets, the rating will be Excellent; if two targets are met, the

rating will be Good; and if less than two targets are met, the rating will be Poor.
4. *Costs.* The calculation of costs will have a special meaning in this report. Because costs will be based on the cost of non-timeloss-compensation claims and the cost of each day lost from work, the cost calculation represents the greatest severity of the three injury measurements (injuries/100, claims/100, cost/100).

Average costs of lost days and non-timeloss-compensation claims can usually be obtained from the insurance carrier or the state compensation bureau. For example, if an organization such as the sheet metal fabrication shop sustains nine worker's compensation claims in a reporting period (month), and three of them result in a total time loss of seventeen days, the following formula for calculating the cost rate will apply. Consider that the average cost of a non-timeloss claim is $175, and the average cost of a lost day is $200.

$$\frac{9 \times \$175 + 17 \times \$200}{\text{Exposure headcount}/100} = \text{Cost}/100 \text{ employees}$$

The use of average cost has advantages. For one thing, it provides a way to get immediate, relatively accurate costs rather than having to wait until actual costs are reported as much as a year later. This average cost formula applied universally to all organizations will furnish a fair and meaningful statistic on accident severity.

The accident experience format described in the previous paragraphs represents a considerable investment in preparation time. Experience with this format, however, shows that the time is well spent because management response is gratifying. While management considers many reports with this title BBR (burn before reading), this configuration, after an initial break-in period, becomes an object of intense interest. Frequently, managers will want to know midway through the month if their accident rate is on or off target.

D. Qualitative Statistics

While accident rate data are a useful tool for motivating managers and employees to act on behalf of safety and health, these data cannot supply management with the information necessary to help it do a better job of accident prevention. To do this, accidents, injuries, and industrial illness must be analyzed and their causes addressed. The purpose of qualitative statistics is to identify problem areas to enable management to make these analyses, make recommendations on problem mediation, select the most appropriate correction technique, and proceed with the scheduling and application of corrective activity. The Safety and Industrial Hygiene Office has access to qualitative data and will prepare quarterly reports for the monthly accident summary reporting organizations. Further consultation and support are available from the safety organization to address safety and hygiene problem areas and effect corrective action.

E. Other Reports

The safety organization will produce special reports on request and will be the sole reporting agency for all external reporting. OSHA reports and special reporting that may be required by the state will also be the responsibility of the safety organization.

F. Visibility

Reporting organizations will receive statistical visibility charts for prominent mounting in the shop. Data for the charts are taken from the monthly accident summary and the quarterly qualitative reports.

VII. Hazard Communication Program

The hazard communication program is designed to ensure that workers have enough information about the chemical hazards of the workplace to make safe and informed choices about the work practices they follow while using chemicals. Specifically the program provides information on:

- The nature of hazardous chemicals used in the company
- The health hazards associated with the use and exposure to those chemicals
- The physical hazards associated with the chemicals and processes found in the work area
- How to detect the presence or release of hazardous chemicals
- How to prevent or reduce exposure
- The storage requirements for hazardous materials
- The immediate treatment of injury due to exposure to hazardous chemicals or processes

A. Program Components

1. Trade Names Index.

The purpose of the Trade Names Index is to provide access to formulation data for commercial products used by the company. The index allows cross-referencing of different chemical names so that the hazards of a substance can be easily determined. Each chemical entry in the Trade Names Index will be listed with the following headings:

- Trade Name
- Generic (chemical) Name
- Effects on the Body
- Storage Requirements
- Flash Point
- Type of Label Used
- Company Bulletin Number
- Emergency First-Aid Requirements
- MSDS Number

2. Labels.

Labeling. All containers of hazardous chemicals used by the company shall be labeled, tagged, or marked with the identity of the material, the appropriate hazard warnings, and the reference to the trade names index, if a commercially named product. The label shall convey the hazard of the chemical in the most direct terms possible, using key words (listed in the next paragraph) as appropriate. All secondary containers except those for temporary use (i.e., used for less than one work shift) shall be labeled in the same manner. Temporary containers should be labeled with an abbreviated version of the more complete label, so long as the identity of the contained substance is not in doubt.

Key Words. Labeling of hazardous materials shall include key words that enable the label writer to warn appropriately of the hazardous properties of the material. Examples of such key words or phrases are:

Causes burns	Irritating
Caution	Combustible
Danger	Causes death
Warning	Flammable
Extremely	Irreversible
Highly	Poisonous
Flash point	Readily absorbed
Reactive with____	Skin (absorption)
Severe	Carcinogenic
Toxic	Narcotic

Label Type and Configuration. Labels used for hazard identification shall be legible, easily visible, and shall remain so for the life of the container. Written standard operating procedures, process sheets, batch tickets, and similar materials may be substituted for labels on stationary process equipment if they contain the same information as a label and are readily available to employees. Safety and health worksite inspections shall include as inspection criteria the presence, suitability, and legibility of hazard identification labels. These labels may be tags, gummed paper, plastic, metal decal, or the special expanding label used for squeeze bottles, depending on the need. They shall be coded and a matching code book developed and maintained to simplify the determination and ordering of labels.

3. Material Safety Data Sheets (MSDS).

The purpose of the Material Safety Data Sheets (MSDS) (OSHA form 174) is to relay detailed chemical hazard information to users of hazardous chemicals. An MSDS must be on file for all chemicals packaged, handled, or transferred by the company. All shipments of chemicals purchased by company departments shall be accompanied by an MSDS, and the receipt of shipments shall not be permitted without it.

Organizational responsibilities are as follows.

1. *The Health and Safety Office* has responsibility for the overall development and management of the hazard communication program. They shall:
   - Design and code labels
   - Develop, produce, update, and distribute the hazardous material bulletin system that will be used as the internal communication medium for hazardous materials and processes
   - Monitor the program periodically to determine how efficiently it is operated
   - Develop and maintain the Trade Names Index
   - Develop program training criteria, and conduct training
   - Serve as technical liaison between the company and chemical suppliers
   - Maintain the company file of material safety data sheets
2. *Materiel Department*
   - Accept no hazardous materials unaccompanied by an MSDS
   - Upon receipt of hazardous materials, affix the appropriate company label, if required
   - Notify vendors that their product cannot be accepted without an MSDS
   - Train materiel personnel in the requirements of the hazard communication programs, and particularly the Materiel Department role
   - Control the sale of overage and surplus chemicals sold to the public through the reclamation section
3. *Plant maintenance*
   - Purchase no chemicals, such as lubricants, cleaners, and solvents, from local outlets without including these materials in the company hazard communication program
   - Train all plant services personnel in the use of the hazard communication program

- Coordinate hazardous material spill cleanup with the requirements of the hazard communication program
4. *All users of hazardous materials*
   - Conform to the labeling, storage, health hazard precautions, on-hand quantity, and emergency requirements of the hazard communication program
   - Refer all questions and problems to the Safety and Industrial Hygiene Office
   - Schedule employees and supervisors for the required training

VIII. Operating Criteria

The section on operating criteria presents technical data on the requirements of law, consensus standards, and reasonable prudence that affect the safety and industrial hygiene of all company employees. Because these criteria are representative only of the most consistently needed requirements that affect current and proposed company operations, it should not be construed that they are the only applicable standards. Many other national, state, and local safety and industrial health regulations are applicable to our operations. (*Note*: The operating criteria presented here are not complete. Since this is a prototype plan, the intention is to show a representative sample and not a complete listing.)

A. Transportation and Handling of Gas Cylinders

The mishandling of compressed gas cylinders can result in catastrophic injury to personnel and property. Because of the severe nature of high-pressure gas-cylinder problems, all personnel involved with their use and handling shall receive a minimum of two hours of training.

Significant Controls

1. Cylinders shall be stored in an upright position, protected from continuous sunlight.
2. Cylinders shall be secured by a rack or an approved device.
3. When not in use, cylinder caps will be in place, hand tight.
4. Acetylene cylinders that have been stored or transported in a horizontal position shall be stored in an upright position for 24 hours before using.
5. All cylinders, full or depleted, shall be handled in the same manner.
6. Cylinders that are lifted or transported by a forklift shall be secured in a manner that will prevent their accidental unloading.

References

1. Compressed Gas Association, Pamphlet #1. "Safe Handling of Compressed Gasses"
2. 29 CFR 1910. 101–105

B. Handling Equipment

Slings, shackles, ropes, and other devices used for handling loads can be subject to corrosion, damage, and misuse, any of which will cause them to fail. A program of inspection, testing and general care should be developed and installed.

Significant Controls

1. All slings must be visually inspected each day before use.
2. A recorded visual inspection must be made once each month.
3. All slings must be identified with the manufacturer's name, load capacity (basket and choke), location, and identification number.
4. All handling equipment—hoists, slings, bridles, cranes, spreader bars, strongbacks, jacks, etc., should be proof load tested at no more than 125 percent of the safe working load.

References

1. 29 CFR 1910.176
2. 29 CFR 1910.184

C. Racks and Shelves

Unless rigidly adhered to, loading requirements for racks and shelves are often overlooked with disastrous results. This is particularly true for power press die storage, where dies vary greatly in size and weight, and are often moved in and out of storage.

Significant Controls

1. Racks and shelves shall not be loaded beyond the manufacturer's specifications.
2. All shelves and racks shall be clearly marked for maximum loading.
3. Height shall not exceed four (4) times the minimum base dimension without extra supporting members.

References

1. National Safety Council, *The Accident Prevention Manual for Industrial Operations* (page numbers vary depending on year of publication)

D. Railings

Working at high work stations presents a special serious risk, where workers usually require the protection of a standard railing. It is extremely important that this protection meet the appropriate standards, since falls from heights are many times catastrophic in nature.

Significant Controls

1. Every floor opening, wall opening, platform, runway, or open-sided floor shall be provided with a standard railing.
2. Materials of construction shall be metal shapes, metal pipe, metal tube, or wood.
3. The top rail shall be no less than 42 inches high, with a midrail provided.
4. Under special conditions, and with the approval of the safety office, chain and/or polyethylene rope may be used for rails.
5. Every flight of stairs with four or more risers shall be equipped with a standard handrail.

References

1. 29 CFR 1910.132–139
2. 29 CFR 1910.261

E. Floor Mounting of Machinery

Machines with high centers of gravity such as drill presses are subject to movement, even upset, under rigorous shop conditions. Generally, if a machine is equipped with floor mounting holes, the machine should be fastened to the floor.

Significant Controls

1. Equipment shall be lagged to the floor if there is:
   • High center of gravity
   • Possibility of tipping due to external force
   • Tendency to creep due to vibration
2. Facilities engineering staff should be consulted if there is a need to mount, secure, or restrain machinery.

References

1. 29 CFR 1910, Part 0
2. Internal Safety Standard #63

F. Human Experimentation

If one employee asks another to try out a new product or process and the fellow employee agrees, this can easily be "human experimentation." Human experimentation is permitted if it is the only way a product or process can be judged as operational, the consent of the subject is obtained, and the test strictly conforms to the company's requirements. The designer of the new product may not be aware of the hidden dangers to the other person's body or psyche. For this reason it is necessary to develop and abide by the company's policy in this matter.

Significant Controls

1. Human subjects volunteering for tests or experiments at the company shall be informed of all risks involved with the tests or experiments.
2. The volunteering employee shall sign an informed consent statement that is specific to the test or experiment being performed.
3. Employee participation is strictly voluntary; any employee may elect to withdraw from a study at any time with no threat of penalty.

References

1. Human Subjects Review Committee Document

G. Welding

Health hazards associated with welding include radiant energy, hazardous fumes, heat, and electrical shock. Welders shall perform their work so as to minimize exposure to these hazards.

Significant Controls

1. Arc welders and gas welders shall receive enough training to become certified in their field.
2. Personnel working in the area where arc welding is taking place shall be protected from flash by an opaque or otherwise approved barrier.
3. The temporary nature of the welding job will not be a reason to relax visual arc protection.

References

1. 29 CFR 1910.252
2. American Welding Society, Publication A6.1, 1966

H. Outside Contractors

Outside contractors may be unfamiliar with company facilities and safety policies, and may have limited safety resources of their own. Because the type of work that they do is usually very hazardous, it is important that all parties to the contract comply with the following rules.

Significant Controls

1. All contractors performing work on company property shall develop an accident prevention plan designed to protect their own workers, other contractors, and company employees.
2. A preconstruction conference shall be held to address the specific dangers associated with the outside contractor's work and the remedial action required to eliminate or safeguard hazards.
3. The contractor's accident prevention plan shall be approved by the Health and Safety Office before work begins.

References

1. Company Document, "Blueprint for Control of Construction Site Safety" (See Chapter 11.)

I. Safety Belts and Harnesses

When a standard railing cannot be used because of the type of work or workplace, then other means of fall protection may be required. Falls from heights must never be taken lightly because of the predictably high severity of these falls.

Significant Controls

1. Any employee working more than four (4) feet from the ground and not protected by an approved guardrail will wear a parachute-type harness with an approved lanyard.
2. Shock absorbers will be used when there is a possible fall of over three (3) feet.
3. Harnesses will be tied off to a static line, capable of supporting a minimum dead weight of 5000 lb, located above the employee.

References

1. 29 CFR 1910.104
2. 29 CFR 1910.28

J. Lifting

Back and musculoskeletal injuries account for 20 percent of all injuries, but over 60 percent of injury cost. Therefore, particular attention to the causes and prevention of avoidable back injuries will benefit both the company and the employee.

Significant Controls

1. When manual lifting takes place the following parameters should be controlled:
   - Physical capacity
   - Body build
   - Medical restrictions
   - Ability to make lift
2. Whenever possible, use mechanical aids.
3. It is important to keep the object being lifted as close to the body as possible.

References

1. "Ergonomics Guide to Manual Lifting." American Industrial Hygiene Association Journal, **31**:511–515 (1970)

2. Grandjean, E. 1986. *Fitting the Task to the Man, an Ergonomic Approach*, Taylor & Francis

K. Confined Spaces

A confined space is one that encloses an employee and has the ability to trap contaminants that will poison, asphyxiate, or otherwise harm the worker. Typical confined spaces are tanks, voids, vaults, pits, underground facilities, and ship compartments (particularly when the ship is under construction).

Significant Controls

1. All confined spaces shall be tested for a hazardous atmosphere before entry is permitted.
2. High-volume mechanical exhaust ventilation shall be used for all confined-space work wherever possible.
3. Supplied air respirators shall be used for tank cleaning.
4. Confined spaces shall be tested before entering after lunch break.
5. A means, such as a tripod, will be provided to rescue unconscious workers from confined spaces.
6. Workers will never work alone in confined spaces, and there shall always be a monitor outside the confined space.

References

1. 29 CFR 1910.252

This concludes the prototype accident prevention plan. The plan is not meant to be closed-ended. Companies that have different needs created by their size or what they do must certainly add, delete, or change the content of the prototype program. Table 10-4 is a guide that will assist in downsizing the participation aspect of the plan for a smaller company.

Table 10-4 Safety Program Activity Matrix

Organization Site	Hazard Class	Executive Safety Council (ESC)	ESC Meeting Frequency	Functional Level Committee (FLC)	FLC Meeting Frequency	Employee Level Committee (ELC)	ELC Meeting Frequency	Hazard Identification Card System	Accident Summary
Large Over 1500 Employees	High	X	M	X	M	X	M	X	M
	Moderate	X	BI	X	BI	X	BI	X	BI
	Low	X	Q	•	•	•	•	X	Q
Medium 300–1500 Employees	High	X	M	X	M	X	M	X	M
	Moderate	X	BI	X	BI	X	BI	X	BI
	Low	X	Q	•	•	•	•	X	Q
Small 0–300 Employees	High	X	M	X	M	X	M	X	M
	Moderate	X	Q	•	•	•	•	X	Q
	Low	X	Q	•	•	•	•	X	Q

Legend: M = monthly; BI = bimonthly (once every 2 months); Q = quarterly; • = nonapplicable.

Chapter 11

Blueprint for Control of Construction Site Safety

INTRODUCTION: THE CONSTRUCTION SAFETY PROBLEM

The construction industry's injury and death rates have long been double to triple that of the private sector. Many proponents of the status quo insist that it is the extrahazardous nature of the industry that accounts for the high rates, contending that current prevention methods are adequate. This contention is contrary to evidence that some companies such as DuPont Construction have been able to consistently maintain injury rates that are even lower than those of the private sector.

The Occupational Safety and Health Administration (OSHA) has made progress toward achieving better safety practices on construction sites, but unfortunately the vast majority of sites will never be inspected for compliance with construction safety law. What is mainly responsible for the unchanging poor accident experience in the construction industry, however, is the lack of a comprehensive and integrated safety program involving all workers on each worksite.

The majority of workers on construction sites are subcontractors hired by a higher tier entity such as a prime contractor, owner, architect, engineer, or construction manager. To achieve subcontractor safety many higher tier entities rely on the subcontractor's own safety programs, while trying to protect themselves from third-party litigation through the contract language. This methodology for handling construction site safety is tantamount to saying, "Ignore it and trust to luck, and if something bad does happen, our contract permits us to avoid liability anyway." General contractors, owners, and architects often hold themselves to be not responsible or accountable for the safety of the crafts (subcontractors) on the site. The crafts themselves are many times too underfunded and underskilled in safe practices to do what is necessary to protect their employees.

The following is a description of one of many actual cases in which I have been involved as a forensic safety expert, and in which only perfunctory safety controls were in place.*

Case Study 11-1

A roofer (working supervisor) was walking backwards while operating a felt machine. His "tailer," the worker whose job it is to lay the felt and call out distances to an obstruction or a hazard, had noticed that the felt machine operator was heading toward an uncovered skylight opening. The tailer yelled "15 feet," then "10 feet," and when he yelled "5 feet," he expected the operator to stop.

Instead, even though he knew that the holes were uncovered, the operator kept going. He and the machine went through the opening, landing 26 feet below on concrete. The operator's luck held, and he was only permanently disabled instead of killed—as had happened to so many others in similar circumstances.

When the facts of the case became known it was found that on the day before, the felt machine operator, in his capacity as supervisor, had requested that the general contractor cover all open roof holes before the roofers began work on the following day. Both the general contractor and subcontractor thought the request was reasonable, since the general contractor had performed this service on two other buildings in the same complex. When the roofers arrived on the following day, however, they found that none of the holes were covered.

Of course, the roofers could have refused to work until the covers were installed, or installed the covers themselves. There are many compelling reasons why in most cases like this, such actions would never be taken. Among these reasons are:

1. The roofers are not equipped with the materials, nor does their contract usually authorize them to perform this work
2. The roofers are working to a deadline and would be very concerned about monetary penalties if they were to stop work
3. The roofing company would be very hesitant to refuse to work for safety reasons because of the stigma of having to walk off the job and the possibility that they would lose future contracts
4. It's not the macho thing to do
5. Most construction workers feel, as this crew felt, that they can do their work efficiently and safely as they have done many times before, even when faced with obviously dangerous conditions

*Hayfield v. Evans. See Appendix.

The primary reason why the felt machine operator did not stop in time was that a worker had distracted his attention by asking him a question at precisely the wrong moment. While the general contractor cannot be expected to control such distractions, or the degree of concentration exercised by a worker, the general contractor can certainly predict that such distractions will be present on all construction jobs. By maintaining control over roof holes and assuring that they will be covered on schedule, the prime contractor will prevent such distractions from having the grave consequences just described.

This chapter is not about roof hole maintenance, but rather is about the prime entity's degree of involvement in the construction site safety effort. The accident described here illustrates how the absence of prime contractor control of subcontractor safety contributes to a construction site where the probability of serious and fatal accidents is greatly increased.

THE DILEMMA OF CONSTRUCTION WORKSITE SAFETY CONTROL

The issues of who should control safety of the construction worksite, how much control should be exercised, and who should be the beneficiaries of that control, are key to the problems facing contractors, owners, architects, engineers, and safety professionals who are concerned about construction safety. On one side of the fence are the defense attorneys who argue that by assuming even partial control of subcontractor safety, the general contractor becomes subject to the following dangers.

1. Being exposed to liability for workers the high-tier (prime) contractor never thought it had.
2. Assuming limited control on the worksite, only to have a court and jury find that it has additional or total control or liability.
3. Assuming control at the worksite by contract or actions and failing to properly exercise that control.
4. Being exposed to a fine, penalty, or an abatement timetable for an OSHA violation dealing with a condition that it did not create.

On the other hand, if the higher tier entity does not assume worksite safety control, or takes only partial control, the following dangers exist.

1. Conditions that produce serious injuries and death will be unchecked.
2. Subcontractors who are unqualified to perform safe work will be hired.
3. In spite of the conscious effort to avoid liability by avoiding worksite control, juries have been convinced that the high-tier entity should

have assumed control. This is because the jurors give credence to the argument that general contractors must not separate control of quality from control of safety, since both safety and quality control require management of subcontractor work practices.
4. Lawsuits will inevitably occur, and in many instances there will be large plaintiff awards.
5. Insurance premiums, legal costs, and contractor time away from the job will increase.
6. Studious avoidance of control will increase costs by creating confusion when trying to sort out where the interface between safety, quality, and production begins and ends.
7. More workers will be killed and seriously injured when safety control by the prime entity is limited.

LEGAL SOLUTIONS MAY NOT ALWAYS BE EFFECTIVE OR ENOUGH

Respected attorney Douglas A. Hofmann and his colleague Robert C. Manlowe wrote about the legal side of this issue from a defense strategy point of view in their article, "Dangers of Assuming Worksite Control." The following is a summary of their comments on how to legally protect the higher tier entity.

1. Require the higher tier entity to read the contract and be familiar with the general contractor's responsibilities on the project.
2. Retain responsibility of initiating a safety program for the general contractor's own workers; ensure (contractually) that subcontractors initiate a safety program of their own. Retain responsibility to inspect and monitor the subcontractors' work and safety program only for the purpose of ensuring completion in accordance with contract plans and specifications. Avoid creation of common work areas.
3. Require that subcontractors be responsible for the day-to-day activities of their workers and their workers' safety practices.
4. Hire competent, registered subcontractors.
5. Require subcontractors to comply with the safety provisions of the owner–general contractor.
6. Use hold harmless/indemnity provisions. Require indemnity provisions specifically waiving worker's compensation protection to the extent of the subcontractor's negligence, and certify that the provision was mutually negotiated.
7. Require subcontractors to provide certification of their insurance and worker's compensation programs. Seek to have the subcontractor's insurance carrier name the general contractor as an additional insured. If the general contractor pays for worker's compensation

premiums, then the general contractor is arguably entitled to the immunity provided by the worker's compensation law.

8. The general contractor should limit control to coordinating construction timing plus supervising and inspecting worksite progress.
9. Comply with OSHA standards and insist that all subcontractors do the same. Do this contractually.
10. Be aware of the following problem areas that may result in general contractor liability.
    • The general contractor retains the *right* to control safety over the entire project.
    • The general contractor directs or controls the subcontractor's daily work activities or safety practices.
    • When the general contractor works with the subcontractor or multiple subcontractors in the same construction area or "common work areas."
    • When the general contractor engages subcontractors for inherently dangerous work that results in injuries to bystanders.
    • When the subcontractor creates a hazard and then leaves the area.
    • When the general contractor ignores obvious safety violations of subcontractors.

Examining these latter six danger areas, we see a glaring and frustrating situation for all construction entities. The frustration is that the mitigation of these dangers requires positive, extensive, and unrelenting control of worksite safety, yet general contractors must avoid this type of control if they are to escape third-party liability for subcontractor injuries.

Woody Allen, noted twentieth century humorist, very aptly described this situation in this funny but perceptive paraphrased quote, "As never before in the history of man we are at a crossroads. One path leads to degradation and chaos and the other path to devastation and utter annihilation. Let us pray for the wisdom to choose the correct way."

Mr. Hofmann and Mr. Manlowe suggest the following correct way in the conclusion to their article. The frustration they experience with the current system is mirrored by the safety and industrial hygiene professions.

To do a good job on a construction site one must be aggressively involved, and take control of all needed aspects of the job. And yet, our present system and court decisions create a trap for those entities who do take control of the worksite. Our courts impose a non-delegable duty to higher tier entities such as prime contractors, and fulfilling that duty may expose them to additional liability to other employer's workers. The uncertainty and inconsistency from being punished for acting responsibly needs to be eliminated.

All those involved in construction should have the same goals. All should want a well-organized and safely built structure that appropriately considers economy and human safety. Yet, our current system actually encourages delegating, avoidance of control, finger-pointing and lack of responsibility. The construction industry needs a 'good Samaritan' rule for construction safety similar to that enjoyed by physicians, so that general contractors for example are encouraged to control safety without assuming extra liability. The construction industry, the workers and the system needs and deserves it.

There is, however, a solution to this quandary that is independent of the immunity provided by worker's compensation. That solution involves the structuring of construction site safety so that it is truly integrated with day-to-day production requirements and is a responsibility of construction site management, which is held accountable for results. The DuPont Corporation follows this formula on its construction sites, and in many instances has been able to maintain an injury rate of from 1 to 3 injuries per 100 employees. This is about one-eighth of the construction industry accident experience and about one-fourth of the entire private sector rate. Consistently achieved on other construction sites, these rates can significantly reduce third-party suits to the point where such actions are no longer a deterrent to general contractor safety control of worksites.

If industry consensus can create a blueprint for construction worksite safety that has a recognized opportunity for preventing construction accidents, then a general contractor who closely follows that blueprint will have a much better chance of avoiding liability suits. It would be far better for all concerned if the general contractor were exonerated by juries who were satisfied that it had closely followed a technically competent safety program. To award blanket immunity based on paying worker's compensation premiums without the assurance that a competent safety program is in place is unfair to workers and counter to our accident-prevention objectives.

A recent unanimous state of Washington Supreme Court decision in the case of *Stute* v. *PGMC* overturned two lower courts that had granted summary judgment in favor of the general contractor. Stute was a roofer who, while working on gutters and equipped with no fall protection, fell to the ground and was seriously injured. This landmark decision by the Washington Supreme Court established that higher tier entities such as general contractors are liable for the safety of *all* workers on the construction site.

The Blueprint for Control of Construction Site Safety details how higher tier entities can organize to accomplish optimum site safety. Under such a safety program there should be far fewer cases that are litigated. As plaintiffs' attorneys recognize that some potential defendants have followed recognized professional safety program standards, there should be a reluctance to proceed with litigation. The Blueprint for

Control of Construction Site Safety is a professional safety plan that, if faithfully followed and enforced, has the potential of generating the accident reductions previously described.

BLUEPRINT FOR CONTROL OF CONSTRUCTION SITE SAFETY

In their paper entitled "Owner's Guidelines for Selecting Safe Contractors," published in the *Journal of the Construction Division of the Proceedings of the American Society of Civil Engineers* (December 1982), Nancy Samuelson and Raymond Levitt, both members of the Construction Institute of the Department of Civil Engineering at Stanford University, state that "The potential savings from managing and controlling safety (about 4% of total cost) are significant and comparable to savings that can be achieved through management of productivity or schedule." The implication is that the prime entity, whether a general contractor, construction manager, owner, architect, or engineer, can materially and beneficially affect safety, costs, and production efficiency by integrating safety into the normal operating routines of each construction activity and all other construction entities. In other words, the construction manager should take control of safety for the entire construction site from the planning stage to project completion. Criteria for control are contained in the following plan.

There are four basic elements to the plan. Three of these elements apply to the higher tier entity—who will be termed construction managers, but could be general contractors, prime contractors, owners, engineers, or architects—and one element applies to subcontractors.

Construction Managers
 I. Qualify subcontractors
 II. Insist on preconstruction conferences that deal with:
   A. The most serious hazards to be encountered
   B. How the subcontractor plans to eliminate or neutralize these hazards
   C. Who will supply the required materials and equipment
   D. When the materials and equipment are to be in place
   E. When the specific safety activities are to be performed
   F. Who will perform the safety activity
   G. The type of cooperation that is required from the general contractor
   H. The activities of other subcontractors that will affect the safety of the worksite
   I. How to handle out-of-sequence or unscheduled work
   J. The date when an approved safety plan is required
 III. Take control of worksite safety
   A. Determine if subcontractors are performing as agreed in the preconstruction meeting
   B. Enforce preconstruction safety agreements
   C. Create and maintain a safety status board to inform all employees of the changing safety status of the worksite

    D. Assure that all crew supervisors are transmitting meaningful and specific safety information

    E. Identify a safety officer

Subcontractors

IV. Write an approved job safety plan

    A. Identify serious hazards that will be encountered by your employees and emphasize changing worksite conditions

    B. Identify a person who is responsible for the safety of subcontractor employees

    C. Detail how worksite hazards are to be eliminated or neutralized; include equipment, materials, and responsible persons

    D. Arrange for appropriate training that deals with the specific hazards that will be encountered on the job

    E. Explain how hazard information will be transmitted; for example, informally, safety meetings, bulletin board, training

There are a number of key individuals who play an important role in construction site safety management, and it is important to understand their safety function before undertaking a safety plan.

1. The project manager must make it clear to the general contractor's personnel and all subcontractors that safety is to be an integral part of the operation from the planning stage to project completion. The project manager must participate in the safety planning process, particularly with subcontractors, and should preside over a regularly scheduled meeting with top project management, that is devoted exclusively to safety. This meeting should convene at least once a month.

2. The safety professionals have a number of specific functions. Among them are:

1. Qualify each subcontractor according to previously developed criteria (see criteria examples below)
2. Maintain a project safety bulletin board that follows project progress by noting day-to-day changes that may affect the safety of all construction workers
3. Convene safety preplanning conferences attended by prime contractor and subcontractor management
4. Along with the subcontractor managers and crew supervisors, develop and perform a schedule of work-practice observations and safety inspections to determine whether all workers are performing in accordance with the preplanning. Report discrepancies to offending contractor management and to project management
5. Approve subcontractor safety plans
6. Assist subcontractor and prime contractor management with the planning, recognition, and control of safety and health hazards
7. Prepare a site safety plan that details the safety equipment and safety activities that are required by all contractors to achieve maximum accident/illness prevention

8. Assure compliance with OSHA and state occupational safety and health regulations
9. Act as organizer and resource person for the top-management-level safety meeting
10. Develop and maintain the hazard communication program (HCP), and assure that each subcontractor's HCP is a reasonable facsimile
11. Develop and maintain the assured equipment grounding program (AEGP), and confirm that each subcontractor's AEGP is a reasonable facsimile. Where ground fault circuit interrupters are used instead of the AEGP, confirm that they are in place at all the appropriate locations

Items 10 and 11 are copiously covered in numerous books, articles, and regulations, and therefore will not be covered here.

3. The subcontractor manager is the safety contact for the subcontractor, and is responsible for the development of the subcontractor safety plan, attendance at preconstruction safety meetings, and subcontractor compliance with previously agreed upon safe working conditions and practices as outlined in the safety plan, bulletin board, and preconstruction conferences. Attend top-level management safety conferences that are held during the period when the manager's company is working on the site.

4. Crew supervisors of both the general contractor and subcontractor must enforce the safe workplace provisions of the site safety plan.

5. Owners need to understand that the safety of all workers must be integrated into daily operations on the construction site and that there will be costs associated with this condition. It is more likely than not that lives will be saved and that accident-reduction cost savings will more than equal expenditures. Savings could be in the range of 4 to 7 percent of the total project cost.

6. Architects and engineers need to integrate worker safety into the planning and design of the construction project. By participating in the safety planning process, project engineers and architects will gain an understanding of how their designs affect worker safety and also how they can contribute to the safety process.

THE BLUEPRINT

1. Construction Manager: Qualify Subcontractors

Establishing the qualification of subcontractors by determining their prior accident experience is the first major step toward a posture of accident prevention on the construction site. There are two primary means for qualifying subcontractors: (1) the state's experience rating system for worker's compensation, and (2) the OSHA incidence rate. Both of these measures should be averaged over the most recent three years. If the subcontractor in question is new and does not have a prior record with the state compensation system or the OSHA recordkeeping system, then some investigation into its owner's past accident record with other contractors for which he or she worked is required.

The experience modification factor is available from the state worker's compensation division, but may be expressed differently in each state. A common method of modification factor expression is to use the number 1 as a basis. As an example, let us say that you are hiring an electrical contractor and the state has established a basic rate for the electrical contracting industry of $9 per $100 of payroll. This means that a new contractor without any accident experience would pay the basic rate for a period of time.

When the contractor gains three years of accident experience, for example, worker's compensation premium rate will be modified by a formula that is driven by the number and severity of compensable accidents sustained during the three-year period. If the rate is poor in comparison to its peers, the experience modification factor will jump to a number greater than one, for example, 1.8. This means that future premiums will be 1.8 times the basic rate of $9, or $16.20 per $100 of payroll.

On the other hand, if the contractor's accident and injury rates are better than its peers, then the modification factor will be a number less than one, for example 0.77. This would result in a premium of $6.93 per $100 of payroll and would be indicative of a superior safety program.

Another objective measure of past superior safety performance is the accident/illness incidence rate, which is the standard by which all industries in this country are measured. This rate is expressed as injuries per 100 employees and is derived by the following formula:

$$\frac{\text{Number of reportable injuries/illness} \times 200{,}000}{\text{Number of worker hours worked during the reporting period}}$$

The number 200,000 in the formula represents the number of hours that 100 employees would work in one year.

Since there are standard rules that govern which injuries and illnesses are reported, the incidence rate becomes a fairly objective measure of safe performance. To arrive at the number that meets the criterion for a safe contractor, the incidence rate can be compared with other electrical contractors or with the construction industry in general.

By using these two objective measurements of prior safe performance to qualify subcontractors, the construction manager can predict who will most likely perform safely, generate greater accident-prevention savings against the total cost of the project, and cooperate with the overall construction site safety plan. As a general rule, the safe contractor works more efficiently. This is a bonus that further reduces total project costs and promotes on-time project completion.

2. Construction Manager: Insist on Preconstruction Conferences on Specific Hazards

It is vital that the construction manager gains an understanding of the specific hazards that each subcontractor will face before the subcontractor begins work. To do this a preconstruction conference is scheduled where the project manager, the safety officer, and the subcontractor manager meet to discuss the following issues.

A. The Most Serious Hazards that the Subcontractor Will Encounter

Many chemical and other heavy-industry plants operate 24 hours a day and shut down only for maintenance. This shutdown may be on a yearly schedule, when all workers except maintenance workers go on vacation. Contract maintenance workers are also usually brought in to supplement in-plant people or to perform specialized work.

Case Study 11-2

In just such a case* a fertilizer plant that contained two huge ammonia tanks was shut down. A major portion of the maintenance to be accomplished was the removal, testing, and replacement of over forty relief valves in the miles of piping that serviced the plant. One of the subcontractors that were hired was a firm that was to perform the valve replacement.

Before work commenced a mass meeting was held to explain to all subcontractors what was going on at the facility and the effects of the shutdown. This was a very general meeting, and no individual preconstruction conferences were scheduled that addressed the specific hazards to which each subcontractor would be exposed. All workers came away from this meeting with the idea that the entire plant was to be shut down and that there were to be no live lines carrying ammonia.

However, because it would cost over $150,000 to shut down, a particular line that carried liquid ammonia would remain viable. The line contained a block valve that had not been replaced in over thirty years of use, and had visible evidence of corrosion on its nipple, which was not only corroded but also undersized considering the weight of the block valve it had to support.

On the day of his injury, a subcontractor employee was replacing the relief valve that was in-line with the block valve, which in turn was attached to the live ammonia line (see Fig. 11-1). While he was working, the corroded nipple gave way, spraying the worker with ammonia. He sustained severe burns and permanent disablement.

*Brown v. Chevron. See Appendix.

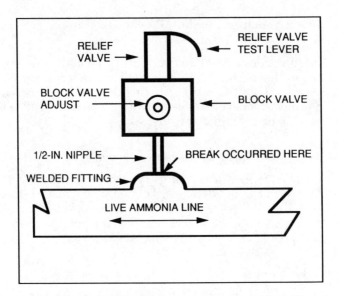

Figure 11-1. Ammonia exposure. While installing the relief valve shown here, a worker was exposed to pressurized ammonia when corrosion at the failure point caused the valve assembly to separate from the live ammonia line. The text discusses the case in detail as well as methods of prevention.

In the absence of a preconstruction conference that addressed the specific hazard presented by the live ammonia line, the injured worker was taken by surprise by the hidden hazard and had no opportunity to take protective measures that would have prevented his permanent disablement. Litigation followed based on the negligence of the owners, who acted as prime contractors, but who did not inform workers that there was an ammonia line still operating in a plant that was thought to be entirely shut down.

Even if it was true that the cost of shutting down the ammonia line was $150,000, the company stood to spend that amount plus a substantial sum to pay for defense attorneys' and employees' time and the cost of settlement or possible judgment against them. (The case was settled for a substantial amount at this writing.) It is reasonable that the total cost would be in excess of one million dollars.

B. How the Subcontractor Plans to Eliminate or Neutralize These Hazards

When the accident in Case Study 11-2 occurred, the breach in the ammonia line was isolated by shutting valves on both sides of the break.

If the live-line condition were discussed and planned for in a precon-struction conference, then one or more of the following steps may have been taken.

1. The double valve assembly (see Fig. 11-1) would have been recog-nized as dangerous to work on because of the undersized nipple and the corrosion, and it would have been replaced. The assembly could have been isolated in the same way just described, and the valves quickly replaced with a prefabricated unit.
2. The subcontractor employees would have been supplied with appro-priate protective equipment that would have prevented ammonia from contacting any body part.
3. The exact amount of torque to apply to the valve assemblies would have been specified and torque wrenches supplied to the workers. This would have reduced or eliminated the possibility that too much torque would be applied to the valves, reducing the likelihood that the valve assembly would disintegrate.

A short job hazard analysis (JHA), or hazard effects and control analysis (HECA), or hazard control analysis (HCA) would have revealed the problem and possible solutions (see Part II of this book). The problem must be aired at a preconstruction conference, however, if meaningful corrective action is to take place.

C. The Materials and Equipment Required and Who Will Supply It

Once the hazard is identified, commitments must be made to the solution. In this case the appropriate protective equipment could be supplied by the general contractor (company), or the subcontractor, or other party, depending on the agreement made at the conference. Torque wrenches and the proper training for their use would be identified as a requirement and a suitable wrench setting stipulated by the company engineering staff.

Arrangements would have to be made with the appropriate company personnel to isolate the corroded valving so that a replacement assem-bly could be installed.

D. When the Materials and Equipment Are to Be In Place

A construction worksite is a dynamic, everchanging place. If a construc-tion safety program is to be successful, it must be integrated into the nature of the construction workplace. In our example protective equip-ment, torque wrenches, training of workers, torque amounts, valve assemblies, and valve isolation were identified as safety requirements. It is essential that sufficient lead times be assigned to each of these requirements so that everything is in the right place at the right time. By doing this in the same way that production-oriented tasks are scheduled, safety will be truly integrated into the normal operating routine of the construction operation.

E. When the Specific Safety Activities Are to Be Performed

In earlier paragraphs we proposed that the isolation of a valve assembly on a live ammonia line was required so the valve assembly could be replaced. As with any construction operation, this is a time-dependent procedure that can make the difference between tragedy and safety. In the following example from a different case* there are at least three violations of blueprint recommendations that resulted in permanent disabling injuries to a dry wall installer. The purpose of using this example is to show how important it would be to accomplish the valve isolation as well as the other safety requirements at the correct time.

Case Study 11-3

During the construction of a ten-story building in a large city, power lines that could not be de-energized were moved across the street to get them out of the way of construction equipment. When the building was completely enclosed except for a line of missing windows in the front, a drywall subcontractor began to cover the building's interior walls.

After completing the first three floors it was necessary to transfer the drywaller's scaffolding to the upper floors. The scaffolding contained 20-ft-long aluminum planks that had to be brought into the fourth floor through the window openings, since it was not possible to use the stairwells or the elevator.

A week before this operation took place the general contractor had negotiated with the city-owned electrical utility to return the power lines to their original position. The return took place on the night before the drywall crew needed to move their scaffolding. No communication on this point ever took place between contractors.

On the early dawn of the day after the power line return the drywall personnel began to move the scaffolding. It was 6 A.M., still quite dark, when the first plank was moved hand over hand to workers stationed on the ground and the second and fourth floors (see Fig. 11-2).

The worker on the fourth floor angled the plank through the fourth floor window, and as he leveraged it over the metal windowsill, the plank contacted the restored power lines. The drywall worker received a severe and disabling shock. It was a twist of fate that the shock from the 7200-volt line was not fatal.

In this case, as with the fertilizer plant, subcontractors were not informed of dangerous conditions that could injure and kill. In both

*Smith v. Gall-Landau. See Appendix.

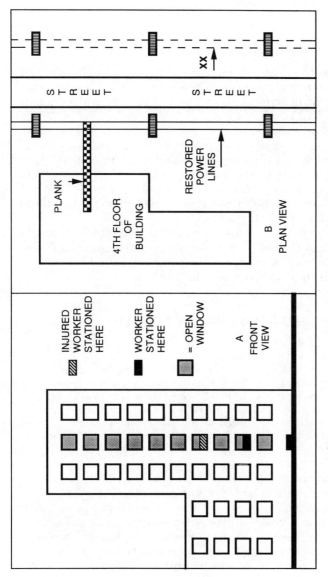

Figure 11-2. Near electrocution. In this accident where a drywall installer was almost killed by a 7200-volt shock, the drywall crew had not been informed that the power lines had been restored to their original position on the night before. The A front view shows how the windows lined up so that the plank could be passed hand to hand up to the fourth floor where the plank was leveraged over the windowsill. Plan view B is an aerial perspective, where the XX position shows where the power lines were moved at the beginning of the project to prevent the type of accident that occurred when they were restored to their original position. The basis for the accident was the absence of communication between the general contractor and his subcontractors, the same as in the live ammonia line case (see Fig. 11-1).

situations timing was critical. If the workers had been informed in time, adequate precautions could have been taken to protect them. The blueprint for control of construction site safety demands correct timing for safety as well as for production.

F. Who Will Perform the Safety Activity

In a previously described case where the general contractor did not cover roof openings when asked to do so, there was no clear understanding, either verbally or in writing, as to who would perform the job of covering the holes. As a result, the general contractor did not schedule the covering operation as it did other production-oriented operations. This set in motion the series of events that ended in a serious injury.

The correct procedure of tracking this problem at a preconstruction meeting of all concerned parties was not accomplished. Had this been done, either the general contractor, the subcontractor, or another contractor, such as the carpenters, would have been officially identified as the entity who would cover the holes.

In the ammonia problem it was necessary to identify who would provide protective equipment, torque wrenches, torquing data, valve assemblies, and valve isolation. Again, the preconstruction conference would have been the appropriate place for this to occur.

G. The Type of Cooperation that Is Required from the General Contractor

Example: In an operation where two million square feet of overhead structure and ceiling were to be painted by a subcontractor, it was determined at a preconstruction meeting that the plant owners (who were also the general contractors) would move the product (aircraft) at scheduled intervals. When this movement was complete the overhead hazard to plant workers had been removed and the area had been made safe and convenient for the painters and their equipment.

The fertilizer plant problem creates a similar condition. The plant owners (also serving as their own general contractor) must agree to isolate the valve or valves involved with the live ammonia lines. Since there may be substantial costs involved, negotiations must take place long before the start of the maintenance operation. Other areas where general contractor cooperation may be necessary are the timely provision of protective equipment, torque wrenches, and torquing data. Certainly, the success of the safety effort in this case also depends heavily on frank and assured communications on the matter of the live ammonia lines.

H. The Activities of Other Subcontractors that will Affect the Safety of the Worksite

When multiple subcontractors are hired on the same job there is often enhanced opportunity for miscommunication. This is because each contractor is intent on getting its own job completed and often resents real or perceived interference by other subcontractors. From a site safety management point of view, the interface between contractors must be examined to prevent one contractor from creating a hazard to another contractor. The best time for this examination to occur is at the preconstruction safety conference where all affected subcontractors can voice their input.

If the electricians were to leave exposed, live wiring available for other crafts to contact, they would be creating an unreasonably dangerous condition. Because accidents occur relatively infrequently, the subject most likely would not be addressed and there would probably be no harmful effect. But because the potential for great harm is present, it is predictable that a serious incident will eventually occur if this practice is continued. Therefore, this is a hazard that must be eliminated or neutralized.

I. How to Handle the Effects of Out-of-Sequence or Unscheduled Work

Unscheduled, out-of-sequence work is dangerous to construction workers because it many times involves hidden hazards. For example, when the floors and walls are completed in a building under construction, few workers may know if an error has been discovered and a floor opening must be cut to correct it.

Such hazards must be managed before the hazard is in place by informing workers through the bulletin board, special meetings with subcontractor management, and by directly addressing its elimination or neutralizing. The general contractor's safety officer can play a key prevention role in this situation.

J. The Date When an Approved Safety Plan Is Required

All subcontractors should be required to file a safety plan to be approved by the general contractor's safety officer. The provisions of such a plan are described in Section 4 of the blueprint. The date given to each subcontractor should allow sufficient lead time so that changes can be made *before* the subcontractor starts work.

Example: In a roofing case where a roofer was catastrophically injured the only blueprint provision that was involved was the submission of a safety plan by the roofing subcontractor. The plan was not approved, but the contractor started working without an approved plan because scheduling demanded that the roof be completed. The worker's injury could be traced directly to noncompliance with the provisions of the blueprint for control of construction site safety.

At the close of the blueprint description a case example will be presented that will illustrate how allegiance to this safety plan can be a very positive force for preventing accidents and on-the-job illness.

3. Construction Manager: Take Safety Control of the Worksite

The construction worksite changes every time a subcontractor completes its work. Without a permanent organization to provide continuity and production control, the project would falter and have little chance of timely completion, if at all. The construction manager, as a permanent entity on the construction worksite, must provide this continuity.

It is well known among professionals that to be effective safety must be integrated into the normal operating practices of the project. It is therefore essential that the safety program be developed along the same lines as production, where the construction manager is the coordinating and controlling agency.

This method of operation does not relieve subcontractors from their responsibility to operate safely. In the same way, the construction manager's control of production does not relieve subcontractors from their responsibility to produce a quality product in a timely way and at the lowest possible cost.

The following are the important elements of worksite safety control.

A. Determine if Subcontractors Are Performing as Agreed in Preconstruction Meetings

The construction manager's safety officer(s) should first sort out what each subcontractor agreed to do in its safety plan and at the preconstruction safety conferences. Some typical provisions may be:

• Use of harnesses and double lanyards
• Covering of roof holes and floor openings
• Marking roof holes and floor openings
• Use of an assured grounding program (or GFCI's)
• Protect the leading edge of floor and roof construction
• Rail all floor openings
• Tie off and stabilize all ladders
• Use proper respiratory equipment
• Use only nailers equipped with pressure interlocks
• Use hand tool tie-off procedures

Once the safety officer understands what is required, an inspection program can be set up so that he or she can determine if each subcontractor is in compliance. Performance of these inspections is as important and should have the same weight as the production superintendent determining if a marble facia is aligned correctly. The construction manager sets the standards for production and quality no matter which employee is involved, and must also set the standards for safety and health in the same manner.

B. Enforce Preconstruction Safety Agreements

The construction manager has the right to stop work if a subcontractor, construction manager, or management representative is not performing safely according to agreements made at the preconstruction conference. The offending employee can be counseled by his or her supervisor, transferred to a less sensitive position, sent home, or even fired, if necessary. Other options that deal with the treatment of the subcontractor as a company may be open to the construction manager, depending on the contract language.

Once subcontractors realize that the general contractor is serious about safety and will not accept crafts that take unnecessary risks, a high degree of acceptance of this policy can be expected. When workers know that they are not encouraged to take risks to produce at a faster pace, but instead are rewarded with psyche income (i.e., "positive reinforcement") for working safely, they will generally cooperate. The end result is faster production, higher quality, and far fewer accidents. The decrease in litigation will more than compensate for the construction manager's acceptance of safety control of the worksite.

C. Create and Maintain a Safety Status Board to Inform All Employees of the Changing Safety Status of the Worksite

Case Study 11-3

In this case* in which two electricians were very seriously injured, a simple communication on the status of the construction site would have prevented the injury. The site was a new shopping mall and the two electricians were working at the 20-ft level in the basket of a mobile manlift. When they finished working on a run of electrical cable they started moving to the next position, which was in an area that contained uncovered structural steel (see Fig. 11-3).

Between their intended work station and their starting point there were numerous holes that measured 4 feet wide by 4 feet long by 4 feet

*Caption not available.

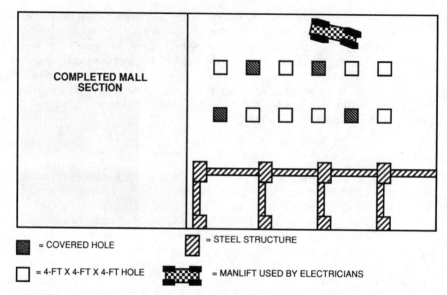

COMPLETED MALL
SECTION

■ = COVERED HOLE   ▨ = STEEL STRUCTURE

□ = 4-FT X 4-FT X 4-FT HOLE   ▦ = MANLIFT USED BY ELECTRICIANS

Figure 11-3. Communication failure on a construction project. Two electricians were seriously injured when the manlift they were using to gain access to a run of electrical cable tipped over. Plans for the shopping mall called for trees to be planted in 4-ft.^{3} holes. On the morning of the injuries the two electricians entered the work platform of the lift and raised it to the 30-ft level. They proceeded to their workstation and completed some wiring. When they attempted to traverse the floor where the holes were located, the lift dropped into an open hole and the whole unit toppled over, throwing the electricians into the steel structure. It seems that the workers were not informed that some of the holes were uncovered that day and that electrical work in that area of the mall was prohibited. See text for further explanation.

deep. These holes were intended to contain trees when the mall was completed. Holes that the electricians had encountered before were always covered. On the day of the injury, however, many of the holes were uncovered because the floor had not completely cured. The general contractor knew they were uncovered and did not want the electricians to work in that area.

Needless to say the word was never received by the electricians, and they did begin working in the danger area on that day. When the wheels of the lift encountered a hole the device toppled over, throwing both workers into the steel structure. They both sustained very serious injury, but survived.

Because construction sites are such dynamic places where project managers often have to handle a multiplicity of problems at the same time it is understandable that sometimes a vital communication is not forwarded to the right people. That is why it is essential that communications systems that will make vital safety information available in a timely manner are installed. The safety status board is such a system.

The safety status board, maintained by the construction manager's safety officer, will each day tell what conditions have changed on the construction site that can materially affect the safety of construction workers. In this case, the fact that the tree holes were uncovered, and that no mobile equipment should be used in the area, would have appeared on such an information board. In that case, if all the workers habitually consulted the status board before they began work, the electricians would have worked in another area that day, would have used another means to gain access to their work stations, or would have waited until the holes were covered.

The safety status board can be an effective communications tool, but should not be the only one. There still must be verbal as well as visual communication between supervisors and crews dealing with hazardous conditions—in this case, warning tape should have been used to block off the danger area.

D. Assure that All Crew Supervisors Are Transmitting Meaningful and Specific Safety Information

Another, equally important communication method is the formal and informal safety meeting conducted by the crew supervisor. Often such meetings are held infrequently, if at all, or the imparted information is nonspecific and therefore of little use as an accident-prevention technique.

If sandblasting were to take place on a construction site and other crafts were scheduled to be working in the vicinity, then suitable safety meeting information should cover the specific hazard and tell workers what they can do to protect themselves. A general discussion of sandblasting weeks or months before the operation is to take place is a far second best. A session where nondescript safety matters are discussed along with pressing production problems is completely useless.

The safety officer should gain an understanding of how craft management is communicating safety information to their people and be able to counsel and assist ineffective crew supervisors on how to improve.

E. Identify a Safety Officer

The construction manager should appoint one or more safety professionals, depending on the size of the job. Chapter 9 contains information on safety staffing that can assist managers who need to determine the quantity of safety staff. At the beginning of the description of the blueprint for control of construction site safety there is a list of duties for the safety officer that can be helpful to the construction manager.

It is important to note that the identification of a safety officer does not relieve the construction manager of his or her participative role in the safety program.

4. Subcontractors: Write a Safety Plan

Each subcontractor on every construction project should make a written commitment to its employees' safety and health. Many subcontractors retain a boilerplate safety plan that they merely reproduce for the construction manager who requires it. This is totally insufficient and should not be accepted. The reasons why such a plan is unacceptable are:

1. The plan is so broad that it cannot cover the specific hazards for every job
2. Such a plan requires no overt development activity on the part of subcontractor management or employees, so few persons will be intimately acquainted with its contents
3. Hazard consequences will also be nonspecific, resulting in inadequate protection for subcontractor employees
4. It demonstrates a general lack of interest in safety, and is indicative of a contractor who may not cooperate with an effective safety plan implemented by the construction manager
5. It does not reflect the agreements derived from the preconstruction safety conferences
6. It may show that the subcontractor has not thought about safety for the particular job

It would not be wrong to use a standard safety plan format, but in general, a plan should be developed for each new job that will accomplish the following:

1. *Identify serious hazards that will be encountered by employees, and emphasize changing worksite conditions.* This section of the plan closely follows the discussions and agreements made at the preconstruction safety conference. By confirming these conditions in an approved written plan, the construction manager and subcontractor manager can reduce possible confusion on safety matters and also have a reference in case a problem surfaces.

Example: A subcontractor whose sole job it is to lay reinforcement rod for high-rise-building floors is subject to a serious slip-and-fall hazard. Before the reinforcement is put in place the temporary high-density plywood floor is sprayed with parting oil so that the plywood can be separated from the concrete and reused. Unless care is taken in the spraying of the oil, oil puddles can form that take a long time to evaporate. The raw puddled oil is very slippery, even when boots with Vibram soles are worn. The dried oil presents no slip-and-fall problem. Under normal conditions a fall on the same level to smooth plywood would not be a problem. On a high-rise construction site, however, the worker is faced with the possibility of being impaled on reinforcement bar, or even worse, slipping through the barrier rail and falling to the ground. This is a hazard that must be identified. It also is a characteristic of changing worksite conditions that should be announced on the safety status board.

2. *Appoint a person to be responsible for the safety of subcontractor employees.* Generally the subcontractor job superintendent is the person who negotiates questions of worker safety and health and is also the designated safety contact person. Selecting this individual as a position rather than as a person has the advantage of continuity. If the person leaves the job for some reason the next person who occupies the position automatically assumes the role of safety responsibility.

This person would be expected to:

1. Monitor employees for safe practice
2. Provide protective equipment and devices
3. Correct unsafe conditions and practices
4. Act as focal point for subcontractor safety matters
5. Attend preconstruction safety conferences
6. Hold safety meetings with subcontractor employees
7. Assure compliance with the subcontractor safety plan
8. Assure that all subcontractor employees consult the safety status board.

3. *Detail how worksite hazards are to be eliminated or neutralized; include equipment, materials, and responsible persons.* Once hazards are identified, the next logical step is to assure that they do not cause injury. In the parting oil example just described, it was found that the oil spray nozzles were malfunctioning. A simple replacement was made, and all was well. This correction was not made until a serious injury occurred, however, while the purpose of a safety plan is to eliminate or neutralize hazards before the injury occurs.

The correction in this example could involve preventing the creation of oil puddles, elimination of puddles once they occurred, or the prevention of workers from walking on the puddled oil. In the first case, checking the nozzles for proper operation and replacing defective nozzles would prevent creation of oil puddles. In the second case, puddles could be vacuumed up. The third solution is the least desirable because it involves work stoppage.

Additional planning would involve the availability of replacement nozzles, identification of the person responsible for vacuuming, and making a vacuum available at the worksite. The series of events that would occur are as follows:

1. The problem and its solutions are identified at a preconstruction safety conference. It is agreed that nozzles will be checked each morning before starting the job and while spraying is carried out. Defective nozzles will be replaced, and if puddles form at any time, they will be vacuumed by the operator.
2. Assignments are made to purchase spare nozzles and to provide a vacuum.
3. All workers who will be in area are to be warned of the slippery conditions that may exist when oil is being sprayed. Warnings will be given at tool box meetings and on the safety bulletin board.

   4. *Arrange for appropriate training that deals with the specific hazards that will be encountered on the job.* It is sometimes difficult for subcontractors to visualize the type of training that is appropriate, because they do the same type of work most of the time and feel very familiar with the equipment and tools of their trade.

   The safety plan simplifies the identification of the training needs because the plan addresses the most serious of the hazards and how the hazards will be neutralized. For example, if a construction organization is building concrete retaining walls, many of its workers will be tying reinforcing bar and will most likely be standing on the bar as the wall is constructed. A harness and double-lanyard system (see Fig. 11-4) will provide mobility for the worker, yet keep him tied off at all times.

   When this hazard and its solution are identified in the subcontractor safety plan, the required amount of training for subcontractor employees, including new hires, should also be indicated. A typical entry for this training would be: "All employees who work on re-bar to demonstrate their ability to use the double-lanyard system. All new hires to receive such training before starting work. Orientation on the need for the system will be held, and employees who do not comply will be disciplined."

   Examples of other types of training are:

1. How to handle solvents
2. How to operate a rented manlift
3. How to de-energize electrical circuits
4. How to lockout/tagout
5. How to operate unfamiliar power tools
6. How to inspect slings and other lifting equipment
7. How to accomplish leading-edge work safely
8. How to safely set up a roof for a reroof job
9. How to recognize asbestiform material
10. How to use the safety bulletin board

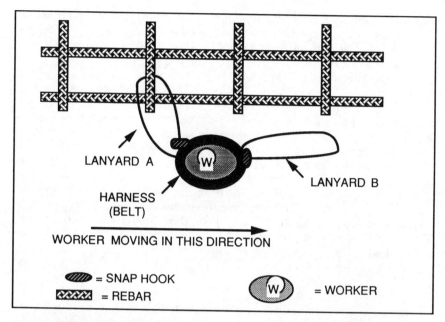

Figure 11-4. Double-lanyard system. The worker, represented by the oval, is standing on the rebar structure installing additional rebar. The hazard is from a fall from elevation and is taken care of through the double-lanyard system. When the worker is stationary he is tied off by means of lanyard A. When the worker must move to the right he must continue past perpendicular tied-off rebar and would not be able to continue without temporarily removing lanyard A. He would then be in danger of a possibly fatal fall. To prevent this problem, a second lanyard is added so that it first may be tied off past the interfering rebar before lanyard A is removed. Thus the worker is tied off at all times.

5. *Explain how hazard information will be transmitted: for example, informally, safety meetings, bulletin board.* Many times the way to perform safety for a particular job is known to the supervisor, to another worker who belongs to another subcontractor, or to the general contractor. If the correct information is not passed on to those who are doing the job, the stage is set for disaster. This is particularly true when there is out-of-sequence or additional unplanned work.

Effective communication is so important that communication methods must be included in the subcontractor's safety plan.

Subcontractor employees should consult the general contractor's safety bulletin board each day before work to determine if the work being performed that day by others will affect job safety. Tool box meetings should be held by contractors, subcontractors, and all crafts to discuss specific hazards that workers will encounter that day. If conditions warrant, subcontractor supervisors should assure that their people are informed of hazards as they arise on the changing, dynamic construction worksite.

For example, if a plywood floor is being laid and a high wind comes up, it may not be wise to continue leading-edge work where four-by-eight plywood panels have to be carried against 50-mph wind gusts. Other less hazardous work may have to be substituted or special precautions taken, such as rigging a static line and harnessing the wood carrier. The safety plan can bring up such subjects so that all parties will understand the importance of preserving life.

This concludes the blueprint for control of construction site safety. The rest of this chapter will use the blueprint in an actual case where, if the blueprint had been in force, the catastrophic accident that happened to a ventilation equipment installer probably would not have occurred. This case* has been briefly mentioned elsewhere in the book, but here we deal with it and its solution in detail.

Case Study 11-4

A large food-processing plant located in a small town in the western part of the state of Washington was to go through a scheduled 22-million-dollar remodel. To save the 10 percent that a hired general contractor would cost, the company decided to use their own experienced facility engineer, who had handled projects similar to this in the past, although not nearly as large.

There were over twenty-five subcontractors hired for this extensive job, and as it proceeded into the first month the construction site was described by some of the workers as "chaotic." There seemed to be little control over scheduling, with many workers, both company and construction types, all over the plant, which was attempting to stay partially in operation.

Three of the subcontractors were a heating and ventilation company that was to install new ventilation equipment; a concrete coring company that was to cut twenty-one holes in the concrete roof for skylights and new ventilation equipment; and a carpenter whose job it was to frame the holes to support the skylights and ventilation gear.

The hole cutters cut their holes and left them without covers, claiming that carpenters usually covered holes. The carpenter claimed that it was not his job. The holes were eventually covered by loose pieces of 4 × 8 plywood. The plywood was not marked or secured in any way. Apparently, the covers just looked like additional debris on an already cluttered construction site.

---

*Wilkie v. Carnation. See Appendix.

On the morning of the accident the ventilation people were bringing in a large unit by crane. The unit was to be set into a four-foot-by-four-foot roof hole. It was decided that the unit would be set down on the roof before placing it in the roof opening. One of the ventilation workers left the site to look for dunnage to place under the vent unit. He was last seen picking up a piece of plywood and then he disappeared from sight.

He had fallen through a roof opening, 28 feet to the concrete floor below, striking food-processing machinery on his way down. This 23-year-old worker sustained catastrophic injuries and will require total care for the rest of his life. The subsequent lawsuit, which settled out of court, recovered very high damages.

During his deposition the engineer in charge was asked who was responsible for safety. His answer was, "Everyone on my staff was responsible for safety." A more perfect textbook example of off-loading safety responsibility had never happened in my career. By believing that all of his staff was responsible for safety, but not organizing or in any way managing the discipline, the construction manager was actually saying, "No one is responsible for safety, particularly me!"

In the analysis of what had occurred, I maintained that the owners had assumed the role of construction manager and therefore they must exercise control of safety on the construction worksite. If they had employed the blueprint for control of construction site safety, they unquestionably would have avoided the fall problem and its unpleasant aftermath. The following exercise shows how the blueprint would have operated in this case.

To simplify the example we will address only the hazards associated with this incident. It is important to understand that many other hazards, such as the roofers' exposure to the roof perimeter or the crane operator's exposure to high voltage, would also be addressed in a complete program development.

This analysis will concern itself with the four major entities that were involved with the injury: the construction manager (general contractor), the ventilation installers, the hole cutters, and the carpenter(s). Each component of the blueprint appears in an illustration that lists (1) the entity (general contractor or subcontractor), (2) the blueprint requirement, (3) how the requirement is fulfilled.

Figure 11-5 deals with the qualification of the three subcontractors. In a small town it may be difficult to get bids from many subcontractors, but on a job of this magnitude contractors will usually come from large cities. Even if there is a short availability of subcontractors the qualification routine will identify the subcontractors that have had past safety problems and need special care.

Table 11-1 illustrates what should be accomplished at preconstruction safety conferences. The importance of these conferences cannot be overstated. It is here that a meeting of the minds occurs on what

ENTITY	General contractor
STAGE	Qualify subcontractors
ITEM	Each subcontractor should be qualified according to its prior accident experience
INFORMATION OR ACTION REQUIRED	The carpenters, ventilation install-ers and the hole cutter subcon-tractors will submit their worker's compensation modification factor and incidence rate for the past three years. The best records will be given priority.

Figure 11-5. Blueprint for control of the construction worksite.

specifically must be accomplished to protect all construction workers on the site. Not only are the definitive hazard-correction methods decided but the persons who will perform the various jobs, the materials involved, and the order that the materials and actions are to be performed are also important subjects of this conference. This is construction safety management at its most efficient.

Now that there has been agreement on specific safety matters, the time has come for the general contractor to take safety control of the worksite. If this does not happen, the effectiveness of the preconstruc-tion conference is reduced significantly. The mere knowledge that it will be held to an agreement by inspections and a disciplined schedule will convince most subcontractors that the construction manager is serious about safety. The actual performance of the safety specifications for worksite control (see Table 11-2) will integrate safety into normal construction site operating routine by demanding accomplishment of production, quality, and safety from all subcontractors as well as from general contractor workers.

The final step in the blueprint is to require each subcontractor to develop an approved safety plan. This plan guarantees that the contractor has committed time, resources, planning, and agreement to the principles of accident prevention. The plan is easily derived from the agreements made and information discussed at the preconstruction conference. The approval of the plan is a job for the general contractor's safety officer (See Table 11-3).

The blueprint for control of construction site safety is now complete. As with any blueprint, changes can be made to fit changing needs and different projects. The vital aspects of addressing specific safety needs, detailing how the needs will be met, and getting it all down in writing will much more likely than not result in superior safety performance.

Table 11-1 Blueprint for Control of the Construction Worksite: Preplanning Conferences

Entity: General Contractor	Stage: Preplanning Conferences—Discuss the Following Items
Item	Information Required or Action Taken
1. The most serious hazards that will be encountered on the job	1. The most serious hazard that the hole cutter, ventilation installers, and the carpenter will encounter is the 20 roof holes that will be cut to receive the skylights and the ventilation equipment. The holes will vary in size from 3 ft × 3 ft to 8 ft × 20 ft.
2. How the subcontractor and the general contractor plan to eliminate or neutralize these hazards	2. Each roof hole to be covered immediately after cutting with a nailed, marked 3/4-in. plywood cover, or in the case where a 4-ft × 8-ft cover will not suffice, the cover will be fabricated. There should be an overhang of at least 6 inches on every side. Covers must meet OSHA standards. WARNING: No roof opening is to be abandoned when uncovered
3. Who will supply the materials and equipment	3. Wood for framing holes and for fabricating covers will be supplied by the carpenters.
4. When the materials and equipment are to be in place	4. Hole covers and framing materials in place before holes are cut. CAUTION: Coordination between contractors is required
5. When the specific safety activities are to be performed	5. Covers are to be installed immediately after holes are cut and immediately after application of roofing materials to hole frames. CAUTION: Coordination between contractors is required

6. Who will perform safety activities

7. The type of cooperation that is expected from the general contractor

8. The activities of other subcontractors that will affect the safety of the worksite

9. How to handle out-of-sequence or unscheduled work

10. Date for an approved subcontractor safety plan

6. Carpenters to install hole covers.

WARNING: Hole cutters will not abandon an uncovered hole

7. General contractor to maintain hazard status bulletin board, provide and maintain a roof-perimeter warning system, and notify all parties of out-of-sequence or unscheduled work.

8. (a) The hole cutters will cut 20 roof holes on 9/6/90 and 9/7/90.
   (b) Roofers will require covers removed to roofover frames on 9/23/90.
   (c) Ventilation equipment installers will require covers removed on 10/10/90 to install ventilation equipment.
   (d) Warning line system to be removed at project's end.

WARNING: No roof opening is to be abandoned for any length of time

CAUTION: Coordination between subcontractors is required

9. All workers will be notified by their supervisors that unscheduled or out-of-sequence work is to be performed. General contractor will notify all supervisors, who in turn will notify their crews. The safety hazard status board will also display this information.

10. The concrete coring company will have an approved safety plan before 8/25/90. The carpenters will have an approved safety plan before 9/1/90. Heat and ventilation subcontractors will have an approved safety plan before 9/7/90.

Table 11-2 Blueprint for Control of the Construction Worksite: Worksite Safety Control

Entity: General Contractor	Stage: Take Safety Control of the Worksite—Perform Following Items
Item	Information Required or Action Taken
1. Determine if subcontractors are performing as agreed in the preplanning conference. Determine also if general safety practices are satisfactory.	1. The general contractor safety officer will conduct two inspections per day at random times. Subcontractor supervisors will conduct one inspection per day.
2. The general contractor and subcontractor supervisors will enforce agreed upon safety activities.	2. After second infraction the subcontractor will be asked to stop work for a hazard-control conference. After third infraction subcontractors will be asked to vacate the premises. This schedule is based on the same or similar infractions (such as subcontractor employees not wearing harnesses and lanyards and being tied-off). If a subcontractor violates six miscellaneous but serious safety rules, the subcontractor will be asked to vacate the premises.
3. The general contractor safety officer will create and maintain a safety hazard status bulletin board.	3. The safety hazard status bulletin board will be displayed at the main entrance to the worksite. All general contractor and subcontractor employees are required to consult the board each day before starting work. Major hazards will be posted as they occur or are eliminated or neutralized.
4. The general contractor safety officer will assure that all supervisors are transmitting meaningful and specific safety information to their crews.	4. The general contractor safety officer will periodically determine if workers are knowledgeable of the existence of major hazards and the methods of controlling them. Supervisors will also perform this function.
5. The general contractor will appoint a safety officer.	5. The number of safety officers should be proportional to the size of the job. Consult the guide for determination of the size of safety staff in Chapter 9 of this book.

Table 11-3 Blueprint for Control of the Construction Worksite: The Subcontractor Accident Prevention Plan

Entity: Subcontractor	Stage: Submit an Approved Safety Plan Covering the Following Items
Item	Information Required or Action Taken
1. Identify the serious hazards that will be encountered by your employees, giving substantial consideration to changing worksite conditions.	1. (a) All subcontractors will be subject to falls through the roof openings. Openings must be covered at all times, but will be uncovered to install ventilation equipment and when the opening frames must be roofed over.
	(b) All subcontractors will be subject to falls from the roof perimeter.
2. Detail how worksite hazards are to be eliminated or neutralized. Include equipment, materials and responsible persons.	2. (a) All openings will be framed and covered by carpenters with nailed, fabricated, and marked covers immediately after cutting. Unframed openings will be either guarded or covered temporarily with prefabricated covers. Temporary covers will be marked and fastened with clamps or other effective means. Roof openings that are in the process of being framed or roofed over will be guarded by a warning-line system to be provided by the subcontractor that is doing the work.
	(b) The general contractor will erect, maintain, and supervise a perimeter warning-line system that will not be removed until the roof is completed.
3. Appoint a person to be responsible for the safety of subcontractor employees. This person will be the focal point for safety contacts by the general contractor.	3. The subcontractor supervisor or job superintendent will be the focal point for subcontractor safety. This person will conduct safety inspections, tool box meetings, and generally will keep employees informed of how changing worksite conditions will affect their safety.
4. Explain how hazard information will be transmitted: informally, at safety meetings, or through the bulletin board.	4. All subcontractor employees will consult the hazard status bulletin board each day before work begins. Safety toolbox meetings will be held every Wednesday immediately before the start of work. Subcontractor safety officers will keep employees informed of immediate safety problems as they arise.
5. Arrange for appropriate training that deals with the specific hazards that will be encountered on the job.	5. All subcontractor workers will receive training in the use of the perimeter warning-line system, how to recognize a roof opening cover, how to guard a roof opening, the safety rules concerning roof openings, and the use of harness protection systems. They will also be trained in the requirements of this safety plan.

Chapter 12

Epilog

The 1980s has been characterized as the decade of the litigation explosion. Nationally, thousands of personal injury cases involving billions of dollars were filed and processed in the United States every year. For 1989, the National Safety Council reported 94,000 deaths, 2.4 million disabling injuries, and costs of over 148 billion dollars attributable to accidental injury.

Although insurance usually pays the judgments when the plaintiff prevails, the cost of defending a personal injury lawsuit is very significant. Even when the defense is successful there is still an enormous cost to the defendant in time, money, and many times loss of public trust through adverse publicity.

This book has demonstrated how to avoid litigation by means of prior preparedness involving the use of an appropriate form of analysis. In addition, Rob Williamson, a skilled Seattle, Washington, trial attorney, has suggested some specific humanitarian steps that can be taken to minimize the possibility of litigation after a personal injury.

1. Apologize for the incident and the injured person's inconvenience and pain.
2. Impress upon the injured person that you are investigating how the accident took place so that you can determine what steps, if any, can be taken to improve the situation and prevent further incidents.
3. Agree to pay medical bills.
4. Follow up to make sure the injured person is doing well.

These procedures should be effective when the responsible party acts quickly, but the more grievous injuries generally will become the subject of litigation.

Another issue to be addressed is the general opinion that I have often heard that many personal injury suits are frivolous, are encouraged by attorneys driven by the lure of huge settlements, or are otherwise without merit. My observation is, however, that when they are confronted with well-presented facts, juries will render a fair judgment that many times will be for the defense. When there is a verdict for the plaintiff, it will reflect just compensation for catastrophic injuries, permanent disabilities, severe economic losses, as well as pain and suffering. Despite large awards in some cases, the victim is usually never made "whole" again.

Harry Philo, well-known trial lawyer, has often stated in very succinct terms that litigation is the best and only remedy when product designers, manufacturers, distributors, and representatives market inherently dangerous equipment and materials. As we have seen, the best way to avoid litigation is through the prudent application of prior analysis to determine the foreseeable accident/injury potential of the product, facility, or design, and then to eliminate the problem through redesign or other corrective action.

When worker's compensation laws were enacted in the 1920s and 1930s, two of their prime purposes were to reduce the need for litigation and to encourage business to reduce insurance premiums by incorporating safety principles into their operations. As a method for reducing third-party personal injury litigation in the construction industry, some persons suggest expanding the worker's compensation laws to cover the construction manager's relationship to subcontractors.

My opinion is that while compensation laws have reduced two-party litigation between workers and their employers, current compensation "no-fault" laws encourage a cavalier attitude toward providing the safest product or facility that the current state of the art will allow. The reason for this is that employers feel protected by the immunity from suits afforded by the worker's compensation laws. Construction managers in particular have been able to contractually protect themselves by using "hold harmless agreements" and other contract provisions based on compensation laws. Harry Philo puts it in less gentle terms when he states that, generally, "worker's compensation laws are a license to maim and kill."

As we saw, a new legal consideration has recently surfaced in the construction industry. In the state of Washington, its supreme court handed down a decision in 1989, *Stute* v. *PGMC*, that is similar to actions in a few other states, and may have far-reaching implications for all jurisdictions. Stute was a roofer who was assigned to work on gutters at the eaves of a steeply pitched roof. He was provided with none of the fall protection required by law. When he fell from the roof he was seriously injured.

A lawsuit was filed in district court against the general contractor, who subsequently applied for and received summary judgment based on insufficient liability. Stute appealed to superior court, where the judgment of the lower court was upheld. The case went to the state supreme court, and there the lower courts were overturned by a vote of 9 to 1. The court held that the general contractor had a safety duty to all workers on the construction site, including those employed by subcontractors.

This means that construction managers (general contractors, owners, architects, prime contractors, etc.) may be liable for the conduct of the construction site safety program as it affects all workers. The blueprint for the control of construction site safety, contained in the previous chapter, details how to effectively do this. Our final conclusion was that if these procedures are followed, and a safety program rigorously adhered to, construction site accidents, and therefore lawsuits, will be substantially reduced. As a general rule: A potential for serious injury or death is always unacceptable if reasonable accident/injury prevention measures will eliminate or minimize the danger.

APPENDIX

Listing of Personal Injury Lawsuits Cited in This Book

Case Type	Agent	Root Cause(s)	Description	Caption	Chapter
Product liability △	Radial arm saw	Lack of appropriate guard	A home craftsman was using a radial arm saw in the rip mode when his attention was diverted. He swung his hand into the unguarded point of operation	*Hollman v. Sears Roebuck* Tacoma, WA	2
Unsafe premises △	Walkway over water	Unsafe design Lack of guardrail Inappropriate management	A walkway leading from a condominium built over water was unguarded on both sides. A young boy and his grandmother drowned when the child fell into the lake	*Wrenn v. Spinaker Bay* Seattle, WA	2
Product liability △	Glue application machine	Poorly designed interlock and improper training	A worker in a laminate plant had her hand amputated when she inadvertantly placed it between in-running rolls. She was in a hurry to leave the plant that day	*Woodward v. Duspohl* Portland, OR	2
Negligent teaching	Table saw	Poor project design Lack of guard	An inexperienced student amputated three fingers when the board she was pushing through a table saw kicked back. No guards or other shop aids were in use	*Snider v. Clover Park School District* Tacoma, WA	2
Product liability △	Binder jack	Improper design	Chains used to bind logs on a logging truck parted with explosive force when the binder jack that held the chains together, slipped. The driver's arm was disabled	Did not reach trial level.	3

254

Case Type	Agent	Root Cause(s)	Description	Caption	Chapter
Product liability △	Panel saw	Negligent design	In this two worker operation a mis-communication occurred and the saw was started at the wrong time. A worker's hand was amputated	*Lytikainen v. Rodgers Machinery* Seattle, WA	4
Product liability	Beer bottling machine	Negligent design	A lever that is routinely used during the bottling machine operation was so close to the machine's point of operation that a worker's hand was amputated	*Brown v. Crown, Cork and Seal* Olympia, WA	4
Unsafe premises	Restaurant parking lot	No maintenance program	A restaurant patron, making her way from her car to the restaurant entrance, tripped over a displaced berm and received serious injuries	Composite slip-and-fall case.	5
Product liability	Electric sign	Mismanufacture Negligent maintenance program	A young man, while servicing an electrical sign, was electrocuted because tripping circuit breakers were negligently treated during use of a defective sign.	*Reich v. A&B Rentals* Seattle, WA	5
Product liability △	Sheet metal feeder	Negligent design	Device stored residual air pressure that was released when the machine was unjammed. Supervisor's hand was caught in the operation of a machine that was shut down	*Meyer v. Coe Machinery* Spokane, WA	6
Product liability △	Bandsaw	Improper design	The knob for tilting the table was located so close to the moving bandsaw blade that the user's hand was severely lacerated	*Hardesty v. Grizzley* Bellingham, WA	6

Case Type	Agent	Root Cause(s)	Description	Caption	Chapter
Product liability	Punch press	Negligent design	Machine operator, while making license plate frames, placed her hand into the point of operation to remove product. Machine double tripped and amputated her hand	Author did not participate in this case.	6
Product liability	Multistation wood working machine	Lack of guard	Machine operator caught in conveyor drive was drawn into the point of operation where his hand was amputated by rotating saw	*Weiss v. Challoner Machinery*, Everett, WA	6
Unsafe premises	Food chain warehouse	Inappropriate access to work station	While delivering pallets of empty soft drink cans, the driver was required to walk on conveyor to routinely unjam the conveyor. Driver slipped and was injured	*Scott v. Safeway*, Seattle, WA	6
Product liability	Articulated manlift	Failure to warn; Negligent design	A tree trimmer was severely burned when he contacted a 13,000-volt powerline. The lift he was using was grounded: the nonmetallic hoses had been replaced with metallic hoses	*Stone v. Asplundh*, Spokane, WA	6
Negligent use of equipment	Rental boom truck	Failure to warn and train	Three workers were electrocuted when the farmer, driving a boom truck with a raised boom, ran into a power line. Workers were holding metal grain elevator legs	Author did not participate in this case.	6

Case Type	Agent	Root Cause(s)	Description	Caption	Chapter
Product liability △	Composting machine	Negligent design Failure to warn	A mushroom farm worker crawled into a composting machine to clean the beaters. Another worker thought he was to turn machine on for lubrication	*Roses-Montes v. Petaluma* San Francisco, CA	6
Product liability	Cattle feed milling machine	Negligent design	A feed mill operator had his hand drawn into in-running rolls after he had shut the machine off. The operator was cleaning the rolls, which had a 24-second overrun	Did not reach trial level.	6
Product liability	Aluminum casting machine	Negligent design	The operator of a Direct Chill Casting machine was severely burned by molten aluminum when the cast exploded. The operator's work station was over the mold	*Johnson v. Bausch & Lombe et al.* Bellingham, WA	6
Product liability △	Heat vent/skylight	Negligent design and deceptive advertising	A roofer, while walking backwards, fell through a heat vent and was killed. The heat vent/skylight had been advertised as being "approved by OSHA"	*Caraveau v. SDL* Seattle, WA	6
Unsafe premises △	Optometrist office	Unsafe design	When a van carrying elderly patients stopped at the prescribed place in the driveway, the passengers were faced with a curb that was difficult to see. An elderly patron tripped	Did not reach trial level.	6

Case Type	Agent	Root Cause(s)	Description	Caption	Chapter
Product liability	Pulp mill conveyor system	Negligent design	A pulp mill worker was assigned to shovel out wood chips at a conveyor pulley station. He caught his foot in the bite of the pulley and he lost his leg. There was no guard	*Taylor v. Atlas Systems* Everett, WA	7
Unsafe environment and procedure	Cutoff saw △	Unsafe production system	A worker was assigned to cut thousands of small pieces of two-by-fours from larger pieces. The factory was so cold that he wore gloves. He lost four fingers when he drew a saw down on his hand	Case not filed.	7
Lack of guardrail △	Balcony in building lobby	Negligent design	A woman fell 20 feet when she stepped out on an improperly railed balcony to water plants	Case not completed.	7
Product liability	Press brake	Failure to warn & negligent design	An experienced press brake operator lost most of both hands when he slipped while holding a part near the point of operation	Case not completed.	7
Failure to warn	Face shield	Improper placement of warning	A casting machine operator had his face shield penetrated by molten aluminum during a surge in the cast process. He was blinded	*Johnson v. Bausch & Lombe* Bellingham, WA	7

Case Type	Agent	Root Cause(s)	Description	Caption	Chapter
Product liability	Automobile child restraint	Management negligence	A child became a paraplegic when she was ejected from an automobile car restraint that had been inappropriately tested. Case explores management's role	Caption may not be released, by court order.	7
Unsafe premises	Department store	Slip and fall and tripping hazards	This is a composite case that covers a number of slip and fall situations that are common in department stores and similar facilities	Composite case	8
Chemical exposure	Wood digester	Negligent management	Two workers were killed and one seriously injured when the digester they were repairing was inadvertently started up. There was a deficient lock-out program	Case not litigated.	9
Fall from elevation	Roof opening	Negligent construction safety program	A felt machine operator fell through a skylight opening on an office building under construction. The holes were not covered in the legally required way	*Hayfield v. Evans* Seattle, WA	11
Chemical exposure △	Ruptured valve stem	Negligent safety program	A live ammonia line sprayed ammonia over a worker who thought that the line was dead	*Brown v. Chevron* Spokane, WA	11

259

Case Type	Agent	Root Cause(s)	Description	Caption	Chapter
Electrical injury △	Contact with power line	Failed communication	A group of workers were lifting an aluminum scaffold plank into the window of an office building when the plank contacted a power line	*Smith v. Gall-Landau* Seattle, WA	11
Fall from elevation △	Manlift	Failed communication	Two electricians were seriously injured when the manlift they were using tipped. Previously covered 4-foot holes had been uncovered	Case not completed.	11
Slip and fall	Construction site	Unsafe procedure	A construction worker was seriously injured when he slipped on parting oil that had puddled on a form for a concrete floor	Case not completed.	11
Fall from elevation	Roof opening	Negligent safety program	A construction manager neglected to specifically treat with the safety requirements of a large factory remodel. Subcontractor employee was badly injured	*Wilkie v. Carnation* Ephrata, WA	11

Note: The justification for this listing is to give the reader easier access to case descriptions that are described in text in detail and with emphasis on the remedy. Illustrated cases are marked with this symbol △ .

BIBLIOGRAPHY

Barnett, R. L., and Brickman, D. B., Safety Hierarchy, *Journal of Safety Research*, Vol. 17, pp. 49–55, 1986.

Bird, F. E., Jr., and Germain, G. L., *Damage Control—A New Horizon in Accident Prevention and Cost Improvement*, Comet Press, 1966.

Browning, R. L., *The Loss Rate Concept in Safety Engineering*, New York: Marcel Dekker, 1980.

Committee on Trauma Research, Commission on Life Sciences, National Research Council, Institute of Medicine, *Injury in America—A Continuing Public Health Problem*, Washington, D.C.: National Academy Press, 1985.

Cunitz, J. C., Psychologically Effective Warnings, *Journal of the System Safety Society*, Vol. 17, No. 3, May/June 1981.

DeReamer, R., *Modern Safety and Health Technology*, New York: John Wiley & Sons, 1980.

Dillon, B. S., *Human Reliability—With Human Factors*, New York: Pergammon Press, 1986.

Ferry, T. S., *Modern Accident Investigation and Analysis—An Executive Guide*, New York: John Wiley & Sons, 1981.

Freeman, S. H., Accident/Illness Statistics are not Effective if They are Confusing, *Occupational Health and Safety*, August 1985.

Goldsmith, F., and Kerr, L. E., *Occupational Safety and Health—The Prevention and Control of Work-related Hazards*, New York: Human Sciences Press, 1982.

Green, A. E., Ed., *High Risk Safety Technology*, Chichester, England: John Wiley & Sons, 1982.

Greenfiels, S., *Management's Safety and Health Imperative: Eight Essential Steps to Improving the Work Environment*, Xavier University: The Minerva Education Institute, July 1989.

Grimaldi, J. V., and Simonds, R. H., *Safety Management*, 4th ed., Homewood, IL: Richard D. Irwin, 1984.

Grove, A., Breaking the Chains of Command, *Newsweek*, October 3, 1983.

Grove, A., How (and why) to Run a Meeting, *Fortune*, July 11, 1983.

Hale, A. R., and Glendon, A. I., *Individual Behavior in the Control of Danger*, Amsterdam, The Netherlands: Elsevier Science Publishers, 1987.

Hammer, W., *Occupational Safety Management and Engineering*, 4th ed., Englewood Cliffs, NJ: Prentice-Hall, 1989.

Handley, W., Ed., *Industrial Safety Handbook*, London: McGraw-Hill, 1977.

Heath, E.D., *Occupational and Environmental Mishaps: Moving Up on the Management Agenda!*, Xavier University: The Minerva Education Institute, July 1989.

Heinrich, H. W., Petersen, D., and Roos, N., *Industrial Accident Prevention—A Safety Management Approach*, New York: McGraw-Hill, 1980.

Hinze, J., *A New Study of Construction Industry Costs*, Morgantown: Excel, West Virginia University Center for Excellence in Construction Safety, Fall 1990.

Hoskin, A. F., *Accident Facts—1990 Edition*, Chicago: National Safety Council, 1990.

Hudson, L., Effective Safety and Health Programming, a Management Oriented Approach, presented at the 44th Annual Conference, South Carolina Occupational Safety Council, Columbia, SC, September 1981.

Johnson, W.G., *MORT—Safety Assurance Systems*, New York: Marcel Dekker, 1980.

Johnson, W. G., and Lowman, G., *The Management Oversite and Risk Tree—MORT*, Washington, D.C.: Superintendent of Documents, SAN 821-2, UC-41., 1973.

Kates, R. W., *Risk Assessment of Environmental Hazard*, New York: John Wiley & Sons, 1978.

Kitchens, C. L., The Probability of "2"—Redundancy and Reliability, *Professional Safety*, March 1980.

Kohr, R. L., Slip Slidin' Away—The Absence of an Effective Slips and Falls Program Can Send Costs to Your Company Reeling, *Safety and Health*, November 1989.

Konner, M., Why the Reckless Survive, *The Sciences*, May/June 1987.

Kvalseth, T. O., *Ergonomics of Workstation Design*, London: Butterworths, 1983.

Layton, D. M., *Systems Safety Including DOD Standards*, Chesterland, OH: Weber Systems, 1989.

Liska, R., *Role of the Educational Institution in Construction Safety*, Morgantown: Excel, West Virginia University Center for Excellence in Construction Safety, Summer 1990.

Lowrance, W. O., *Of Acceptable Risk—Science and the Determination of Safety*, Los Altos, CA: William Kaufmann, 1976.

Marshall, G., *Safety Engineering*, Monterey, CA: Brooks/Cole, 1982.

McGlade, F., Accident Prevention as a Management Enterprise*

Mintzberg, H., The Manager's Job: Folklore and Fact, *Harvard Business Review*, July/August 1975.

Mishan, E. J., *Cost-Benefit Analysis—New and Expanded Edition*, New York: Praeger, 1976.

Nothstein, G. Z., *The Law of Occupational Safety and Health*, New York: The Free Press, 1981.

Peters, G. A., *Product Liability and Safety*, Washington, D.C.: Coiner Publications, 1971.

Petersen, D., *Analyzing Safety Performance*, New York: Garland STPM Press, 1980.

Petersen, D., *Safety Management, A Human Approach*, Englewood, NJ: Aloray, 1975.

---

*Francis McGlade is former chief of U.S. Army Safety and the title cited was published but taken from a presentation by Dr. McGlade. A copy is available on request from the publisher or from S. Freeman.

Philo, H., *Lawyer's Desk Reference*, Vols. I, and II, Rochester, NY: Lawyer's Cooperative Publication Company, 1987.

President's Commission on the Accident at TMI, *Report of the President's Commission on The Accident at Three Mile Island*, New York: Pergamon Press, October 1979.

Revelle, J. B., *Safety Training Methods*, New York: John Wiley & Sons, 1980.

Ridley, J. R., Ed., *Safety at Work*, London: Butterworths, 1983.

Robertson, L. S., *Injuries*, Lexington, MA: Lexington Books, 1983.

Rodgers, W. P., *Introduction to System Safety Engineering*, New York: John Wiley & Sons, 1971.

Roland, H. E., and Moriarty, B., *System Safety Engineering and Management*, New York: John Wiley & Sons, 1983.

Samuelson, N., and Levitt, R., Owner's Guidelines for Selecting Safe Contractors, *Journal of the Construction Division of American Society of Civil Engineers*, December 1982.

Simonds, R., and Shafai-Sahrai, Y., Factors Apparently Affecting Injury Frequency in Eleven Matched Pairs of Companies, *Journal of Safety Research*, Autumn 1977.

Smith, M., Cohen, H., Cohen, A., and Cleveland, R., Characteristics of Successful Safety Programs, *Journal of Safety Research*, Spring 1978.

Tarrants, W. E., *The Measurement of Safety Performance*, New York: Garland STPM Press, 1980.

U.S. Department of Health, Education and Welfare, Publication No. (NIOSH) 75-173, *Machine Guarding—Assessment of Need*, Washington, D.C.: Superintendent of Documents, 1975.

Viscusi, W. K., *Employment Hazards—An Investigation of Market Performance*, Cambridge, MA: Harvard University Press, 1979.

Waller, J. A., *Injury Control—A Guide to the Causes and Prevention of Trauma*, Lexington, MA: Lexington Books, 1985.

Wang, C. C. K., *How to Manage Workplace Derived Hazards and Avoid Liability*, Park Ridge, NJ: Noyes, 1987.

INDEX